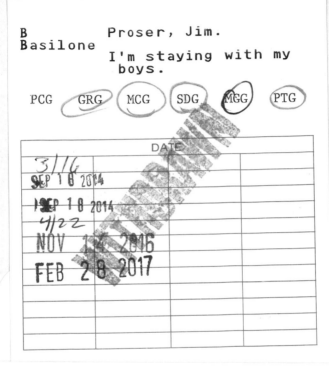

65-0081   B
                   BASILONE
Proser, Jim   PBK.
I'm staying with my boys

I'm Staying with My Boys

The Heroic Life of Sgt. John Basilone, USMC

★

Jim Proser

with Jerry Cutter

St. Martin's Griffin
New York

www.stmartins.com

PHOTO CREDITS

Photos throughout:

Courtesy of the author: JB cover photo; p. 8 Raritan Bldg; 31 Pvt. Basilone; 33 street in Manila; 54 Fort Jay; 76 JB with MofH; 96 laundry truck; 111 JB with baby; 123 JB open shirt; 253 JB with woman; 288 four GIs.

Courtesy of the U.S. Government: p. 1 Marines on Amtrac; 26 Amtracs in water; 65 Army group; 87 Marines on beach; 149 USS *Chicago*; 159 two Marines; 168 coconut grove/swamp; 170 coconut grove/camp; 170 Bloody Ridge Trail; 182 Matanikau River; 182 Lt. Col. Chesty; 185 1/5 Marines on trail; 191 two Marines in hole; 197 Bloody Ridge field; 222 dead bodies; 223 Marine patrol; 238 1/7 band; 295 tank; 322 Iwo beach.

Eight-page photo insert:

Courtesy of the author: p. 1 children; 1 family; 2 16th Infantry; 3 JB receiving MofH; 3 JB sideways hat; 4 thirty thousand attend parade; 4 JB at church; 4 JB wedding; 4 JB with mayor; 4 JB in car; 5 JB on car; 8 JB statue.

Courtesy of the U.S. Government: p. 2 Bloody Ridge; 2 battle map; 3 graves; 3 Marines dig in; 3 Marine carrying MG; 5 Iwo aerial view; 5 Marines on Iwo; 5 Japanese Iwo view; 5 Marines on beach; 8 satchel charge; 8 Japanese bodies; 8 Marines advance; 8 JB rucksack.

Colliers Magazine: p. 6 cover image.

Medal of Honor: p. 7 JB image.

Technical advisor: Col. Ken Jordan, USMC (Ret.)
Research: Jerry Cutter

LIBRARY OF CONGRESS CATALOGING-IN-PUBLICATION DATA

Proser, Jim.
    I'm staying with my boys: the heroic life of Sgt. John Basilone, USMC / Jim Proser with Jerry Cutter.—1st St. Martin's Griffin ed.
    p. cm.
    ISBN 978-0-312-61144-6
    1. Basilone, John, 1916–1945. 2. United States. Marine Corps—Biography. 3. Medal of Honor—Biography. 4. Guadalcanal, Battle of, Solomon Islands, 1942–1943. 5. Iwo Jima, Battle of, Japan, 1945. 6. World War, 1939–1945—Biography. 7. Marines—New Jersey—Biography. 8. Soldiers—New Jersey—Biography. 9. Raritan (N.J.)—Biography. I. Cutter, Jerry. II. Title.
VE25.B36P76 2010
940.54'5973092—dc22
[B]

2009039994

First published in the United States under the title *I'm Staying with My Boys . . .* by Lightbearer Communications Co.

First St. Martin's Griffin Edition: February 2010

10 9 8 7 6 5 4 3 2 1

To Monte, Jane, and Tim—the stars I sail under

Contents

★

Author's Note

★

In this book I have attempted to include every historical fact known about Sgt. Basilone and many personal stories that cannot be verified. It is my hope that I have created a more accurate portrait of him in the process than has existed before. I have attempted to re-create his story in his own voice based on hundreds of hours of interviews with people who knew John well and spoke with him frequently. I also grew up near his hometown of Raritan, New Jersey. The speech of that area is second nature to me.

John Basilone was a man of extraordinary courage. He was in many ways a simple and ordinary young man, but he had at least one unusual ability: He could see into his own future. This paranormal ability might seem speculative in the story of a hero whose actions in battle are already well known and documented, but I believe that it is this "gift" that sets his extraordinary courage apart, beyond even most human understanding.

These premonitions are documented in his sister Phyllis's book *The Basilone Story*. This book is the only authoritative account of John as a child and young man. I personally confirmed the fact of

John's premonitions with Phyllis and with John's older brother and closest confidant, Carlo, who heard John correctly foretell his own future on three different occasions.

The last of John's three premonitions foretold his own death. By this time, he had received the Medal of Honor and was strongly encouraged by his military superiors to stay out of the fight, to stay home and promote the sale of war bonds. In spite of his superiors and his fatal vision, John wanted to protect the young men who had volunteered to face a desperate and fanatical Japanese enemy—his beloved Marines. And so he returned one final time to the battlefield explaining simply, "I'm staying with my boys. They need me."

In the writing of this book, John Basilone has become a personal hero of mine. I hope that I have done him justice in this account.

—JIM PROSER

Preface

★

I owe a debt. In my time, among my peers, it was seen as dishonorable to go to war in Vietnam. So I did not go. I used my cleverness to dodge the draft. But some young man, perhaps less concerned with his peers or more committed to the call of his country or maybe just a little less lucky, went in my place. To that young man of thirty-five years ago I owe a debt I can never repay.

I am not going to debate here whether that war was right or wrong. I am only going to acknowledge what I have come to feel about those who sacrifice some, or all, of their young lives to defend the rest of us. They are our ordinary citizens who have forced themselves to extraordinary service. They do not answer the call to arms lightly, but weigh it against the safety and comforts of life at home. Yet they do answer. They answer because when the call does come, and they then look into their hearts, they see the delicate flame of freedom begin to flicker. I chose to write this book to offer what small payment I can toward those defenders of freedom. For them, I can offer no greater inspiration than the subject of this book.

Now, well past my prime as a warrior, the warrior instinct is stirred by threats that bear down against my country and her principles. I am moved to take my place in the line that will not be crossed. But these are vain fantasies. My place in that line will be taken once again by others. For these new defenders as well, I dedicate what talents I have in honor of their service with the certain knowledge that they will continue to risk all they have and all they will ever have, to keep the delicate flame alive.

I'm Staying with My Boys

★

★ 1 ★

D-day, Iwo Jima
0700 Hours

We heard the diesels fire up. Metal groaned as the bow of our ship split down the middle and the two twenty-ton doors swung open to the black sea. Behind the doors, amtracs were lined up inside the belly of the ship like green, steel beetles.

On deck, the sound of the ship waking up got our minds focused on the assault ahead of us. We were going to be in the first waves of men to hit the beach. It all made sense, if you were a war planner who calculated schedules, machines, casualties and such. But we were the ones they made their plans on, so no matter how much sense it made on paper, you're never quite ready to be in that first group—even Marines like the boys in my platoon. They were mostly teenagers, a few were in their early twenties, and inexperienced, except for a few vets like me who rode herd. They were gung-ho and itching to get into the fight but even so, I could read their faces, being the first to face enemy fire was making them think things over. My younger brother George, a vet of Saipan and Tinian, saw these kids back in Hawaii and asked me, "Where the hell are the vets? You're gonna get yourself killed. Y'oughta come over to the 4th with me."

"Nothing doin'," I told him. "I'm stayin' put."

"Stubborn fuck, always were." George spat on the deck. Seemed like he didn't give a shit about anything anymore. I guessed it was from Saipan—where they say things got pretty rough. Over three thousand men, including most of his friends, got killed.

We were the 5th Division. Like George said, we had a lot of the younger legs in our outfit. Those young legs would get us across the beach faster to the airfield, our first objective. But we both knew that these youngsters would take the brunt of the dying. When you know how war works, like a wolf pack on the hunt, it made sense. But it still wasn't right. These boys were the bravest we had. They didn't wait to get drafted, they joined the Marines, and that should count for something. But of course, in the logic of war, it didn't.

The boys finished their prayers and the chaplain blessed us. The swabbies powered up more diesels and set to work getting the landing craft–medium (LCMs) and landing craft–personnel (LCPs) that would bring in the supplies after we hit the beach, hoisted up on the davits and swung over the side. All the activity set the boys murmuring to each other, "Here we go," and "This is it." For a second some of them looked down, bit their lips, like kids anywhere who were about to be punished. Inside I know some were panicking, feeling their nerve fail, even after all the training and preparation. Their instinct for survival was taking over. They wanted to beg for their lives, or hide in some cubbyhole or ammo crate of our huge transport ship, but they didn't do it. They sucked it up and believed they were ready. They weren't. What can I tell you about these young guys standing out on the cold deck with me? I loved them as much as my own brothers. Some were skinheaded young boots when they came into my platoon, some were fresh out of paratrooper school and were pissed off to be humping metal through the mud instead of floating down from the air under green silk. But all that was over now. The last six months of training together every day made them as tough and tight-knit a fighting platoon as I ever knew. They were the kind of heroes I wanted to be, not the Medal of Honor showboat that Topside wanted me to be.

Then a strange thing happened. As I watched them, I felt something release, all of a sudden. I can't really explain it, but it felt like a knot in my chest, that was there all my life, suddenly came loose. I was free somehow and quiet inside. The voice that had been inside my head since I can remember, the one that whispers all the time and gets loud when you do something wrong, was suddenly gone. When that voice in your head suddenly stops, you notice. At least I did, because I had learned to listen to it. It sounds strange and I don't go in for any sort of mumbo jumbo as a rule, but the voice told me the future, and did it more than once. Three different times I heard it clear as a bell, and it was right all three times. So I guess I learned to listen a little closer than most people. The voice was definitely gone. Maybe I just didn't need it anymore.

It was half-light, just as the sun was crowning over the horizon behind storm clouds. It was February 19, 1945, Monday, the beginning of the workweek. We were scheduled to hit the beach at 0900. Christ almighty, Monday at 9:00 A.M. just like we were starting a new job, punching a time clock. It made you wonder if God didn't have some kind of dark sense of humor. The heavy seas of last night had calmed down to gentle swells. I was standing there on deck and must have looked like a tourist with nothing to do. I looked up. Storm clouds covered us like dirty wool. They changed their mind every ten minutes whether to rain or not. At the horizon, the clouds broke up. Behind them was a red-orange sky and I remembered, ". . . Red sky at morning, sailors take warning," but it was too late for warnings now.

Then the boys heard the amtrac engines firing up belowdecks and they looked at me like, "What do we do now, Sarge?" Fear was already beginning to numb them. It was a natural reaction. They were like deer sensing the hungry wolves were already too close. They knew it was too late to run so they froze, hoping the wolves would miss them. And there they stood, my platoon of fifty-eight young warriors, still as sticks, looking at me. I told them to get down the gangways and get going.

I knew what was about to happen to them. They didn't know and so they were afraid. But I knew. "All Marines prepare to disembark!" The loudspeaker backed me up. The boys gathered up their things, all in a rush, like they were going to miss something. They weren't going to miss anything. They packed up the heavy .30 cal. Brownies, the air-cooled .30s, the mortars, the razor-stropped Ka-Bar knives and bayonets. They wouldn't need any of these things right now. They would just need their young legs to carry them as far and as fast as they could, across the beach, straight into a nightmare they would never wake up from. The guns and the knives would come later, for those of us who were left to fight back.

They would need me even more, very soon. They would think that hell had opened up a back door just for them. They wouldn't know which way to go. Some wouldn't be able to move and would be surprised that their legs didn't obey. You couldn't tell which ones by looking at them. The bravest ones in camp sometimes buried their faces in the sand and wet their pants. You just couldn't tell and neither could they. That's when they'll need me. They'll need me to pull them or kick them to get off the beach. Maybe that's why I'm calm, because I know I'll save some of them.

We filed down the gangways into the ship's steel belly. Half of my boys loaded into amphibious tractor 3C27 with me. Amtrac 3C27 was an armor-plated, rectangular tub made for delivering men onto a beach. It rode low and slow in the water. The best of them couldn't take much more than a two-foot ocean swell. What we found out was that if they didn't sink in the water, they sank in the loose, volcanic sand. It seemed like war plans never went according to plan.

We climbed into the hold of this steel tank. The engines thundered inside the metal walls of the ship. We rolled down the ramp and plopped into the open ocean. The driver gunned the engine and we churned away toward the island just over a mile in front of us.

The fellas were hunkered down in the hold and some were starting to look as green as the olive-drab metal around us. There was already an inch of water on the deck. Some of the boys were worried about that. We all heard the joke about these things capsizing if two men farted in the same direction. Then the big Navy guns opened up. They threw the big 16-inch shells that weighed as much as a jeep. They threw them a few miles and we could see them hit the side of Mount Suribachi on shore with a little red flash and gray blossoms of debris thrown up. The force of the cannon fire pushed six-foot waves out from the battleships. These concussion waves rode up under our keel, tossing us up higher and flipping our steak and eggs breakfast over in our bellies.

"It's gonna be alright, boys. They're gonna be dizzy as shithouse rats after we get done pounding 'em," I lied—just like Topside lied to us when they told us it would be over in seventy-two hours. All of us vets knew that seventy-two hours was pure bullshit and said so. It was like an involuntary reaction. The minute it dropped from the CO's mouth, it sounded like a dozen men coughed at once. But it was a dozen mumbled bullshits jumping right off the lips of us vets. We couldn't help it. There were twenty-two thousand Japanese jungle fighters straight ahead who had been digging in and calibrating their guns for the past three months. That meant they had coordinates for every square inch of beach and could put Japanese steel on any point almost instantly. Maybe they thought we were all young boots who hadn't seen action yet.

We also expected mines and railroad ties raked at a 45-degree angle in the shallow surf that could punch through the bottom of our amtracs like a tin can. Before we got in the boats we smeared white flash cream on our faces, a thick grease that smelled like a garage floor. This was to protect us from the drums of gasoline that might explode under our tracks as we got close to the beach.

We didn't know it at the time, but the Japs also had new weapons: an array of huge mortars and an early version of a buzz bomb—a rocket-propelled aerial bomb. They were dug so deep into the lava and coral rock that even the 16-inch navy shells weren't touching them. We didn't know that at the time either.

But I got the boys' minds off the mess around their feet. The ones who were staring straight ahead were the ones I worried about. They knew they were about to run up and knock on the main gate to hell. But there was nothing much I could do for them until they did. They had heard all the horror stories—the Japs didn't take prisoners, they tortured you, then cut your head off. Some of them ate your liver. These boys weren't innocent like we were before Guadalcanal. And they were still ready to face whatever came at them.

Once we got up to speed, the side-to-side heaving mostly stopped and the engine noise cut out most of the opportunity for nervous chatter. It was all business now, everyone in their own thoughts. These poor boys. For a moment they each thought they were going to be the lucky one, in the next they'd remember a time when they got hit by a foul ball or tripped in the obstacle course. They'd remember a time when they weren't lucky and then they'd worry. Once you know for sure that no one is lucky, that luck has nothing to do with you personally—it's either your time or it isn't—you just get on with it.

We had time to think about what we were up against and pray while our floating tank churned through the swells. The tension and the bobbing up and down caused a few of the greener-looking boys to finally lose their steak and eggs breakfast. That started up a healthy round of cursing as the puke mixed with the seawater around our feet. Threats and counterthreats flew back and forth. It broke some of the tension. Those who didn't have one already, lit up a smoke to cover the smell.

We reached the line of departure about a mile from the beach and started circling. The clouds had lifted a bit and the big navy guns let up while the flyboys came in with rockets and 500-pound bombs. The island started sprouting mushrooms of gray dust where the bombs hit. The beach of black volcanic sand was just a wavy pencil line under the dishwater sky. Off to the left, Mount Suribachi squatted—its old, busted volcano top was just 550 feet above the beach.

We circled to the left, counterclockwise. The sea was crowded with our armada of 880 ships. In convoy, our formation stretched for seventy miles. We continued circling, and to the south were ships laying out ten miles toward the horizon. We continued around and more ships stretched out to the east. A week ago we sailed from Hawaii to take Japan's front porch. Now, as our amtrac completed its first circle, the front porch was right in front of us. The Japs called it Iwo Jima—Sulfur Island.

The swelling mushrooms of dust and smoke thrown up by our firepower made it hard to see anything of the island. We started the next go-round. It was like everything else in a Marine's life, going in circles, waiting and trying to stay comfortable while hoping whatever was next wouldn't hurt too bad. When you get tired of worrying, your mind goes back home.

Raritan

★

I saw the Raritan Valley Country Club for the first time and knew that was what I wanted. At least I thought so when I was sixteen. It had been carved out of New Jersey cow pastures and cornfields and was still surrounded by them. In the early morning, the fairways were silver with dew. Cowbells clanked in lazy time as the big Jerseys and Holsteins were let out of their barn and wandered to their grazing spot. That was my time. It was like the place was all mine then and sometimes I would just take off walking the fairways. In a few weeks I knew every tree and dimple in the grass by heart.

When I first started caddying, I thought that was it. I thought I could carry bags for the rest of my life, live on tips and be happy. After a few weeks, the bags weren't even heavy to me. I carried two bags without a problem. The only thing that interrupted my daydream was the fact that by the third hole, my feet were soaked. I wore the twice handed-down shoes from my older brothers Angelo and Carlo. The tops were so creased and cracked that the water soaked right through. The soles were split. I looked like Li'l Abner in Dogpatch. I hated those goddamn shoes.

This one day the double bags were already cutting into each shoulder but that didn't bother me as much as waiting for these damn slow players I drew. They knew me and considered it some kind of ritual that they pick me every time. I thought it was a good luck, superstitious thing but I found out later they were concerned that I would be insulted if they picked someone else. Insulting somebody was a very big deal to these guys. Don't get me wrong, they were nice enough and treated me well but that didn't make up for it. They were just so slow—I wanted to throw the bags down and start hopping around like a crazy Indian just to get a rise out of them, but I didn't, of course.

They played golf like they were building a bridge. Weighing, measuring, consulting. They took three and four practice swings. They sighted along the shaft of the club for the lay of the land. With this crew I only ever got in one round before lunch. I guess they realized this and so they over-tipped me. They were real considerate but by the time we got around to the back nine, I was ready to run off howling across a cornfield. Then one time, everything was pretty much normal—I was being nice, they were being nice—one of them saw me tapping my foot. Some song I'd heard on the radio was in my head and the boredom got to me and I was tapping my foot. That's how stupid life is sometimes. You're just tapping your foot and suddenly you're the shitbird. The guy who looked at me wasn't even shooting. He sort of raked his head to one side then straightened up and looked a hole in me. I thought he was looking beyond me for a second because he was real still, like he was looking at something far away. But it was me. When a guy looks at me like that, it usually means he's looking to get his ass kicked, but I let it go because I was still just a kid.

Tapping or no tapping, they weren't going to be rushed. Old ladies played through. The sun came up and dried the dew off the grass. These guys just smiled and bowed and kept playing. They couldn't help it—the politeness and the bowing. It was their religion, or something. And the endless chatter, in their strange hard language—Japanese. It sounded like a flat tire flapping. What were they laughing about?

That was the first time the voice in my head showed me the future. It said, "Wake up!" but I wasn't sleeping. I got the feeling that I was looking through a telescope, seeing something I wasn't supposed to see. It came over me in a snap and since it was the first time, it went away before I knew what to think. But I saw it and I never forgot it. I saw that I was going to have trouble with these guys—these Japanese people. I didn't know how or when or anything. But it was clear enough that I went home and told my big sister Phyllis and of course she didn't know what the hell I was talking about. I told George, who never paid a bit of attention to me anyhow, and I told Carlo, who was just a year older than me. Carlo was a sweet kid, wouldn't hurt a fly. He listened to me and said, "Whatta ya think it means, Johnny?"

"Beats me. But it's gotta mean something."

"Maybe you were just day-dreaming. That can happen, you know."

Trouble with anybody was just about the furthest thing from Carlo's mind. He couldn't picture it. But I could. It seemed like plenty of things were cause for trouble if you asked me. Not that I asked for it, or that I wanted trouble, but when things just don't go your way and you start tapping your foot or something stupid like that, things are just naturally going to go wrong. It just seems like nature is set up to make certain people fight.

I had nothing against Japanese people then and the truth is I got nothing against them now, but I knew for sure, ten years before it happened, that there was going to be trouble. So don't tell me people only know what they can see and hear, I know better. There are things in the world that are so mysterious that there aren't even words for them.

★

Caddying at the country club, I'd make a dollar a round, maybe. Not bad for a kid in 1933. It paid enough to keep me in movies and ice cream and sometimes enough to make a contribution to the family coffers. But it wasn't a real job, like working in a garage or in one of the shops around town. I just couldn't stand the idea of that—being cooped up in a box all day. I had to be out and mixing it up. I don't know, I just wasn't cut out for regular work like most people. As far as I could tell none of the other nine Basilone kids had this problem. Maybe it was wanderlust like Phyllis said, maybe it was something else.

How did people do it? It was the same in school for me. I couldn't sit still. The words went in one ear and out the other. The numbers just sat on the page and teased me. While all the time my legs were twitching to get up and run. What was I supposed to do? The clock on the classroom wall was some kind of Chinese torture device. It sometimes went backward when I looked down for a second. Then I'd look out the window and suddenly the thing would leap ahead fifteen minutes and the teacher would be calling on me for my answer. It didn't matter what I said. I knew some of the kids would laugh. I wasn't that smart in school, but I wasn't dumb, not by a long shot. I knew what was going on. I just couldn't sit still and pay attention.

No matter what I did, I was always getting into trouble. The nuns at St. Bernard's would warn me, "Johnny Basilone! If you don't settle down, we're going to take points away from you!" We had points for conduct, points for grades, points for everything.

"Take them all away," just leaped out of my mouth. I wasn't really a bad kid, just talkative. But for me school was hopeless. I hated how it made me feel. I didn't want to be a bad student and embarrass everybody, so I quit. I didn't see how it was doing any good. So to hell with it. I figured I'd get a job and be just fine.

Pop didn't like the sound of it when I told him, but he wasn't one to put up a big fight about things. He wasn't going to let me off so easy, so we went a couple of rounds at the dinner table.

"Johnny," he said to me, "what is it? Somebody bothering you at school?"

"Nah, Pop. It's just not for me. I can't keep my mind on things. I gotta be out, outside. I want to get a job. It's just not doing me any good in school."

He came at me a dozen different ways and I came back with the same reasons. I just couldn't make it work. After a while he could see it was just making me mad and he let off. He knew I was stubborn and so did everybody else in the family. That's the way it is when you're at the bottom of a pile of older brothers. If you don't stand your ground, you're gonna end up in the shit. So that's the way I am and I make no apologies.

He said I could try working for a while, maybe I'd change my mind. I was a lot like him, so he understood what I was going through easier than Mom did. He had only finished enough school so that he could read, then went to work as a tailor's apprentice when he was still a kid. He worked all his life as a tailor in hot, cramped little shops. First back in Naples, then in the States when they came over. He never complained once. In fact, he thought he had the greatest life anyone could wish for. To him America was a dream that he couldn't even imagine for the first part of his life. America had given him the ability to raise ten children in a home that he owned. He was a simple tailor, uneducated but ". . . look at my life," he said like he was showing off a castle. "Look at what I got. No man has more than me." That ended most conversations because all you could do was agree. After work on some days, he'd walk to his Italian club a few blocks from his shop, drink coffee, play dominoes and speak Italian to his buddies from the old country but that was as close as he wanted to come to Italy. They'd talk mostly about families and whose kid was doing what. They'd lie to keep up with their big hopes. One would say his kid was going to be an electrician, the next would top him about how his kid was learning everything about radios. The topper of all was somebody going to college ". . . like Mr. Roosevelt's boy." There was no place more American than Pop's Italian club. In or out of the club, nobody could say the hint of a bad word about America in front of my old man. He loved to say nobody was better than anybody else in America. So he didn't worry about my future too much. If a poor, uneducated immigrant tailor like him could live well, anyone willing to work hard could do the same.

We didn't know from nothing as kids. Raritan was in the middle of New Jersey farm country so we didn't have a lot of news like city kids. We only had what we could get off the funnies and the radio sometimes. So we were always playing Lone Ranger, fighting bad guys and Indians. One of the older guys would claim to be the Lone Ranger and that left Tonto, if you wanted to be a good guy—and I always wanted to be a good guy. I didn't mind playing Tonto because he seemed to be the one who always knew how to get out of a jam. I don't know how we kept it up for hours and hours but we did. That was mostly what it was like growing up—endless battles against bad characters and long adventure hikes into neighboring farmlands.

My stubborn streak started to show early on in life. I got it in my mind one day to tame a bull. It wasn't like I hadn't seen a bull before and didn't know what I was getting into. I knew what a bull was. I just figured other people didn't know how to handle bulls and I did. I was twelve and stubborn even then. I figured to make this bull, Archie, my pet. I could give my friends rides on him and people would be amazed at the things I could make him do. I had it all figured out. So I climbed the fence into Archie's pasture where I was warned never to go because Archie would kill me. To hell with that, I'm going to make Archie my pet, I'm thinking.

"Hi Archie," I started casually so he wouldn't catch on that I was the boss right away. He lifted his head to look at me as I crossed the pasture. I figured he would remember me since I was the kid that threw him apples sometimes. The closer I got, the bigger Archie got. I started to think maybe this wasn't such a great idea. Archie was huge. That silver ring on his nose was thick steel and dented and covered with snot. And it wasn't on his nose, it was through his nose— piercing the soft part. Now right away I figured that's why he was as mean as everybody said. Archie didn't take his eyes off me. His head was as big as a hundred-pound pumpkin and flat in front like a rock. I right away sympathized with him about the ring. I explained that when he became my pet I would get rid of it. ". . . Right boy?" I said and reached out my hand to pet him on the head. He tossed his head and looked me in the eye. Damn, now I was scared but I wasn't going to run. He was going to be my pet and that was that. I just kept talking to him soft and slow, telling him how we were going to have fun when he became my pet. I'd get him apples every day. While I was negotiating, Archie started to lower his head, keeping me in his sight at all times. He blew hard out of his nostrils. I knew he was getting mad but I also knew all animals were like that. They don't want to do anything until you make them and then they like it and everybody gets along fine. I'm just going to keep up coming here, I told Archie, so you better get used to it. You're going to be . . . I don't think I got the whole sentence out before Archie took two fast steps at me, caught me between his horns and threw me about twenty feet over his back. It happened so fast. One second I was standing there explaining to Archie how fine it was going to be when he became my pet, the next second I was ten feet in the air. I hit the down side of a little slope next to the creek that let me roll out of my fall instead of splattering flat on the ground. I rolled over and onto my feet, which were already spinning. I never ran as fast as I did that day. I was over the fence and a quarter mile down the next field before I slowed down. Archie never did become my pet.

Country life was beautiful now when I think back on it. We didn't carry our worries around like some city people you see. We swam in the creek in the summer. We swam naked because nobody had special swimming pants, so no girls were allowed except on special occasions like the Fourth of July when we reluctantly covered up. We called our local resort Bare Ass Beach. We made snow forts in the winter. We got used to being quiet. We got used to the quiet that comes over a little town when the sun quits and everybody goes inside for supper. That's how it was. We were poor. Practically everybody we knew was poor. We didn't even have a nickel to spare for candy most times but we didn't care at all. Sugar on buttered bread was just as good. We were Americans so everything was possible.

★

Older brothers throw their weight around. It's just the way things are. Shit rolls downhill so by the time you are third or fourth in the line of older brothers, you can get buried in it. One or two, maybe I could have put up with that. But me being as far down as I was, it was just too much. I fought back. I wasn't going to put up with shit from Angelo, and I wasn't going to let him boss Carlo around either because Carlo never fought back. So I took him on for both me and Carlo even though Carlo was older than me. He wasn't going to steal our stuff and make us do chores he was supposed to do, not on my watch. So I learned to fight. The older I got the better and tougher I got. At first I just took on the scarecrows I'd find in the fields. I'd shadowbox and wrestle with Carlo just to get my moves down for when the big showdown came. He'd put up a fight knowing it was all just pretend, that I wasn't really going to hurt him. But at around thirteen I started putting on muscle and that's when I started caddying. I also worked summers baling hay for the local farmers.

Now that was my kind of work. I'd stand up in the wagon as the others walked behind and snatched bales off the ground and chucked them up to me. It was usually me and a few of the farmer's sons or cousins, sometimes even his wife. These farm people were tough. I once baled hay with a sixty-year-old woman, a granny, who was throwing the bales up to me. I'd swat them on the ends with the baling hooks and hoist them up to the next guy who would stack them in the wagon. Sometimes we'd have two above me in the wagon when the stack got over six feet, one in the middle passing the bale up to the top man. There was a rhythm to the work and I laid into it, feeling the power in my arms and back. After the first day or two, when the soreness left, I could feel the bales getting lighter. It might sound boring but it wasn't. It was the group of us working together. Around noon we'd break and sit under the wagon or a tree for shade. We'd get a farm lunch brought to us—fried chicken or baloney sandwiches and lemonade. If there was a creek along the field, we'd be in it. Of course, if the female cousins or sisters were haying with us, that added a lot to the picture. The pay wasn't too good, couple of bucks a day, but I liked it and it built up my arms and shoulders so that I could swat like hell with either hand.

I wasn't near to being able to square off with any of the older guys. It seemed like they were going to torment me forever until I found out the secret; I could attack and scare the hell out of them. Even though

I was smaller, I could put on a show like I was some kind of wild Indian and get them to back down. It was a miracle to me and I remember telling myself, this was how I was going to be. If anybody bothered me, I could take care of it by getting down to business first—going on the attack. It must've first happened some time around that summer when I was fourteen. The particular incident isn't very clear but it was after I was starting to have trouble in school. We were playing cowboys and Indians or cops and robbers as usual. I had one of the few decent toy guns we owned. It might have been the one we made out of a piece of pipe. Anyway, Angelo came up and tried to bully me out of it, snatching it out of my hand. That was it. I went to work on him in a way that scared the hell out of all the kids in the neighborhood. He tried to fight me off but I had the drop on him and knocked him over to where gravity and a few rocks on the ground did the rest. He landed like a sack of potatoes and I jumped on him to get in my licks before he could get up. The other kids dragged me off but not before I had added a few bruises of my own to him. That was it. He didn't say a word at the dinner table that night and Pop could tell something had happened. Later on, George spilled to him what had happened. There was no discussion after that and he didn't bring any trouble toward me or Carlo ever again. Maybe that's how I learned the power of the attack.

I wanted to test this new power, of course, to see how far I could go. I wasn't going to pick fights with anybody or that kind of thing, but I had a real feeling I could lick almost anybody near my size. At first I just played around with kid stuff—charging over walls at people or challenging two guys to wrestle me at once. That didn't work great because I was getting too rough and it ruined the game. I was getting too big to play kid games anyway.

Before I left St. Bernard's to find my way in the world, I found a heavy bag in the school gym that almost nobody ever used. Like I said, this was about the time I was starting to have trouble in school, so the bag came in handy. After school, or even sometimes if I didn't care about being late, I'd go into the gym and take a few swats at it. I've got to tell you that felt good.

I hit that bag and I felt the power shoot from my chest, through my shoulder, down my arm and WAM!—into that bag. The thing didn't move, didn't even dent at first. It was like I was a fly beating my wings against the thing and that gave me the concentration. I just wanted to make a dent, even a little dent in that big, stupid bag. So that's where I started, trying to make a dent in a dusty, old, heavy bag. After a while I could make a dent by hitting it in the same place four or five times.

I started listening to the fights on the radio with Pop. He wasn't a big fight fan until the Italian giant Primo Carnera knocked out Ernie Schaaf in thirteen rounds in New York. Carnera was six foot, seven inches tall and weighed 270 pounds. They called him "The Amblin' Alp" because he was as big as a mountain. Pop took a lot of pride from the fact that Carnera was a new hero in America. He said if I wanted to be a fighter like Carnera, that was okay with him. That's when I really started to get to work.

Carnera was 23-2 and had even knocked out Jack Sharkey, who most people thought was going to be the champ. So he became my hero, I guess like a lot of other Italian guys. I started working hard at the heavy bag, still trying to make a little dent in it. I got to where I started to be able to make the bag move. Again, it was a slow start because I just didn't have the power yet but I was starting to get the thing to swing on its chain a little bit.

Then a surprising thing happened. Angelo decided he wanted to be my trainer and sparring partner. He'd seen some movie I think on top of being all excited by Carnera. Maybe he was thinking he wanted to be a fighter too, I don't know, but he put together a training routine from what he saw in the movie. Mainly it was running and jumping rope—we used an old piece of clothesline—and for some dumb reason, chopping wood. It was in the movie, so that's the way it had to be. I could see the problem coming again with Angelo and me. But for a while I followed his lead. We ran in the morning before school and again before dinner. He worked push-ups and sit-ups into our routine and kept track of everything in a little black notebook he kept. I've got to give him credit, he taught me discipline. He never missed a training session and wouldn't let me miss one either. It was about this time that things were taking a bad turn for me at school.

★

I don't know how much women had to do with the fact that I couldn't sit still in school, but ever since I started noticing them I've been what you might politely call a ladies' man. They liked me too, which made the problem worse. They started coming up to me and asking which one of the Basilone boys I was, which they already knew, or if I was going to go out for the football team. They would've helped me with the schoolwork if I'd asked them, I'm sure. But I would never do it. I wasn't going to pretend to know something if I didn't. I didn't care if I flunked out, I wasn't going to do it. I guess that's the bad part of being stubborn, but that's the way I am.

Marion Brown lived down the street from us. I'd known her most of my life, at least since we were little kids. We played together in the whole mix with the other neighborhood kids. When we got a little bigger and our roughhouse games got a little too rough, she stopped playing with us. I forgot about her for about five years and went on with my muddy, bloody boyhood scrapes and scrambles. As I was growing out of cops and robbers, she still stayed away. That lasted until I saw her in school when the first change of life, when we changed from kids to teenagers, came over us. She was still quiet and gentle, just the way she was as a little kid, but she was a woman. It seemed like it happened that quick. She walked around a corner one day and, there you go, she was as grown up as anything you'd see in a fashion magazine. Jesus, she was fine as china.

I couldn't keep my eyes from drifting to her and teased her when I could, just to get her attention. I sort of took up where we left off as kids, poking her arm, tickling her. The honest truth was I'd do just about anything to touch her but she put an end to that with a swat at my face that let me know where the line was. She could never hit me since I'd been practicing my head bobbing and weaving for my match up against Primo Carnera one day, but that fire in her eyes let me know where to get off. And that fire just made it all worse. I'm not saying I never looked at another girl, not by a long shot. But Marion was that special one that sort of put the others in the shade when she came around. I came right around to my polite side after I felt the wind from her right hook come across my nose. She had a pretty decent swing for a girl, you could tell there was some power behind it. I apologized right away just so she knew I wasn't one of those guys who don't know when to quit.

"You keep your hands to yourself," she said.

She looked at me, more like straight through me, getting a read on my face to see if I was some kind of joker. That was the goddamnedest five seconds of my young life. I thought I was going to fall over.

When I could, I made sure I left school at the same time as she did so I could walk with her. It wasn't like we were total strangers, so talking to her was pretty easy compared to most girls. We fell into a natural friendship again and I felt good being close to her. I wanted her to feel like she could count on me, like I could take care of anything that came up, so I bragged a little bit on the sly, letting her know I was training to be a fighter like Primo. She thought that was pretty funny but I didn't see the humor in it and got pretty hot.

It got to be where I was carrying her books home pretty much every day and being invited into her parent's house for a cider or hot chocolate as winter came on. We never made a big deal out of being together, like her having a ring or her wearing my varsity sweater—I didn't have a varsity sweater. But people knew, and we knew and that was enough.

It came to a point in my training as a fighter that I was ready to start sparring. At least that was the opinion of my manager, Angelo. I worked at first practicing bare-fisted against the palms of his hands, like he'd seen in the movie. I think it was Pat O'Brien who was in the movie and sure hoped they got it right, otherwise I might be learning all the wrong things. Anyway, I was just working on the basics of trying to hit a moving target with my fists. One thing became clear right away, I had more stamina to stand there and swing than Angelo had just to stand there and get his palms slapped. It was just like in school. I had more energy than a normal person but if I ever got in a real ring with a real fighter, that wasn't going to be the problem it was in school.

I started to dream about fights and saw all the moves—the feints, the jabs and the shot to Primo's gigantic chin that would send him sprawling like Goliath in the Bible. I was spending more and more time training and less time on my schoolwork. Maybe if Mom and Pop'd had more school themselves, they would have been able to help me more. But in our house, school was something that was supposed to help you get a good job. I could already read and write as well as anybody, so I didn't see the reason to keep beating my brains against algebra and French grammar problems. I was going to be a fighter. My fists could do the talking. I think that was something Angelo heard in the movie, because I got it from him.

It was time for real sparring. We took ten-pound flour and potato sacks, filled them up with wadded-up newspaper and tied them over our hands. It took a few minutes to form the sacks and paper into something that looked like boxing gloves but it did the trick eventually. That was when I thought the real fun would begin. I could really get a feel for the contact and see if I had what it took to get in and scrap with another fighter, even though it was only my brother. I had what it took all right, but I wouldn't use it until I got good and mad. All those years of holding back against my brother so nobody would get hurt—which would make Pop yell, meant I couldn't connect with any power. It was a tap fight, which was okay, but it didn't let me unload, which was what I was itching to do. My sisters didn't like to watch us spar, they thought it was stupid, so it was usually just us and maybe Carlo when he wanted to referee. We thought it was the height of entertainment and considered building an outdoor ring where we could charge admission to the neighbors to watch us spar. The tap fighting was good for a while. We were getting our reflexes tuned up and maybe just as important for new fighters, we were getting over the shock of getting hit. A tap on the nose, the cheek or in the gut sent the message but didn't do the damage. Our minds were getting adjusted to the idea that pain was coming and we would have to overcome it. Angelo still had the reach on me and the weight, so whenever he wanted to he could up the ante and let one of his stingers fly. I couldn't afford to get in close unless I was willing to get another stinger even worse, so for a while I stayed outside and took the occasional swat. It didn't bother me because I knew it was all part of the training. I was building up my tolerance to pain and I knew that was part of the whole picture.

It was only a matter of time, as anyone who has been around competing brothers knows, before they would have to have it out to see who was going to be the top dog in the pack. Our time came during a sparring session that was set up especially to be an official, scored event. We had a referee, probably Carlo again, and a judge or two to count the blows and time the rounds. It was billed as a three-round main event with the decision of the judges final as to who would be the new welterweight champion of Raritan, New Jersey. We didn't know what welterweight meant but it sounded better than lightweight and we knew we weren't heavyweights. So we guessed that we were welterweights. The first round started out with lots of mean looks and fancy footwork, feints, jabs and bobbing and weaving, all on display to show the crowd that we were trained professionals who knew what we were doing. Then all hell broke loose. Angelo stepped into me and walloped me with a right hand that left my ear ringing and my head spinning. I backpedaled to get away from him but he was coming right after me. Then he hit me with a combination that nearly crippled me. I wasn't ready for this attack. I thought it was going to be an exhibition match that got scored on points and skill but it looked like Angelo was going to try and knock me out. The fear and pain turned around in me when I saw what he was up to and I played possum, like I was hurt and ready to hit the deck with his next swing. I let him close in so I could get inside his reach and then I exploded on him. He walked right into the giant killer shot on the chin that I had seen in my dreams. He was Primo Carnera, the Goliath that always beat the hell out of me until I unloaded on him with an equalizer. I'm surprised that shot didn't take out a few of his teeth because we only used bubble gum as pretend rubber mouth protectors. I was mad as hell and went after him while he was still reeling. I took him apart. Apparently a few in the crowd had their problems with Angelo bullying them as well and their cheering brought Pop out to the backyard to see what the ruckus was about. He saw me whipping the living piss out of his oldest son. I didn't really know what I was doing but I was doing what came naturally to me and it landed Angelo flat on his back. Pop jumped in and pulled me away. Then everybody got real quiet. There wasn't anybody raising my arm and proclaiming me the new "Champeen of the world!!" like in my dream. It was just that sickening quiet time after any battle when the adrenaline fades and you wait to see who is going to stand up again. Angelo was just shaken up and had the wind knocked out of him. I think it was the only time I saw Pop lose his temper. After he knew Angelo was going to be okay, he wheeled on me like I was the bully after his innocent boy.

"Whatta you trying to do!" he yelled at me. "Kill somebody!" He tore the bags off my hands and sent me into the house to tell my mother what I'd done. It was the end of the Basilone Boxing Club and Training Camp. From now on if I wanted to box, I'd have to do it in a proper gym.

The Approach,
0830 Hours

★

We were about a mile offshore, still at the line of departure and I could see racks of five-inch missiles being fired from LSMRs (meaning Landing Ship Medium Rocket) that ran parallel to the beach. We were unloading the whole arsenal on them now; battleships and heavy cruisers blasted dents in the slopes of Suribachi. Navy Hellcats and Marine Corsairs flew in low and laid blankets of flaming napalm just beyond the beach and down the side of Suribachi. There was so much goddamn smoke and noise you couldn't see or hear anything. Then the guns let up, the planes flew off and there was nothing but a dust cloud where Iwo Jima used to be and the droning of our amtrac engines. This was it. A few of the boys looked up. Their faces were covered with the chalk-white flash cream. They looked like the Mexican Day of the Dead figurines they sold in some of the Mexican fruit stands around Pendleton. The line control boat waved the diagonal-striped signal flag and our driver gunned the engine. We swung out of our circle and headed straight for the beach. I don't want to give the idea that this was any kind of high-speed dash. Amtracs don't do anything at high speed, especially when they are loaded down with twenty-five men and a thousand pounds of supplies and weapons. The thing more or less waddled around and started grinding toward the beach. It didn't give you a lot of confidence that you were going to come in fast and low. Amtracs didn't move fast and they didn't turn well. They were just tanks that floated a little. If you were lucky they stayed above water and went straight ahead.

A few more of the boys tossed their steak and eggs as we came around. Tension had been ratcheting up as we turned around in circles at the rally point. This was it, we were going in.

I got up behind the .50 cal. machine gun mounted by the driver. Orders were not to fire unless we saw enemy, but I knew we wouldn't see any. After three months of waiting for us, they were dug in too deep, and the Japs were too good at camouflage. We wouldn't see a damn thing. So I planned to shoot everything, just to be sure. I chambered the .50 and squeezed off a few rounds. The driver reminded me of orders not to fire unless we saw something and I gave him my opinion, "Fuck orders and fuck you, Mac."

Except for me squeezing off a few rounds at a time, it was a quiet ride. That terrible kind of quiet. Just the engine grinding away and no other sound in the world. We got to within range of their guns and still no incoming. I didn't want to think about what might be waiting for us in the shallow surf. They'd had plenty of time to mine and booby-trap every inch of shoreline. They could impale us on steel rails just under the surface so we would block the approach, or take long, steady aim as we wallowed in at six knots and blow us out of the water. I fired off a couple more rounds into the breakers where the mines might be.

Some of the other gunners got the same idea so that "No firing until you see targets" order went all to hell real quick.

We were closing in, less than two hundred yards to go. This is where things can turn ugly fast, but still nothing. What the hell were they waiting for? I touched the little pocket Bible in my breast pocket for luck and a reminder of Lena back in San Diego. We got married a few weeks after we met at Pendleton. We'd only been married a few months and I didn't even know her that well yet, but she was a Marine, a reservist working at the mess hall. At least we had the Corps in common. I let myself see her face once, in her bridal veil, and that's all. I put her beautiful face out of my mind and got back to work. Sometimes people just pop up in your mind when you're going into combat. You have to just block them out and focus on the job. You hear what they said from years ago and you want to answer. Your mind is telling you to answer them, start the conversation again because that's where you should be, not here, riding in a tin can down somebody's gun sight. So you force your mind back to the job because that's the only thing that might get you back to that conversation someday. But you can hear some of the boys answer out loud or see them shake their heads as they talk to their mother or a brother. If you multiplied the twenty-five guys in the metal gut of this machine by all their special people, there was a decent-sized crowd that was about to hit the beach.

A hundred yards and still nothing. What the hell were they waiting for? We were lumbering through the water in these steel bathtubs and nobody's taking a shot? I opened up with the .50, sending rounds into Motoyama One, the airfield, our first objective, which was about four hundred yards inland. Even though I couldn't see anyone to shoot at, I knew they were there, dug in deep, twenty-two thousand of them. I knew their commanders' names. I knew they were going to fight to the last man. I knew they'd been there for three or four months digging in. But they weren't firing. They had to be waiting to draw us in. I fired more bursts at the airfield, cursing the sons of bitches to come out of their holes and fight.

We hit the beach and rolled up to the first terrace. The angle was too steep, we bogged down in the loose black ash. This stuff wasn't even sand, it was cinders. We were up, over the sides and onto the beach in a few seconds. We sank up to our ankles in wet black ash that tried to suck our boots off.

In front of us were terraces, fifteen-foot black mounds covered with the three previous waves of Marines. Twenty yards of beach to the water was in back of us. Our amtrac backed out into the surf, going back for the next load. I didn't recognize any of the men in front of us. Jesus, we were in the wrong sector. The plan was going to hell already and half of us hadn't even landed yet. Here we are like Spam out of the can, waiting up against a wall. The next wave was coming in behind us. The black sand mound was like quicksand. You'd take two steps and fall back one. We started to crawl up the first one. The fifth wave landed and started coming up behind us. We were bunching up. The radios were crackling with orders, whole units were landed in the wrong sector. I had no idea where the rest of my C Company was. We still had no targets and no incoming fire. We sucked air slogging up these black cinder mounds. It was useless trying to dig in. The loose sand just filled in as fast as you scooped it out. Marines with their Doberman war dogs tried digging together. The dogs were throwing out more sand than their masters but the holes weren't getting any deeper. Getting over the first terrace and up to the second terrace was like running through dry cement up to your knees.

"Fix bayonets!" I ordered my boys. The Japs would spring the trap any second now and I could imagine them swooping over the terraces on top of us. Banzai! would be the last thing we'd hear on this earth. But still nothing, just the sound of amtracs beaching behind us and officers yelling to find their units. Maybe Topside was right. Maybe the thousands of shells and bombs we threw at them did the trick. Maybe we'd just move in and mop up. Maybe this really was a seventy-two-hour operation. The fifth wave was practically on top of us. We were getting packed in like sardines. This was bad, real bad. I looked over to my left, up at Suribachi towering over us. Something on the burned lava wall moved. Jesus Christ, they were still there. We hadn't even touched them. They were looking straight down at us, sighting us in.

★ 2 ★

Manila John

*Pvt. John Basilone and friends, Manila,
Phillipines, 1935*

This match was for all the marbles. I wasn't really looking forward to twelve rounds with this Danish farmer, a machinist's
mate on a Navy destroyer, who looked like he could bend horseshoes
in each hand. I was 18-0, over half were knockouts but these were
against guys in the outfit. The Dane had a dozen pro fights, at least
that was the rumor. My CO and every man in camp had laid down a
month's pay on the bet that I was going to take this swabbie apart
like the other guys I fought. But this big shitkicker looked like he
enjoyed his work. I'd heard he stove in a guy's ribs with his right

hook and that soldier never walked straight again. He was that raw-boned kind of farmhand I used to toss hay bales to. The kind that worked all day in the hot sun and then tossed hay bales up into the hayloft half the night. These guys didn't feel pain. They were all baling wire and leather. You have to kill them to get them to stop.

After three years of garrison duty in Manila, these Army buddies of mine were near stir-crazy and would have bet their left nut on a roach race. Jesus Christ if there wasn't a war soon, these guys would start one. I could hear them screaming for blood—mine, the Dane's, they didn't care. They just wanted to see someone get the shit beat out of them. My hands were getting taped when the CO came in. I made a move. "At ease," he said. "Basilone, you are a bastard breaker of hearts and killer of men. Am I right?"

"Yes, sir."

"You are going to teach this swabbie son of a bitch something about pain, are you not?"

"Yes, sir."

"That's good, son, how you feel?"

"I feel like getting into a fight, sir."

"I'll bet you do. I've got fifty bucks that's saying you're going to knock this guy out. Should I get my money back?"

"No, sir."

He clapped me on the shoulder and left trailing cigar smoke, and I went in to my hunker-down before a fight. I see the punches landing. I see the Dane swing and miss. I see my combination find its mark and the big Dane hit the canvas. Soon it's going to be time to go, so I say an "Our Father," hoping this Danish shit-shoveler doesn't break my neck.

Street in Manila, circa 1936

Lolita

So far Army life had been okay by me. Since we steamed into Manila Harbor in 1936, we'd been chasing bandits all over the islands who had been harassing the local police and terrorizing the countryside. I was a specialist machine gunner so I had the privilege of humping a Browning water cooled over ten miles of jungle trails and back when it came time for duty. The only good thing about it was that my arms and shoulders got to be as hard as the steel I carried. I could crack a walnut in the crook of my arm. And my legs were used to carrying the extra seventy pounds up hill and down. I could run all day long.

When we weren't chasing these poor, raggedy-assed bandits through the jungle, we tended to chase local skirts around Manila. I was in a leaky nipa hut one day after the clouds opened up with the regular afternoon monsoon rain. A girl ran in to get out of the rain. Her hair was black, long past her shoulders. Her wet sarong clung to her and that was just about the last thing I remember, except her

name was Lolita. Or that's what she called herself. She was trying to
be a whore or a housewife to a willing GI, either one probably would
have been okay. She was the most beautiful woman, still to this day,
that I've ever seen. She had the almond Oriental eyes with light,
honey-brown irises. She never did tell me her last name. I guessed
she didn't want me dropping into her parents' house one night. She
was Catholic, like everybody in the barrio, where I guessed she
came from, so that helped, giving us something in common. She was
Oriental mixed with Spanish dark skin and hair—lips tan on the
outer rim with a line of rose pink next to her teeth. I just kept looking
at her—I think we were together almost every day for the next four
or five months. Those first few weeks were like a fever-dream where
things seem real but aren't. I'd see the shape of her in a drying
blouse on a clothesline. I thought I could hear her just behind me
sometimes. I was eighteen years old and crazy as a raped ape for
pussy and target practice. Target practice was just about the only
thing that got my mind off of her. I'd load up a belt in a heavy—this
was what we called the Browning .30 cals—and I'd tear the hell out
of something. Sometimes I'd cut down a tree with it. I'd be laughing
like a hyena, firing lots of tax dollars' worth of ammunition at an
innocent palm tree. Anybody who has a feel for automatic weapons
knows what I mean. You don't want to be on the wrong side of a
poontang-crazed eighteen-year-old with a machine gun, that much I
know for sure.

I don't know if she was seeing other GIs, probably so, but that
was the game unless I was going to pop the question, take care of
her. Maybe I should have. For the time being it was okay. I wasn't
about to settle down. I'd just got away from that racket back in Raritan and I wasn't about to be boxed in for a while yet.

Once in a while, laying on my bunk in the mosquito farm we called camp, I'd think about making it official with her. But how would it work? I'd be shipped out most of the time unless I bucked the Army and got a 9 to 5. I just didn't see it. So half the time, when I was with her, I was okay—the other half, I wanted to drown any son of a bitch who looked at her. Jesus Christ on a crutch, sometimes I thought I was going Section 8, meaning crazy in G.I. language. Lolita, goddamn beautiful Lolita.

Round One

So this fucking Dane comes out of his corner in a crouch like he's expecting incoming fire. I circle with him and he's ranging me in, then starts trying to hook me. Then he unloads like a steel piston into my ribs and I almost lose my mouthpiece from the force of it. Goddamn that hurt. I came off my stance and crouched low with him, tucking my elbow over my sore ribs. Now I'm off balance. I hear Albie screaming from my corner over the thousands of other men screaming at me. He's yelling, "Box! Box him!" I know he's right so I come up a little and then I'm looking down at this sweaty farm animal in front of me with no target except the top of his Scandinavian cement head. I test him with an overhand right, he counters with a straight shot that nails me just under the heart. Shit, that hurt too! I saw his opening so I go at him again, same overhand right. He counters but I'm ready. I slip his counter and come up and across with my left, pay dirt. His thick head bounces off the end of my fist and he loses a step. I figure I could probably punch this cow-humper in the head all night and end up with nothing but sore hands but it's all I've got to work with. We stepped around each other for a while swatting, dodging—him trying to hook me and me trying to upper-cut him. Not much happens except we fend off each other's punches. The bell rang and I walked back to my corner thinking, goddamn, this is going to be a long night. I saw Lolita, second or third row back, hands over her mouth. She looked scared as hell.

★

When the black silk kimono arrived from the Philippines I heard Mom didn't know what to do with it. It was too exotic for any occa-sion she could imagine. I know Lolita spent half the money I gave her on it but I couldn't stop her. She was something. That's when I guessed that she wasn't whoring, but you never can be completely sure. Or maybe she stopped because we were starting to like each other. She made an awful convincing show of going to church and saving her money from working in her uncle's bicycle shop. I wanted to believe her.

Round Two

Round two was when we got into it good. I wasn't going to make twelve rounds with this meat-grinder, I already felt my ribs turning purple. One more good swat at them and he'd break one for sure. I knew I had knockout power, so I was determined to turn the lights out on the Dane. The goddamn guys were yelling so loud you al-most couldn't hear the bell. The place was full of smoke from thou-sands of cigarettes that glowed in the haze around me. Albie screamed in my ear to box him, stay away from him. I heard him and said to myself, fuck that, I'm ending this right now. I nodded so Albie would think I was taking his advice. I walked out, stepped into my range and threw a straight right at the Dane's head. It went through his gloves and boom, right on the kisser. Shit, he was mad now and came at me like a windmill, hooking left and right. He caught me with a left and just about caved my head in. He saw me go weak and was on top of me looking to finish me off. I roped in his arms and hung on for dear life. I should've listened to Albie. He wrestled to get free but I got him clinched in good and rested on the ropes. The ref came to break it up and I took a couple of swats from him before I let go. Albie was screaming, "Stay away! Stay away!" as I backpedaled out of range. The Dane kept coming, throwing whistlers past my nose, but I slowed him up with a few hard, quick shots to his gut. Round two ended and I was sinking fast. I looked around and didn't see Lolita. I guessed she couldn't take it.

★

Practically all we did in camp was gamble and swap lies about the girls in Manila. So with Lolita's connections in town and my understanding of my brothers-in-arms, we created a kind of a nightclub in her uncle's shop. We'd move the bikes outside in front and string up a line of colored lights. When the sun went down the bikes made it look like half of Manila had pedaled over to see where the action was.

In a few weeks the place was doing good. We rigged a few boards on top of her uncle's oily workbench and that was the bar. We had local beer and stuff made out of cactus and palm fruit. I didn't know everything that was in it, I just knew that if you drank enough of it the next day you wanted to shoot yourself. So we called it Mother's Milk. We sold a lot of it because the boys were generally in a hurry and beer took time. Gambling was illegal, so we staked the crap games outside, technically off the premises. Lolita arranged for the local musicians to come by some nights and some of her girlfriends made it a regular stop when the fleet was in.

I had to keep an even keel and didn't drink any of what we sold except a beer now and then. I was in training all the time for the camp bouts that were the main entertainment in camp. This fight training also came in handy when some hophead missed his point out back and comments about the shooter's mother started to fly. After a while, we got to be able to hear whether it was serious or not. Generally a couple of swings would quiet one or another of the gents and then peace would be restored. The clicking of dice against the back wall would start up again and the guys would start up squawking about their good luck and cursing the bad.

Round Three

The goddamn wheels came off. I've always been as stubborn as a constipated mule and round three is when it cost me. I'm really not enjoying fighting this sailor and I still figure I can end it quick. I come out of my corner the same way, ignoring Albie. I walk right up to the Dane like I'm going to box with him and then nail him with a shot, right in the chops. I wade in figuring I'm going to clean this fella's clock and then hit the showers. But he's a cagey kind of Dane and he's playing possum. He dances away like he's hurt and I fall for it. I chase after him and he swings to keep me off but he had no power, or he didn't put any behind the punches to throw me off, which is more likely. Beer bottles are starting to fly across the ring and I see the MPs coming in out of the corner of my eye. Now I'm winding up because I figure this is good-night for the Dane. The soldiers and sailors watching us were getting to the point where they were going to finish the third round themselves if we didn't start fighting again and end this square dance. I figure the Dane is about out of steam so I wade in and throw my right, my knockout punch. I must have telegraphed it because from somewhere a bolt of lightning hits me in the left side of my head. I go down hard and the lights are flickering. The place roars even louder so that it sounds like another typhoon is hitting. The floor is vibrating, I feel my head bouncing on the canvas. Around the count of three I wake up and see the ref throwing fingers at my face. I can barely hear what he's saying. I crawl over to the ropes and get on one knee. Albie's screaming at me to take a nine count so I stay down. Six, seven, eight, I hear the ref. I wobble up on nine and stand there as the ref looks in my eyes.

"What's your name?" he yells into my face.

"Basilone," I answer. He wipes my gloves on his shirt and is about to unleash the Dane on me again when the bell rings.

In the corner, Albie works on me with the smelling salts. He's hopping mad. "What'd I tell you? Y'can't trade punches with this guy!" He went on and on about me staying away, backing off. I figure he's probably right, he's trained pros stateside so I should probably listen to him. It sounds like the place is coming apart with all the yelling. The ref kicked a piece of fruit off the canvas that somebody had thrown in. Albie puts in my mouthpiece, gives me another shot of salts. The bell rings.

Round Four

"Stay away from him," Albie yells for the last time. I know it's good advice and the right thing to do. But to hell with it. I'm going in just like I did it the last three rounds. That's what I mean about being stubborn. I just can't stop when I get something in my head.

This time the Dane comes out looking for the kill. No more playing possum. He's got a cut over his eye and he's looking to end this match too. I started in again with a combination and he came back with a counterpunch that missed. I went at him again and connected. It rocked him back and he jabbed but didn't have any snap on it. I figure he wasn't faking it this time and stepped inside his hooking range. I went to work and then he started falling back fast. He whacked me a couple times and I gave it right back to him. This fight wasn't going to round five. Somebody was going to be kissing the canvas here real quick. He hit me as hard as he could and I hit him back as hard as I could. There wasn't any art or skill left in it. It was a bar brawl. We just went at it, toe to toe, both fists working, hitting each other with everything we had left. Somewhere in all the sweat and blood flying around, he came up out of his crouch finally and I let my right fly. It landed dead center on his nose and kept going. His head rolled back. He rocked back on his heels and then went over like a tall tree.

The ref waved me off to a neutral corner and gave the Dane the full ten count. The Dane was flat on his back, not moving. The ref pulled his mouth guard and the doc and trainers jumped in the ring. The yelling stopped. I joined the crowd at center ring. I see the Dane's eyes flutter. He came around. They helped him up and over to his corner.

Albie didn't know whether to shit or kiss me. He was so damn mad. This was my nineteenth fight. Maybe I wanted to prove something to myself, that's why I traded punches and took the chance of getting knocked out. I'm not sure, but it was over now and I made it. There was nobody left in the Army or the Navy to fight unless I wanted to go up a weight class. I figured there had to be a better way to spend an evening. This was my last fight.

★

That weekend Manila was crowded with soldiers spending all the sailors' money. The only thing I got besides sore hands and a busted-up face was the nickname "Manila John." Guys were coming at me from all directions just wanting to shake hands and say hello. I was a hero. For the first time in my life, I was somebody special. I had shot glasses of Mother's Milk lined up on the bar from one end to the other. Everybody who came in bought me a drink. This particular night we were extra loud and the cops came around to shut us down. The party was just getting going so we took to the streets to see who else might have us. Down on the docks were a few mean little dives for sailors who didn't want to attract attention—the kind of place where you could get someone's throat cut for the price of a bottle. We'd been warned in camp about these kinds of places but we were in the middle of a party and didn't much care what the Army had to say at this point. A few more rounds of drinks and I was pretty numb. I got it into my head that I ought to marry Lolita. How that came over me, I'll never know but it was important to show I was serious. A few of the drunks who were going to be my best men, got me over to a tattoo parlor to seal the deal. On my good right arm I had the picture of a Lolita tattooed. It was a picture of a dance hall girl, somebody from the Wild West days, which was as close to Lolita as the one-eyed artist had available. A week later when the scabs fell off and she could make out the picture, Lolita took a good look at it and didn't like it much. It really didn't look like her at all.

The attention was good for a while, everybody looking up to me like that. It made me feel like I finally found a place in the world, like I wasn't secretly some shitbird who wouldn't ever amount to much. It was one of those times when you could be in a room with presidents or generals and you knew for sure that you were as good as they were. The voice stops, the voice in your head that keeps you on your toes. It's got nothing more to say for a while because you are at the top of a mountain. There's nowhere else to go for a while and you can be quiet and just enjoy the view. It was like that for a while after the fight—quiet in my head.

The more I thought about it the more I knew I was good at only one thing, fighting. I don't just mean boxing. All through duty in Manila as I was coming up from welterweight to light heavyweight, I was getting letters from fight managers in the States telling me I should sign up with them when I finished my bit for the country. That wasn't it. I could get by like a lot of the jokers in the Army who go back to jobs in factories and offices when their stint is up. I could make myself do that somehow but I would never be good at it. I'd be faking it like most of them do. A lot of them, if they could handle the discipline and the shitty food, would be like me. They would be fighters. That's the only way I fit into the picture. They'll go back to their world of sofas and Sunday dinners. They'll get old and get soft white bellies from working all day at a desk. But not me. I won't make it in that world.

There is another, darker world that most of them didn't see. But I did, and I learned not to talk about it. I knew what was coming. I saw it years before in Raritan. I saw trouble with the Japanese and everybody said I was crazy. The GIs thought it was an accident that they were in the Philippines, but it wasn't an accident for me. Like Father Amedeo Russo said, God had a plan for me. I guessed the Philippines was part of it.

The news came from time to time while I was in Manila—the enemy was on the march. Then the news came about their tactics. I hadn't imagined anything about the cruelty that was reported. They used bayonets and swords on civilians. Why would they do that? I didn't understand it. If this was part of God's plan for me, I didn't want any part of it. I could be a soldier. I could fight. I just didn't understand the cruelty of the enemy. Why the cruelty against civilians?

THE EMPIRE OF JAPAN

In over two thousand years of warfare, Japan never lost a battle on land or sea. For generations, the Japanese military dominated Asia. The military grew to dominate Japanese civil society, even to dictating the terms of a new war to Emperor Hirohito. In 1905, they wrested Korea from a weak and disorganized China and by 1910 after three years of warfare officially annexed the country, enslaving thousands of Koreans into the service for the emperor. By 1932, the need for conquest moved the Japanese to invade Manchuria. After Manchuria, they crushed China completely. In each place they conquered by arms and ruled by terror; beheading, raping and torturing civilians. Brutality toward the weak was seen as a virtue. Weakness was despised as much among themselves as among their enemies. Soldiers considered themselves dispensable under a new, fatalistic interpretation of the ancient warrior code of "bushido" which stated that ". . . death was lighter than a feather but duty was heavier than a mountain." The suicidal "banzai" charge and the kamikaze tactics were a direct result of these perverted teachings of bushido. The "Spirit Warriors" of the new Japan, as they called themselves, were simply cynical, bureaucratic military officers whose true concern was only for their own grip on power. They inserted their bizarre, militaristic death cultism even into the primary education system of Japan that taught strict marshal values, the insignificance of the individual and devotion to the new God they created for Japan, the living Emperor Hirohito.

As an infant, Hirohito had been taken from his mother and raised by an admiral, a hero of the recent Russo-Japanese War, a victory of Japan over Russia. The boy's father, the weak and feeble-minded Emperor Taisho, was dominated completely by the military commanders who had served his own father, the Emperor Meiji, in decisively defeating the Russians at the battle of Tsushima. This stunning victory announced to the world that Japan was no longer an isolated backwater like its neighbor, the flaccid China that had been exploited and subjugated to Europe and America. Japan was now worthy of inclusion into the club of dominating military powers of the world that included the United States. The decorated admiral raised the young Emperor Hirohito in the traditions of the newly powerful Japanese military class that claimed legitimacy from the ancient ways of the samurai warriors. But these new militarists were not samurai. They were commoners who had studied European strategy and tactics and then graduated to become career military men. They issued orders from the comfort of their offices in Tokyo to thousands of conscripts fighting on the muddy, bloody battlefields of distant territories. They issued orders as well to young Prince Hirohito, who had learned only war from them. At their command, he became the living God of Japan. At their command as well, the soldiers and citizens of Japan gave their full devotion and lives to serve him.

Technologically, the armed forces of Japan were considered the most advanced in the world. The powerful Mitsubishi "Zero" airplane was the fastest, most maneuverable fighter in the sky. The navy boasted the largest battleship in the world, the *Nagano*, with a supporting fleet of modern aircraft carriers and battle groups.

They believed they were invincible, they believed they were commanded by a living God—the Emperor, they believed they would control the entire Pacific up to and including the Panama Canal. They believed they would eventually strangle the United States and that a defeated enemy was weak and did not deserve mercy. They were merciless even to their own fighting men who were ordered to commit suicide rather than surrender and if wounded in battle were expected to kill themselves rather than burden their unit with their care.

The Japanese military was being starved of resources, particularly oil by America and her allies, who wanted to reign in Japan's power. Without imported oil, the nation of Japan faced economic collapse. Its military could not operate. To survive, the armies of Japan infused with yamato damashii, the spirit of Japan, and under the spiritual guidance of their own living God, were forced to attack.

At Loose Ends

I hadn't thought much about what happens to a caddy between November and April. September came around and a lot of the other caddies went back to school somewhere so those of us who were left got more trips around the greens. By mid-October the wait between trips got longer and longer. I felt pretty stupid when I realized I was going to be out of a job soon. The only thing worse than waiting on a slow player, was not waiting on a slow player.

The wind started smelling like snow and the world moved on without me. People went on about their business and I was sitting it out in the caddy shack. I'd walk home some nights with a buck or two for the whole day. Then I felt like a real fool. I was embarrassed to talk to anybody, especially Marion, in case she would ask me how I was getting along outside of school.

Pop was on my back. "Johnny, why don't you go back to school?" he'd say. It must've been hard for him to watch me. I was getting hunkered down and quiet like I do when I have to figure things out. I don't know why but I just can't talk. I just got nothing to say.

"It's just not for me. I'll be all right," I told him. He never rode me about it. Stubborn as I am, it would've just made things worse, and he knew it.

I started going by St. Ann's on the days when the weather was bad. I'd sit by myself and pray, asking for a sign to let me know what to do next. Father Amedeo Russo saw me and knew I was in some kind of trouble. He came up and asked me if I wanted to talk. At first I didn't, I still felt too ashamed of being so dumb about quitting school and having no job. After a few days of coming in and getting no answers, I was getting worried that I'd never figure it out. I must have stared at those stained-glass windows for hours trying to figure out if there was a message in them. Stations of the Cross. All I got was how Jesus must have felt like me carrying that big, wooden cross. He must've thought I really don't know what the hell I am doing to be in such a mess. Or maybe he was above it all, but that's not the way they showed it in the glass. His head hurt from the thorns. He was in agony and nobody could help him. He lost hope and not even his Father, who was God, could help him, like me. Those were some of my worst days. With the weather closing in I couldn't stay outside but I couldn't stay in the house either. I had to find a place to hide until I sorted things out in my mind. I tried the diner and the library and the hardware store but everywhere I went I was just wasting time. It's a terrible feeling when you know that there is something you could be great at but you just don't know what it is. It made me kind of sick with worry and maybe even a little crazy after a week or so of wandering around like somebody who'd lost his marbles. Father Russo would keep things private, I knew that, so I just walked up to his office one day and knocked on the door. That was about the smartest thing I did that whole year.

He was a great man and a smart man. He could have been a lawyer or a judge or run a big company but he gave it all up, everything, to be a priest. All he wanted was to help other people and didn't want anything for himself. That got me thinking right away. How do you just do that, give up everything for other people? And why do you do it? It didn't make much sense to me because I was just a kid and I wasn't thinking about anybody but me.

He gave me my confidence back because he didn't talk to me like I was some stupid kid who didn't know what the hell was going on. He talked to me like I was as smart as him and he talked first so I wouldn't have to. He didn't know what he wanted when he was a teenager either, so right away I knew I didn't have to go into the whole sad story of why I couldn't figure anything out. He kept talking and came to a point in his story where he said he got the calling. That's when it all started to come into view in my mind. A calling. I needed some kind of calling.

He had finished college on his own dime. Nobody gave him a thing. He had a girlfriend then and probably could have gotten any job he wanted. I could see him as a young guy, kind of the bookworm type. But then he got his calling and he gave it all up. My mind started spinning. I knew I wasn't supposed to just sit around and waste my days. Then I started talking. He listened a lot and asked me a few questions like Pop did only he told me I didn't have to have the answers. He just asked me questions so I would think about what I was supposed to do. It wasn't what I wanted to do, or what I thought I should do. It was what I was supposed to do, what I had to do in my heart of hearts, the way he put it. He let me know that I didn't have to figure out everything myself. I was just supposed to sit on it and stew while God tried to get through to me with my calling. All I had to do was watch and listen and I would know what was right for me. You could see Father Russo smiling as he got to that part because he knew it was the greatest gift he could give me. It was Christmas Eve and he was Santa Claus. I guess it was a bigger deal than I thought because it hit me like a ton of bricks, all of a sudden. I felt like I was going to cry. I felt so good, like I'd just been let out of jail, or what it must feel like, because I'd never been in jail. It was confusing. I felt like he'd saved my life, but I wanted to cry. I thought to hell with that, I'm not crying. Only women cry when they're happy, so I left. Didn't even say thanks.

The next day I was changed completely. I went looking for any other kind of job, a clerk, or anything. There wasn't much in Raritan

that I hadn't tried before. I told myself it didn't matter I'd only finished eighth grade but deep down, it still bothered me. I was looking
for my calling so I could ignore most of the chatter in my head that
kept telling me I still didn't know what the hell I was doing, Father
Russo or no Father Russo. It got to where I would get up early and go
out like I was going to the golf course but I'd walk the streets of
Raritan trying to think of what I could do. I'd hitch a ride up to Bound
Brook and Somerville, sometimes all the way to Newark. I figured I'd
land something up that way. It was Depression times, 1933, so nobody was handing out jobs on the corner.

People liked me. They liked my looks. I was a damn good-
looking kid and that's the truth. So I had a leg up when I walked in
the door most places. I didn't put on airs. I spoke straight and respectful to people so they tended to give me a break. On my second
or third trip, I found a part-time job stocking plumbing fixtures in
Newark. It looked cold as hell in that stockroom, piles of iron on
four sides. Not much company there. Not like the caddy shack
where at least I could play poker all day with the old duffers and
stay in the country. It was dark in that stockroom and small,
crowded all around with walls of cold iron in steel bins. It looked
like Hell after it froze over. I knew I should take the job. It was a
gift. But I knew I couldn't take it. If this was my calling, I was really in one hell of a big mess. I wouldn't last a month. But I couldn't
come right out and admit it to myself. When you're young you can
bullshit yourself better. I told myself, if I found that job, there had
to be others. Also, I'd have to move to Newark. I don't remember
exactly what all I said to myself but it was enough. I never went back
to Newark again.

So there I was back at Pop's kitchen table with another few weeks past and me with nothing to show for them. It got to where he didn't want to say anything and I didn't want to hear it anyway. I was going to have to go back to school or make good somehow. Sometimes I'd go out in the morning to spy on the kids as they walked to school. It was just up from the corner of Clinton Street where they all turned up toward school. I was looking each of them over, imagining how they'd treat me if I decided to go back. I'd be admitting I was wrong and I'd be no better at school than when I left. It was dead-on winter now of 1933, heading toward 1934. I only did the spying a few times, mostly to see if anyone was carrying Marion's books. Nobody was. It didn't matter. What would she want with me now anyway, who couldn't even get a job?

She wasn't one to call it quits though, I found out. She always wanted to know how the job search was going—always wishing the best for me. I knew that if I was in school we could go to dances and games together. But now, I didn't think it would be such a good idea. When I ran into kids they'd ask me how I was getting along in the big, bad world. I didn't let on how things really were.

"Never better. Working on my first million." I'd say something like that, never getting into the whos and wheres of it. That's when I'd really start to feel bad. Seems I could bullshit myself easier than I could bullshit other people. I'd hear every lie come back to me at night when I was trying to get to sleep. I'd hear it until my head hurt. That's when I began to hear the voice, my voice, telling me where I was going wrong. I didn't know if I was cracking up or if this was God trying to get through like Father Russo said. Anyway, that's the way the voice started to come to me and I just let it come. I needed all the help I could get.

The Science and Art of Card Playing

Of course the truth was that I wasn't doing any better out of school than I had in school. In spite of Father Russo's great help, it was hard for me to wait around for God to tell me what to do. I was never that religious to begin with, so after a few days I started having real doubts. Just when I was beginning to think that maybe I was just a misfit, that I didn't have what it takes to have a normal life or that maybe God's plan for me was to sit around and go nuts, I became a student of the art and science of card playing.

Since it was always God's plan that I become a soldier, there was no better preparation for that life than learning to play cards. Gambling has always been the main source of entertainment for soldiers and I was about to get my higher education in that art.

The games rotated from pinochle to tonk to poker, stud and draw. Once in a while some oddball would come in with a new game like night baseball that had to do with variable wildcards, that nobody much liked. The caddy shack was my classroom for this course of study and it had all the comforts of home if you lived in a cave on the run from the law. The management of the country club provided us with a round dining table that was perfect for our purposes. An old canvas tarp covered it so we wouldn't burn it with our butts or nick it up. The caddy shack itself wasn't really a shack at all but the root cellar of the old farmhouse that was now the clubhouse of Raritan Country Club. It was bermed into the side of the little rise the starter's office sat on so no matter what kind of weather was outside, it was always that same root-cellar cool.

The math of cards caught me. That's the only way I can explain it. I could figure the odds and read people a whole lot better than I could read a textbook. If they had made a way to teach lessons with card games I would have done a lot better in school. I wasn't much of a talker anyway, so cards suited me. I could sit quietly for a long time in the company of the caddies, some young and some old duffers, who had been through a lot in their own ways. I could slip in questions that got them to talk about how they figured out what they were supposed to do in life. Mostly it was a lot of baloney because, after all, they'd wound up sitting in this root cellar with me all day. But still, once in a while, we'd get onto a subject that gave me a picture of another life I could choose. So that's how it went for a while. Me sitting with the caddies talking about anything that came into our heads, playing cards, while it rained, snowed and hailed outside. I made a bit of money some days, which I gave back the next, so it looked at home like I was at least doing something useful. The club let us stay because most of us had nowhere else to go and they always liked to have extra hands around for work on the grounds or repairs on the clubhouse if they came up. We put in a potbelly stove and had our very own gentleman's card club, complete with an icebox, a sink, garden tools and a few hundred-pound bags of fertilizer for the putting greens. We feathered our gambler's nest with a cast-off couch and a reading lamp. We were planning to keep the game going until spring, and I believe many of the original members made it. I didn't.

I think it was some time in February when I looked down and noticed I was sharing my upholstered chair with a field mouse. This mouse was as determined to stay out of the weather as I was, so unless I was going to eat him, he was staying put. He was either the bravest or dumbest mouse I ever met. Either way he became our mascot and soon was making a good living in peanuts that were always part of our game. For some reason the mouse began to get to me. He was always around, always hungry and always looking to us to take care of him. He wasn't going anywhere and after a while I knew that neither was anyone else in that cellar. I began to feel a stirring, that cooped-up feeling, and the cards lost their shine. What the hell was I doing sitting out the days and weeks in some root cellar with a mouse! I said to hell with it. I thanked the fellas for all their money that was now mine and told them I was joining the Army. And that's exactly what I did.

★ 3 ★

In the Army Now

Fort Jay, Governor's Island, New York

After the first couple of days, basic was a game to me. I never had trouble with the physical training. I was already a pretty good athlete. When it came to following orders, well, that's what I joined up for. The truth was I wanted somebody to tell me the right way to do things. I wasn't about to be a failure at soldiering too, so when they told me to do something, I gave it everything I had. If the drill instructor wanted twenty push-ups, I gave him thirty. If they wanted volunteers for a detail, I was first in line. I was the perfect recruit. I was there to learn. I was there to become a soldier and that's all I cared about.

When our DI realized I wasn't putting him on, he took a shine to me and had me demonstrate the way he wanted things done. Basic training was the only school where I went right to the head of the class. It made me feel like I was finally doing something right. And where some guys only found things to complain about, I just remembered sitting in that root cellar with the starving mouse. Maybe they came from big, fancy places somewhere, but I came from nothing and nowhere. Not that I didn't love my family, but I had nothing to go back to.

My first unit was the 16th Infantry, Company D, stationed at Fort Jay on Governor's Island in New York Harbor. This place went all the way back to the Revolutionary War. It guarded the approach to New York City. To me it was a country club—172 acres of greens, training grounds and beaches. It was out in the middle of the harbor so the sea breezes kept it cool through my basic training that summer of 1934. The old granite and brick fort was low and thick, laid out in the classic six-pointed defense perimeter. It gave you the feeling you could make a stand here against anybody. There were even a few golf holes on the island so I could keep up my short game. All through the summer, I worked on my two specialties, machine gunning and poker. I also had a very active hobby across the harbor in Manhattan when we had passes off the base. This involved young ladies who seemed to be attracted to men in uniform. All in all, the Army was shaping up to be the kind of life that was tailor-made for me.

Even my specialty, machine gunner, suited me down to the ground. When I imagined myself in some future battle, even though I had no idea what a real battle was like, I only knew what I'd seen in the movies, I knew I wanted to be behind a machine gun. Outside of a tank, I figured that was the most powerful weapon on a battlefield and I'd be damned if I was getting into a tank if I could help it. I couldn't even stand being in a room all that much. I wouldn't last ten minutes inside a tank.

The first time we rolled our 1917A Browning water-cooled .30 calibers out of the old fort's magazine on their caissons, they looked to me like something I could handle. They were human sized. They weren't complicated.

We rolled them out to the gunnery ranges and spent the next six weeks of our boot camp learning the weapon. You could see the rest of the boys getting excited as the Sarge went through the ins and outs of the machine. He seemed to go on forever. You could see he had given this instruction a hundred times, exactly the same way each time—by the book. The name and army designation—everything had an Army short name. The 1917A, its military purpose, capabilities, operating procedure, safety procedure, parts and assembly—it went on all day. By the afternoon, we were ready to get our hands on one and try it out. Sarge went on, the strategy of infantry assault, interlocking fields of fire, trajectory, care and maintenance. Just before chow, we set them up on the range and squeezed off our first rounds. For me it was a God-given moment. It was pure thunder in my hands. The most awesome personal weapon ever built. With correct technique, the gun could fire almost continuously for days before the barrel had to be replaced. It could fire in all weather, in all directions and accurate at 150 yards. It was like a living thing, like the bull that nearly killed me. It was that overpowering. Suddenly I was safe against a hundred bulls or a thousand men or anything else. I was safe, but nothing else was. I was like the God who throws thunderbolts.

We went in to eat and it was like the whole unit got hit by the same bolt of lightning. It had passed through them and out their arms. We were different people than we had been that morning. We had earned the power to destroy. After some chat at the start of dinner, nobody talked much. At lights out, the Devil came to visit me, wanting to share my new power. I saw visions of destruction and felt the temptation of glory. Father Amedeo's had warned me of all types of temptations, in particular glory. In a whisper, I told the Devil to go away. I didn't want anyone to hear me and think I was nuts. I was too tired to pay attention anyway.

★

We were all youngsters, practically all of us under twenty. So naturally we turned everything into a game—target practice, memory of weapon parts, blindfolded assembly. Then, being soldiers, we bet on the games. It made things more interesting. It also made things more clear. It showed us that our bad gunners were more likely to wind up dead, so they might as well give us their money first. I won quite a few bets putting the Brownie together blindfolded. Nobody could beat me. It wasn't that I was such a great mechanic; it was just something I put my whole mind to. I was going to be good at this soldiering, no matter what. I'd take the thing apart and put it back together again dozens of times while a buddy timed me. We figured we had to get paid for all the time we were putting in practicing so we'd find some blowhard to go up against me. I'd do the old dopey routine with my pisscutter, Army-speak for peaked cap, off a bit sideways on my head. The mark would take one look at me and I'd stare him in the eye with my hat on sideways. He wouldn't know whether to piss or go blind. He'd go for it. We never lost. Barney, from Rutherford, roped them in and I beat everybody by a full ten seconds. I started to think I could beat some of them with one hand. The only problem was there were only a few hundred men on base, and word got around pretty fast.

The whole time at Fort Jay, I was still only forty miles away from home. With a two or three day pass, I'd get to show off my uniform back in Raritan, prove to people that I wasn't an aimless dropout. Everyone made such a fuss you'd think they never saw a soldier before. I think they were just happy I'd made something of myself.

I always managed to squeeze in at least a few holes at the country club when I was back. I'd poke my head in the caddy shack and grab a partner, break up the card game, so I wouldn't have to go out single. It was a great feeling knowing that in an hour or two I was going to walk out of there and not have to come back. It was good to see the faces of old friends. They still carried bags for rich men and old men and any lady. They were the escorts of people enjoying themselves. It seemed like such a carefree life now. I imagined that I'd soon be in places where I'd want to be back in the cellar playing cards with these guys. But I signed the paper, the Army gave me my food and my clothes, they gave me a job. I had a dangerous job and I was happy about it. The danger seemed far away.

Then, for the second time, there on the fairway of Raritan I saw my future clearly. The picture wasn't complete but it was clear. I saw that I would be in a war against Japan, and soon. Maybe it was just common sense but I saw what I saw and said so. This time people didn't say I was overexcited. The papers had the stories about the Japanese attacking the Chinese. Over the last four years the stories got longer and more sickening. They used poison gas on civilians. They were made out to be monsters—the most savage killers since Attila the Hun. They enjoyed beheading with ceremonial swords. They tortured soldiers and civilians publicly. They killed children. General Tojo just signed a deal with Mussolini and Hitler. They called it the Anti-Comintern Pact. It said they were against Communists but meant they were against everybody. The newspapers started calling them the Rome-Berlin Axis, the Axis. No one was surprised when I mentioned my vision. Many people were seeing signs then. War was on everyone's mind and we hoped it would stay on the other side of the world. The Japanese men who played their round of golf at the club every Thursday afternoon still came. I remembered these men. I liked them. But I wondered about them now. Everyone did. Now on Thursdays, they carried their own bags.

★

After I'd seen everyone, played a few holes of golf and spent time with Mama and Pop, it was time to go. Except for Marion. I was never quite finished with her. I'd stop by her house. If her old man was home he'd make a big fuss, want to know everything about my time in the Army and her mother would try to make me eat something. When it came to Marion, though, we couldn't just sit around in the living room and catch up on the news. I had to get out. We always went out for a walk. She was excited about her plans for college. I kept my news to activities in camp. If she knew what I'd been up to in New York with all kinds of girls in all kinds of places, she'd probably never speak to me again. So it came down to a sidestep kind of talking, which I wasn't good at. She said I'd changed and I just let it drop. I let her think that. Like I was a grown man now with a lot on my mind, instead of what I was really doing, which was chasing tail like a fireman at a barn burning. I let myself imagine, in years, we would be sitting on a porch here in Raritan. Then I got the idea she was seeing someone else. I asked her and she didn't say exactly, so I let that drop too. It seemed only fair. So it was like that between us, round and round, talking around the edge of things. She was right in one way, I was different, older. I had my confidence back. My feelings toward her were even stronger than before. I knew we were about to go our own ways in life and if I wanted her I'd have to do something, say something to let her know. I saw her now as a grown woman and so my mind kept going toward some kind of future with her, trying to see it. But I couldn't. Maybe deep inside I knew I was already going in a different direction. In the end, all I had was my feelings for her, the words just wouldn't come.

When we got to some hidden spot, an alley or behind a tree, we just went at each other. If there had been a place to lie down, we probably would have ended up married. As it was, it was some kind of good-bye. After all those years growing up together, we wanted to be together. Maybe we thought we should be. But it just wasn't enough somehow. Once we stopped kissing, there were still no words. I couldn't tell her I would wait for her. She couldn't tell me that either. I walked Marion home and we didn't say a word the whole way. I didn't see her again for years.

Being home for two days was enough. The last day and night I spent in the city. That night I'd be up late. I'd be knee-deep into the pleasures of being a young stud. The next day I'd be close to base and might have time for an eye-opener before reveille. My appetite was constant and not too particular. I gobbled up women like salty peanuts. I was a starving man at a picnic. Life was so, so good.

In July, there was a machine gun competition on the base. My unit, D Company, walked away with the pennant. I was in a company of fifty-eight winners. I could easier spend a year with these guys than a weekend at home. They were my family now. This was my home and the Army was my life. I was a soldier.

★

We shipped out to San Diego on the Super Chief out of Grand Central Station. You might have thought it was the Wild West by what went on in the saloons in the station. The closer it got to "all aboard" the wilder things got. Fellas who had never smoked or drank in their lives were doing two at a time. That went for women too. I'm not proud of the way we acted but I won't pretend we were choirboys either. We were warriors and likely off to war. Orders were for the Philippines. Soon enough the MPs cleared the places out and got us on the train. They were some of the roughest sons of bitches I ever met, those MPs. If you didn't hear them the first time they said something, you might never hear anything again. They used those white batons like Ted Williams used a ball bat. Five or six boys got dumped into the train bleeding or doubled over with the wind knocked out of them. I hadn't really seen that kind of rough stuff before. In camp nobody ever got beaten like that, that bad. In a way, after all the ceremonies and speeches after basic training, this was the real graduation. We were trained for violence and suddenly here it was. Every one of us who could still walk wanted to jump off that train and smash those MPs in the face. That's who we were now. We were violent men. We were a hunting pack and our blood had been spilled. We were ready for our first kill.

★

A long train ride with soldiers holding full pay envelopes was like a dream come true. The first crap game started before we cleared Grand Central. I was in no hurry since the money wasn't leaving this train for the next four days. I wanted to see the country since I'd never been outside of New York and New Jersey.

We slept in our seats and washed over a basin the size of a soup bowl with one foot wedged against the bathroom door so we wouldn't get knocked around by the swaying of the train. By the second day, we were starting to smell like goats. Civilians who got on the train didn't stay around us long. We were irritated as hell from not getting any decent sleep and arguments were breaking out every hour or so. If it weren't for gambling, I'm sure we would have been at each other more than we were. The fact that we still had three days left to go didn't help.

We got our choice of three kinds of sandwiches: ham, cheese or ham and cheese. Pretty soon we weren't a crack fighting force, we were a gang of squabbling chiselers and malcontents. The Army made sure we were going to get to California alive, but they weren't worried about morale. The unfunny joke going around was they were going to put down straw for us and give us hay instead of sandwiches at the next stop. I lost interest in the passing scenery. It all looked the same. I just wanted to get off that train and away from my brothers-in-arms. After the third day of sleeping sitting up and eating stale sandwiches, we were all miserable. Liquor bottles, puke and cigarette butts covered the floor in some cars. The porters wouldn't come near us anymore and neither would any civilians. We were stuck with each other in our filth and stench. We sat shoulder-to-shoulder, unshaven and hungover. All we thought about was getting off that train. Fights broke out and almost nobody bothered to stop them.

★

The Pacific Ocean slid into view and I'd never seen anything quite as beautiful before. The open spaces and mountains of the West were inspiring but the Pacific was a new world completely. Some of the boys never saw an ocean before and for once there was no arguing or shouting. Everybody was nose against the glass. Some tough soldiers these were. We were like kids looking into a candy store. We could have been a baseball team or a college class on a trip together. So many of us had never been off a farm before we joined the Army.

The trip was almost over. We were just outside of Los Angeles on our way to San Diego. The rumors started up again. Some said we were on our way to China, some said the Panama Canal. It was clear that no one knew a goddamn thing about where we were going or why.

THE HISTORY OF THE PHILIPPINES

In 1898, after years of suffering under Spanish rule, Filipinos fought on the side of America during the Spanish-American War and against their oppressors. It was America's first war of conquest and it gained the colonies of Cuba, Puerto Rico and eventually the Philippines. When the Spanish were defeated, Filipino General Aguinaldo declared the Philippines independent. The United States, however, had other plans. They bought the islands from the defeated Spanish for the bargain price of $20 million. General Aguinaldo realized his American allies were now the occupying enemy. He continued his war for independence against his homeland's new oppressors. For the next thirty-five years, the Americans fought a bloody guerilla war with the Filipinos for control of their land.

By November of 1899, Aguinaldo and his forces had been pushed into the interior of the main island of Luzon. He realized he could not fight the Americans with conventional military tactics and ordered his troops to use guerilla tactics. The war became a savage bloodletting of ambushes, massacres and retribution. Villages were destroyed, civilians murdered, prisoners were tortured and mutilated.

"Talk about war being 'hell,' this war beats the hottest estimate ever made of that locality. Caloocan was supposed to contain seventeen thousand inhabitants. The Twentieth Kansas swept through it, and now Caloocan contains not one living native. Of the buildings, the battered walls of the great church and dismal prison alone remain. The village of Maypaja, where our first fight occurred on the night of the fourth, had five thousand people on that day—now not one stone remains up on top of another. You can only faintly imagine this terrible scene of desolation. War is worse than hell."
—*Captain Elliott of the Kansas Regiment,*
   February 27th

Aguinaldo was captured but armed attacks against Americans continued. After over three decades of continuous guerilla warfare, America recognized the right of the Philippine people to be their own independent nation. Manuel Quezon was sworn in as President of the Philippine Commonwealth in 1935 as part of a transitional phase pending full independence.

John Basilone arrived in Manila Bay in March of that year on the troop transport ship USS *Republic*. He joined the 16,000 American troops stationed on the main island of Luzon. This was

America's most distant outpost—7,000 miles from San Diego, 1,800 miles from Tokyo and less than 1,000 miles from Japanese-controlled Formosa directly to the north.

U.S. Army instructor teaches Philippine Army regulars .30 cal. machine gun, circa 1935

Garrison Duty

We didn't have enough soap. We didn't have any gasoline most of the time. Some of us didn't even have weapons. I understood the gas and weapons, they were expensive, but soap was cheap. Some of us slept in makeshift tents, we didn't even have the lumber to put up barracks. We'd go on patrol with twenty rounds and old Enfield rifles from the First World War. They stuck us out here on this island surrounded by local Filipino hostiles and a short cruise away from the Japanese, who were slicing up Chinamen like the Christmas goose, but they couldn't give us enough weapons. That's the first time I started to wonder about my decision to go into the Army.

Major General Grunert had his hands full whipping the Filipino forces into shape, so our health and safety fell to Mac, General Douglas MacArthur. Mac seemed to be all business and didn't mind getting in close to us. It embarrassed the hell out of him to be out in the camp and see boys wearing Navy dungarees that were meant for some swabbie outfit but arrived on our supply list. He was always coming around for inspection so we got to know him pretty well. Why the hell this old guy wanted to take this command after all he'd done, he'd been the Army's chief of staff stateside, was something none of us could figure out. Maybe he liked a challenge. Or maybe, like me, he knew the Japanese would be coming soon and the Philippines would be their first stop.

It didn't seem to matter much to Topside because the plan was to retreat to the rock peninsula of Corregidor in case of a Japanese attack. That took the crease out of our new recruits' trousers. We were drilling for retreat. That and the ragged look of the outfit, the slum conditions of the camp and the fact that there was nothing much to do after we'd policed up the butts on the ground, took morale down to sea level. It was the same kind of aimless Life of Riley that I'd left in the Raritan Country Club. The same characters were there and just like before all they generally did all day was play cards. If it wasn't for cards, I'm not sure how any of us would have spent that first year. Maybe just staring at the sky.

We couldn't look forward to chow usually. Some of the men used the little money we had to stash food around the base that they'd bought in Manila. Private cook fires, against regulations, would spring up around base at least once a week when a certain smell came from the mess. The smell was boiling goat. The Army bought their meat from the local suppliers. They got good prices on goat meat, so we got boiled goat at least once a week. The cursing would start as the stink from the kitchen spread across the camp. We risked the stockade to cook our own food on those days.

"Fuckin' goat!" You could hear the comment from one end of the chow line to the other. The cooks were threatened and retaliated by spitting, or worse, into the boiling pots of meat. In the monsoon months, when the rain came down for days and the heat made you want to tear your clothes off, the smell of boiling goat pushed us as close to mutiny as we ever came. Eventually the cooks took to frying the meat, which made it smell better but we had to bring our Ka-Bar assault knives to cut it.

We were told not to go anywhere alone off base and never to go into the countryside, even with other soldiers. It seemed like we still didn't have control of the place even though we'd been here chasing bandits and guerillas since the turn of the century. It was depressing. It got to some of us. Certain GIs went "native," mixing with the locals in Manila, wearing nonregulation Filipino clothes, taking up with Filipino families and starting up businesses off base. For the first year or two, I didn't go in for any of that. I was still U.S. Army and kept my nose clean as far as that.

It was a pretty island in most parts and even though we weren't supposed to go anywhere, we all did anyway. I was still knocked out by the ocean, looking at it, being near it. Me and Warburton, from Muncie, Indiana, rented a motor skiff and set out on tours of the rock—Corregidor, Cavite and the points just up from the harbor. It was a peaceful feeling out on the water. We'd take our fishing poles and usually come back with something. They weren't like any fish we'd ever seen before but they tasted about the same.

That's when I started training as a fighter. At first it was just sparring and horsing around with the guys but a lot of steam had been building up in my head. I didn't like sitting around waiting for an attack, just so we could make a run for it. And I didn't like that we were stuck on this island and we weren't even important enough to get soap.

Sparring let me blow off steam and kept me sharp. Being a fighter got you privileges sometimes, like an inside bunk and credit at card games—which I didn't usually need. Once I started winning, I started getting steaks and pork chops stolen from the Officer's Club. My fellow soldiers started to see me as a moneymaking enterprise. There was always a group that wanted to be part of my training and sparring team because they didn't have anything to do all day either. I think I had ten corner men, two or three medics lined up to be my cut man, dozens of trainers and managers and at least two hundred sparring partners. It's always good to have a lot of friends I found out more than once.

We were in town, Manila, when one of our group—Smits from Canton, Ohio—got a serious load on. News from home or something set him off. He was talking quietly to a young lady negotiating a price for personal services and then suddenly he's pushing a Filipino scout's face into the floor. This kind of thing happened all the time so no one was very surprised, but Filipino scouts were on our side so it was looked down upon and could draw stockade time. We were just breaking it up when another whole crew of Filipinos jumped us and started windmilling with batons. We fought them off as best we could until another dozen or so jumped in. Pretty soon they had us laid out on the floor and busted up pretty good. They were the Manila police. I don't know why soldiers and police, especially the military police, never seem to get along. It seems to be some kind of competition is the only way I can make it out. The Manila cops got the background story from the lady who attracted all the attention in the first place. They hauled Smits away and we got marching orders back to base with a serious warning from the top cop. We were limping back to camp, which took about an hour when we could walk normally. We were beaten, spineless things who couldn't even call ourselves soldiers. We'd left a man behind, a captive of hostile forces, and we were retreating in defeat. This wasn't what I signed up for. It was a disgrace.

Five-ton trucks were kept at a motor pool off base. The motor pool was on the way back to base and was being guarded by at least one soldier I knew well. This young boot was unlucky at cards and owed money to men all over camp. I could take care of some of that debt for him if he was willing to help us redeem ourselves as soldiers. He was willing to help. Specialist 4th Class Edmund Caisie was deployed to a forward position as a truck thief. He performed with distinction.

Smits was dead drunk asleep in his cell at about 3:00 A.M. Everything was quiet since it was Sunday morning and the Filipinos are devout Catholics, most of them. Pfc. Gerald Conner's recon of the jailhouse had determined that a deputy or two were in the station house. They looked to be asleep.

We sat in the truck, lights off, engine running about fifty yards from the jailhouse. We discussed a tactical feint to draw the deputies from their position but in the end it was too late at night for such subtleties. Pfc. Martin Warburton jammed the five-ton truck into gear and aimed for Smits's cell. We hit the wall of Smits's cell at about twenty miles an hour, which gave us all a hell of a jolt. We guessed the deputies might have thought it was an earthquake, or rebel mortar attack because they never did show up and probably ran for help. The enemy line was not quite breeched so the five-ton backed up and hit the wall again. This time the headlights shined right through the wall and into Smits's terrified face. We backed the truck out of the hole in the wall and pulled Smits through it. The operation was a great success—well planned and executed with daring. We returned to base, heads held high, mission accomplished. Since then I always liked having a lot of friends around me. You never know when you might need a few.

Twice a month fights were organized and became the most important things in our camp life. They gave us something to look forward to. Without them discipline might have broken down completely. Even with the fights to hold our interest, there were so many men AWOL and drunk on duty that we couldn't have stood up to an attack of pissants. I trained hard, building my legs up by running in the deep sand by Manila Bay and up the sides of hills that had been cleared of all life by tank training.

It was a good life then. I won my first matches, knocking out two of my first three opponents. That's when I got the name Manila John. It's a fighter's nickname like Kid Jersey or Amblin' Alp—the nickname of my old hero Primo Carnera. The brass came around and even old Mac himself would wish me luck before a fight. He was probably the only man in uniform who didn't have money on me one way or the other.

We still patrolled the interior from time to time. Mostly there was no one home by the time we got to where we were going. Reports came in that guerillas were massing in a distant camp, or some farmers lost their cattle to them. Every few months, shots came into camp from beyond the perimeter. Once or twice mortars were fired at us from the bush. We'd chase them but never catch them. It was just enough to keep everybody pissed off. While I was there a contingent of the Filipino Scouts was formed. Mac took that on and built it up to 16,000 men, about the same number as us. We heard that Mac was a real scrapper, getting us more supplies and equipment. We even got soap eventually.

Every six months or so, we'd get rotated out to New Zealand for two weeks. This was to give us a rest from all the card playing and drinking we had to do in Manila. The New Zealanders called themselves Kiwis, after this little bird that ran around over there. The thing couldn't fly but they were proud as hell of it and made it the national bird. They were great people and would do just about anything for a good time. I could always get a rise out of them when I explained why the kiwi was the ugliest bird I ever saw and was a disgrace to all birds. A few of us GIs would take part of the two weeks out on one of the sheep ranches working. It was more like being home. We could do the things we were used to and eat the food we were used to. I could have stayed in New Zealand and quite a few of the boys went back there to live when their time was up in the Army. The time in New Zealand made me think that I wasn't doing a whole lot in the Army except beating up other guys who were in the Army. I could do that at home. As far as being a soldier, there wasn't much I was asked to do. New Zealand made it harder to go back. I didn't know what I was anymore and I sure didn't feel like I was a soldier.

I kept racking up the wins. I was 11 and 0 with seven knockouts when the letters from the States started coming. The news of my fights was going out in the Army newspapers. Soon professional managers stateside got wind of the welterweight, Manila John. They promised me big fights in New York, Chicago, all the best places against real big-time fighters not just chowhounds looking for a quick payday. The temptation for glory—here it was again. I saw the way they wanted to make Manila John Basilone something they could sell like canned goods. Some even talked about their connections with the finest hotels where I'd live like a king. I could have my own car and enough money to retire in a few years. I didn't believe a god-damn word. It was tempting though. I wanted to believe them. I wanted to be like the great Primo Carnera. Pop would bust his buttons, he'd be so proud. Something just told me, it must have been Father Amedeo's voice again, not to believe them. I didn't answer the letters.

Things gradually improved under Mac. He was a fighter for us, for the things we needed, and that got him the respect of the guys. We got regular uniforms, more weapons, even soap. The thing he couldn't do much about was malaria. After the rains of monsoon season, clouds of mosquitoes descended on the camp. Within weeks, almost a third of us were down with fever. They'd dose us with quinine and those that came back got the reward of returning to regular duty, boiled goat and long days of swatting bugs. Those that didn't come back got a ticket home and the shakes for the rest of their lives. The mosquitoes were bad in camp but in the bush were also chiggers, leaches, stinging spiders and snakes. The guerillas were not our biggest problem. I don't mean to say it was all misery, just most of it. If it weren't for the camp bouts, my guess is I would have ended up fighting somebody anyway and wound up in the stockade. The stinking food, the boredom and the malaria were the worst of it and sometimes they all added up in the wrong direction, so you had to be careful what you said.

A couple of weeks into monsoon season was when things got really bad. Everything got covered with sticky mud. The latrines would overflow into the camp and jungle rot fungus grew on everything, even between toes. I developed a hatred of Army wool socks. When Army socks got wet they itched like a colony of chiggers got into my boots. I'd go around barefoot during rainy season and would catch hell regularly when I got caught doing it. I wrote home for cotton socks but they took weeks to arrive, if they ever did. Once I got them, they rotted in a few weeks so nothing seemed to work for long. The guys thought I was going native so I had to make myself clear to a few of them. The safest way to do that was in the sparring ring. I tangled with a few that made me sorry for the invitation, but generally they were good practice to sharpen up my skills.

All the sparring and training put me over the weight limit for welterweight. I moved into light heavyweight during my last year in the Philippines. This was definitely a rougher class of people and forced me to train even harder. I was getting a reputation now outside our command. Fights with champions from other units were set to see who would eventually be going up against the other services, like our traditional rival, the Navy.

I kept racking up wins in the ring and got my lumps in the process including a broken nose. Along the way, Mac latched onto me as a kind of mascot for the shabby outfit he had promised to whip into shape. Somehow me beating the tar out these other GIs gave him the moxie to pry better support for us from Topside. I became the symbol of our outfit, light in our weight class but real scrappers.

He was trying to get us into a better tactical position than having to run for the hills at the first Japanese shot, which looked more and more likely to happen as time went on. We were the tip of the spear pointed at Japan. He could see it was just a matter of time before the Japanese would attack us. By 1939, the rest of the brass saw what he was seeing too. That's when the supplies started coming, like a hundred tanks in one shipment. As it turned out, Mac was too late. Our 16,000 and another 16,000 Filipino scouts weren't nearly enough. That's why the names of Corregidor and Bataan became lessons written in our blood.

My time was almost up on the island by the time Mac started to get his way but I was sick of the way the Army operated by then. I didn't sign up to run backward when trouble came. They had the wrong guy for that detail.

★

I was coming up on eighteen wins, ten by knockout, when I met Lolita. That monsoon season I stayed warm and got to see the beauty of the islands finally. We were wild together and maybe I could have stayed with her if things were different. Being a short-timer and not knowing if I could take the Army anymore, it made it tough to make plans. I loved the Army once and now it broke my heart. I was mad and I was sick about it. It had given me a life when I didn't know which way to go. But now it looked like the Army itself was confused. I didn't know what I could do now or where I could go. The time came when the staff sergeant asked me to reenlist. I turned the Army down. It wasn't my life anymore but there was nothing to replace it. I didn't have a career to go back to. There was no family that depended on me. All I had was my beautiful Filipino girl,

Lolita, and the little nightclub we made in her uncle's bicycle shop. Maybe I could have been happy. Maybe I could have made a life there, with her somehow. But I had lost the life, the calling I had found. I wasn't a soldier anymore. I was lost.

⋆ 4 ⋆

Back Home

Ididn't tell anybody I was coming home. I didn't want a phony hero's welcome, like I did something important. I just wanted to slip back into civilian life and find a way to forget about the Army for a while. Maybe Marion was still around. On the way home, crossing the country again, I thought sometimes that I'd get off that train at some place where I liked the sound of the name, like Sweetwater, Kansas, or Carefree, Indiana, and disappear completely. I could find a job in Kansas as easy as I could in New Jersey and save the effort of lying about being in an outfit with standing orders to retreat. At home, there would be a thousand questions and what the hell was I going to tell them? I'm not a slick talker so I thought I'd get tripped up for sure. I'd have to tell them eventually how I really felt and then everybody would feel bad and worry about me. That, I wouldn't allow. Nobody was going to feel sorry for me. I just needed time to figure out what the hell I was going to do next, get my mind off the past. There's not much use for a machine gunner in New Jersey.

I kept wondering about Fort. Jay. I was a warrior with a purpose there. What if I had stayed in that old fort guarding New York Harbor, in a crack outfit? Maybe I would have stayed in the Army. I wondered if the DIs even believed anything they taught us? They must have known about places like Manila. What was all that malarkey they taught us about being a soldier?

It was these kinds of black thoughts that were in my mind. Nobody really believed that the U.S. would ever get involved in another war overseas. Not after the last trench and poison gas war in Europe. Civilians didn't believe in having soldiers anymore. They didn't need us and I think most of them didn't even like us. Soldiers reminded them of how stupid the last war was. We were treated like field hands after the hay was put up. We were useless. We were only good for dressing up and marching in parades. They didn't even care enough to send us soap.

In my frame of mind, I wasn't going to make anyone proud. I thought I'd just slip away and start over somewhere, where I wouldn't feel like such a fool. My school friends were mostly through college by now. They were starting careers and families. They were building their own businesses. The only thing I could build was a Browning machine gun. My circle of friends was mostly misfits and Army loafers. My prospects for a wife were mostly whores, with the exception of Lolita. I was all-around feeling like I didn't deserve anything, like I was ashamed of the wasted time I'd spent.

The bus dropped me in Raritan. I walked through town. When people recognized me, they treated me like I was a hero. That made me feel like a real phony. Al and George came walking up First Avenue. When we saw each other, the party really started. You could hear the yelling from one end of town to the other. Three years is a long time to be away from a small town like Raritan. Little boys who used to run around the block for a nickel's worth of candy had grown up to be shy teenagers who were so awkward they couldn't give me the time of day. They stared at the marksman medals and service ribbons on my chest like I was really something. The people my age were off to college. Both Al and George had become solid citizens, especially Al who acted like an old married man even as a kid. George was wild, like me, but quieter and so didn't have as many friends. I seemed to pick up friends everywhere. They just seemed to come as part of having a good time. We first stopped in at older brother Angelo's tailor shop where the party became three. Angie closed the shop and joined us.

We walked toward the house while George chattered on about joining the Army too. I didn't say anything good or bad about it. I knew he was so bullheaded he was going to do exactly as he wanted anyway. But just in case he accidentally was listening I said, "Think about it." I didn't want him blaming me for his decision later on.

Mom went over the moon when we walked in the house. The air was full of garlic and tomato. Gravy had been on the stove for hours. She was worried that maybe I got my face cut up in the ring so she looked me over like a surgeon. She felt the bump where my nose got busted and made a little face. I got big, wet kisses on the face and then got turned loose.

The rest of that night the family and food kept coming in waves. Everybody had read all about my record as a fighter from the base newspapers I sent back. I wanted everybody, especially Pop, to know I was somebody who could take care of himself. They didn't have to worry about me anymore. The older boys wanted to hear about the ladies of the Philippines. I didn't mention Lolita by name, I just said I knew a girl. I described her as typical of all the island ladies, which wasn't even close to true. I knew she was rare, in the Philippines or anywhere. I was missing her badly. Speaking her name now seemed disrespectful, like she was just one of the sights or just someone I had fun with. She was part of my private life. Three years ago, when I left home, I didn't even have a private life. Everybody knew everything about me. Now I had all kinds of secrets, good and bad.

The girls wanted to know about everything else. I tried to make it all sound like a lot of fun but it came out that the Army was a mess. That took some of the gas out of the party. When I told them I was home for good, I got a quiet kind of smile, like they weren't sure of what I was saying. Then the questions started that I had no answers for. I didn't have a plan. I could tell Pop was worried, he'd seen me go through this before. The older ones, Angelo, Catherine and Mary were well on their way in life. Angelo was already married, the girls had steady boyfriends and regular jobs. It didn't strike them right away. Pop could tell I was not saying everything. At least he wasn't the type to make a big deal about it. I knew we'd have a talk later on.

★

Even though I couldn't imagine a thing I could do in life outside the Army, the thought didn't panic me. I had waited for God to tell me my direction before, I'd wait again. In the meantime, I meant to eat, sleep and enjoy a quiet country life. That idea lasted about two days.

Almost the first question everybody wanted to know was, "What're you going to do now, Johnny?" Of course, I didn't have a good answer. I didn't have any answer. The Depression had eased up and just about everybody had a brother, a son or a cousin who was doing this great job or working for some great company. Everybody was doing something, and they wanted to give me a hand, get me started. I don't know if that's how things are in every small town, but Raritan was like that, almost a big family. They all wanted to see me do well. At least most did. There are always one or two no-accounts who make things tough. I'd seen dozens of them in the Army. Especially Manila seemed to bring out the no-account even in good soldiers. They find their little place in the world and spend the rest of their time complaining. They were a disgrace as soldiers by my lights. And there was no use arguing with them, they were all set up for that and would argue until you were both blue in the face. All I could do was try to avoid them. It wasn't even that they were wrong. Everything they said made perfect sense—the Army was a half-breed organization with the brain of a chicken and the manners of a goat. They trained us to be fighters, but treated us like convicts; nobody cared about us. It was all true. That's what made it hard to ignore.

The same was true at home. The layabouts who had left school before me or just made it through, settled into their little places in town like the feed store, the grocery and from there they made their hard luck complaints part of the everyday conversation. It was hard to avoid them. They were the new generation, the up and comers. They weren't that different from the no-accounts in the Army or, I suspect, from guys in lots of other small towns. But to me they were

poison. They poisoned my mind because the things they were saying, that Raritan was a dead-end town and that any job was just trad-
ing your life for a paycheck, were true. They had made their peace
with this kind of thinking but if I lived to be a hundred, I knew I
never would.

So here I was, older and still no wiser. Raritan was even smaller
than before because now there were places I had to avoid. There were
conversations I didn't want to have and people I didn't want to have
conversations with. After the hell raising I'd been up to for three
years, Raritan now seemed like a desert island. But the Army was
over for me, so here I was—on a desert island or the North Pole—
and I'd better get used to it.

I started sparring again. I traveled a few days a week up to a Newark gym just to blow off steam. At least I had that and I could tire
myself out so I could sleep at night. But I wasn't getting any further
up the mountain.

The boys at the country club made room for me in the lineup.
Toting bags got me out of the house earning a little money while I
was getting my head on straight. I couldn't figure out why it was so
hard for me. Almost everyone else seemed to be able to pick a direction and go. I just didn't understand how one day they could say,
"Okay, I'm going to be a cop for the rest of my life," or "I think I'd
like to be a plumber." What the hell kind of thinking was that? But
I wanted to be sure, like them. I wanted to know what I was supposed
to be doing. I wanted it to be easy like it was for them. I wanted
people to stop asking me what I was going to do.

I was facing it again. The same thing I thought I'd licked when I
joined the Army. It was here and bigger than before. I was losing this
fight. What was I going to do with the rest of my life? There was

something I was supposed to be doing and goddamn if it didn't start to tear me up again. I tried to remember the vision I had once but it was all part of being a soldier and that was over. Even though I had faith in God and even though I talked it over with Father Russo, this problem of who and what I was supposed to be was the mountain I would have to climb if I was ever going to rest easy. There was no way around it.

To other people, I made it look like I was just taking it easy while I made up my mind. But Pop remembered this act from before and I caught his look, the kind where he was trying hard not to have a look, at the dinner table. I could tell he didn't want to have the conversation any more than I did but it was coming. He had to say something.

"What's your plan?" he asked one night, a few weeks after I'd been home. "You can't be a caddy your whole life."

I had to tell him I didn't know. I pretended like I wasn't in any rush. "Aw come on, Pop. I'll get on to something here in a while. I got prospects." I had no prospects. None that I could stand to think of.

He pretended like that was okay. Mom wanted to know about the girl in the Philippines who had sent her the beautiful black dress. She wanted to know about any girl I was interested in. I told her stories, talking sideways, not really saying what was on my mind. So I told stories about the beautiful girl who couldn't leave her parents in Manila. She smiled and looked at Pop. God almighty, she knew too. I wasn't fooling anybody. I was just a Charlie McCarthy, a ventriloquist dummy, talking nonsense.

The crazy idea came into my head that I could get a job and then send for Lolita. That would make everybody happy. I thought, that must be what I'm supposed to do. It seemed the only thing I could

do. I'd buckle down, get a real job and start living the life I was supposed to live. The rest of my days would be happy and it would be
enough for me. I felt like this was progress. I felt like I was finally
being responsible and facing the music.

In a big family like mine with ten kids, you don't stay the center
of attention for long. Soon I was just one more clown in the regular
circus in our house. Phyllis was married already and living in Reisterstown, Maryland. Angelo, Catherine and Mary were out of the
house as well but that still left the others: George, Alphonse, Delores
and Donald as well as me and Carlo, so there were still plenty of
people left to take the attention off of me.

Everything was going to be okay. I was going to change my way of
thinking to accept the way things really were, not keep dreaming of
some life of adventure like before. I'd seen adventure. It turned out
to be a lot of boiled goat with not even enough soap to wash the smell
off. Then late one night as I was falling asleep, the voice started in
on me again. It had been mostly silent the last few years, just the
normal background chatter like everybody else. Now it was more
like a drill instructor, not as rough but just as pushy. It was asking
why couldn't I just be happy and live like the others? But I was older
now and had my own way of thinking. I talked back. I said to myself
I was happy, I was living just like everybody else. And then it asked,
like nothing I just said mattered—Was I too good? No, I wasn't too
good, I told myself. I wasn't too good, I was going to get a job and
send for Lolita. I was doing what I was supposed to do. I wasn't putting up with any second-guessing, even if it was my own. I rolled
over and went to sleep.

Everyone living under the same roof, but going in different directions, kept my mind from spending too much time on me and then

overheating. There were always half a dozen friends, boyfriends, girl-friends, cousins or co-workers in the kitchen and living room. In the first week or two, Pop took me to his Italian-American club where I had to tell all my stories over and over again as each member showed up for his nightly game of backgammon or dominoes and glass of anisette. Is this where I was going to end up forty years from now? Would I be telling these same stories to the sons of these old men? Nothing against Pop or his friends but I couldn't stand the place. I didn't even like the smell of it, like a barn for old men. I made ex-cuses so I wouldn't have to go anymore. Pop didn't press me about it. He knew I didn't have anything in common with these old gas bags. He was proud of me though. That was clear and that was enough.

I figured it would only be a matter of time before something came up for me. I'd stay busy until then. Whenever I had a spare minute I'd be running an errand or helping to load coal or put up firewood with a neighbor. People could actually afford to pay now so I had no trouble paying my way at home. The card games at the club helped boost my income between rounds.

It was only at night, like before, when my mind would race and I would see everything past, present and future. The voice didn't come every night. Mostly it was just pictures. I had the vision of myself as a fighter, a real fighter. More powerful than even the great Primo Carnera in his prime. These days it seemed like Primo and me were on the same track. The only difference was that he had been losing ground for years, I'd only been backsliding for a month since leaving the Army. There were a dozen young fighters now who could whip Primo. The Amblin' Alp was starting to stumble. It was sad. I thought about how deep the hurt must have been for him. Did he even know that his time had passed? Or did he still think he had a shot? He knew he couldn't whip half of these new fighters but he kept showing up and taking his beatings, so I had to wonder and hope he was still the champ in his own heart. Every time he fought the crowd got smaller and the place got dirtier until he was doing exhibition matches in local gymnasiums. Did he still have his vision, was he still a champ in his heart or was he just getting a paycheck?

When you love someone like that, someone bigger than real life, like I loved Primo, they become a part of who you are. Since I was a young man listening to his fights from Madison Square Garden in front of the Philco with Pop, I was Primo Carnera. In every sparring match or training exercise, I was the champ. Just like him, I was the overpowering force. I was a king among my people and a source of pride. But what were we now—me and Primo? Where did we fit in?

I played golf. I played cards. I made a few bucks. In a few weeks everyone forgot I'd ever been a soldier, including me. I was just Johnny again. I was the brother of George or Delores. Marion was gone, off to college and I was glad for that. There was nothing to say anymore between us. I made my choice and she went on and made hers. Besides, I was going to bring Lolita over when I got myself squared away.

Marion's dad told me there was factory work up in East Orange. He could get me on if I wanted. I had to pretend there was something else I was waiting on so as not to hurt his feelings. He would've thought I had some crust on me to turn down a steady job, a union job, with him. So there I was again, hiding, trying to stay out of sight. He wanted me to come by the house, have a beer and talk about it. The way I understood it from Marion, was that he always wanted a son and I was as close as he was going to get. I didn't go to the house. I didn't want to talk about a factory job.

Every week I'd try again to write a letter to Lolita. They were ridiculous. Reading them aloud you might think some kid wrote them. I tore them up. She would never want to come after reading a letter like mine. I didn't have much hope she would come even if I was William Shakespeare. Why would she believe me or forgive me after I left her there with just a good-bye? I asked Carlo to help me write. Carlo was smarter than me as far as writing. And he could keep a secret.

★

Sleeping was starting to be a problem again and that particular day I wasn't even going to go to the gym, but something got me going. That's when I hurt some boy sparring. On the bus up from Somerville everything was spinning in front of me—like what had gone wrong in Manila? Why were we left out there in such bad shape? Didn't people see what was happening? Didn't they care? The place was full of Japanese businessmen looking over every square inch of the island. They didn't fool us, especially Mac. He knew they were measuring the place like a new suit they were about to try on. But there we were, with orders to run for high ground on Corregidor at the first shot! Why?

By the time I got off the bus my jaw was tight as a drumhead. In the gym, I worked the jump rope like I was trying to break it. By this time, a couple of old guys who kept an eye out for fresh meat had heard of me. Maybe they heard about my 19-0 record in the service and started pissing in my ear about the bright lights and big money. That day I wasn't listening to any of it and moved off as soon as they started on me.

I hit the heavy bag for a while trying to fight off the visions of

Manila when a spot opened up to spar. Somebody's partner hadn't shown, so they picked me because I looked to be in about the same weight class. This guy had a few people in his corner. It looked like he was on his way to turning pro. I had nobody in my corner. One of his people rewrapped my hands and put my gloves on. We were going to go one or two rounds and we were supposed to take it easy. We came out to center ring and touched gloves. One of his corner men was shouting to him every second—watch this, do that.

I'll give him credit, he had style and speed. I don't know exactly what happened but he must have hit me and all of a sudden it wasn't a sparring match anymore. I lit into him. He wasn't ready but he got ready after I tagged him a few times. All of a sudden it was a bar brawl. I don't know why the corner men let it go on as long as they did. Maybe they saw their boy was dishing it out pretty good too. It was a bad decision. He tried to swing at my head but he couldn't hit me while I rocked him from side to side with body shots. I didn't care if he hit me. Nothing could stop my attack. I would have beaten him until his whole body was one big bruise. Pretty soon he couldn't lift his arms and I was just trying to crush his ribs. I didn't want him

to fall. I don't know what I wanted. It didn't matter because pretty soon all three of his corner men were on top of me dragging me away. They were all yelling in my face. The boy had the wind knocked out of him. That's when I decided to see Father Russo again.

IWO JIMA
0930 hours
D plus 30 minutes

They finally opened up on us with everything they had, blasting big, bloody holes in the crowded beach. Cannons spit fire down from Mount Suribachi directly to our left. Mortars whooshed in and crumped in the sand. The Navy's rolling barrage that had walked up the beach and across the airfield before us only made the enemy pause. We were on our own now—a few inches of sand and a green dungaree uniform between us and showers of hot steel splinters. The black sand shuddered and bucked like a living animal as the men dove into any hole they could find and held on.

The Japanese defenders had waited until our six assault waves had piled up on each other. Then from the high ground on the sides of Suribachi and just beyond our first objective, the Motoyama One airfield four hundred yards inland, they unloaded on us. We hadn't even taken fifty yards of the island. We were sitting ducks and being cut to pieces.

Me and Lou Plain, the executive officer of the 27th Marines decided that was enough of that shit. Men were scattered from three or four different outfits. We started down the line kicking asses and hauling men up by the scruffs of their necks.

"Move out! Get the fuck off the beach you dumb sons of bitches!" we yelled over the incoming fire. My Charlie Company, with C-1-27 stenciled on their gear, were now mixed in with Able and Baker companies. We didn't know how many men we had at that moment or what their specialty was but we dragged them out of that bottleneck on the sand terraces. The men moved up over the top of the last terrace and dashed to the nearest shell hole. A glance told me I was a few dozen men short. The gray clouds moved off, bringing on the heat of the day. The beach below us was jammed with thousands of men and tons of equipment. A big league cluster fuck if I ever saw one.

Fifty-caliber bullets stitched a line across the sand in front of us but came from behind. A Navy torpedo bomber, the pilot dead at the controls, was in his death dive toward the ocean. The burst must have come from his reflex as he was hit. The plane angled down and hit a transport about three hundred yards out to sea. Debris exploded toward us, taking down more men on the beach. Close support bombardment was called in, which didn't do much to cut down on the incoming Jap shells, but it meant our big shells whizzed just overhead and exploded less than a football field away. We were now practically under the bombardment meant for the enemy as well as the bombardment the enemy prepared for us. One thing most soldiers who fought them agreed upon was that the Japanese were professionals. They were disciplined and fierce. The big guns up on Suribachi zeroed in sector after sector. Wherever they found a concentration of us, it would be rags and smoke the next second. But they only had moments to live themselves. Each shot exposed their position. They knew that we would get to each one of them very soon. The only hope was to try and outgun us first.

Motoyama One airfield, our first objective, was four hundred yards ahead and to our right. But before we got anywhere near it, a reinforced pillbox that guarded the approach with a 75 mm cannon would have to go. It was tearing the hell out of George's 4th Division directly to our right and would be getting to us next. Direct hits by Navy shells had only dented the bunker's hardened concrete walls and flat roof. I whacked a machine gunner on his helmet to get his attention and pointed at the bunker. There was a small sighting aperture in its side. That was the target. The PFC gunner finally saw what I was pointing at. The smash of cannon shells and rattling small arms fire made it almost useless to yell. We were pretty much down to hand signals. The gunner slammed his gun tripod into position, his buddy snapped the .30 cal. body onto the legs and opened the breech. He laid in the ammo belt, slapped it closed, chambered a round and click. Nothing. It didn't fire. Sniper rounds kicked up the black sand around us and whizzed by my ears like hornets. Enemy mortars were raining straight down on us with a sickening whisper, "whish whish," like snakes falling out of the sky. They landed close enough to throw sand into my eyes and mouth. We were dying in packs, all around me. The gunner rolled over and went to work cleaning the gun. It wasn't healthy for me to stand there and watch him. I needed metal on that target fast and wanted to grab that gun out of his hands. I could clean that goddamn thing in half his time. His buddy was digging the cleaning kit out of the gunner's pack, another cluster fuck. If this gunner didn't get himself and his buddy killed, I'd come back when he was firing. I needed a gun and demolition team fast. I went up the line looking for them. More men were coming over the top terrace chased by the cannon fire ripping up the beach behind us. I moved my men forward to spread us out and open up holes for the new men to take cover in. I ran in a crouch down the line kicking asses to get them up and out of their holes, looking for my gun crew. Some boys were shaking so badly they came up on rubbery legs and had to be hauled up and pushed. Others sprung out of the ground like jackrabbits. The adrenaline pushed them another ten yards up the beach until they found another hole to flop in. I found a corporal and his demolition-assault team hugging their holes. I picked out the young satchel man and helped him strip off everything but his satchel of C-2 explosive. I pointed out the aperture and he looked back at me, nearly paralyzed with fear. But he nodded quickly, letting me know he was ready. He was one of the greatest heroes I ever met, this boy who couldn't have been more than twenty years old. He had about a fifty-yard dash ahead of him over shell holes through sniper, cannon and mortar fire but he nodded at me and got ready to run, very possibly to his death. Can anyone be more of a hero than that? This is where we needed those young legs. They could save us because we were sure to die very soon if we didn't take out that bunker.

I looked back at my gunner. He was cleaning the breech of his gun with a toothbrush. He was pretty cool under fire, I had to give him that. I could tell he was taking his time and wasn't going to make the same mistake twice, if he lived long enough. My gunners, the boys I'd trained from raw boots, were scattered across the beach mixed in with everybody else. I knew we had to lay some fire and mortar rounds into the airfield where the snipers and enemy mortar crews were operating.

"Get them fucking guns set up!" I screamed out to the next hole, "Pass it on!" The order went down the line while a hailstorm of mortars started falling all around us. The mortar crews had us bracketed.

"Move up!" I ordered. Holes were sometimes no defense against mortars. They came straight down and if they landed anywhere near the rim of your hole, you were going to have a real bad day. I had to get the men out of this area. Down the shells came, blasting red-hot steel needles in a thirty-yard circle when they hit, leaving little three-foot smoking craters in the sand. The men moved up. Four or five were cut down instantly by snipers and exploding mortar shells. The screams went up to heaven as my men got blown apart.

The Navy started finding their targets on the sides of Suribachi. A few of the bastards that had been killing us a dozen at a time were now quiet, their blackened steel muzzles smoking, their camouflage burned away. The weather was turning quickly. Whitecaps were whipping up on the surface of the gray water. It was getting hard to make a landing on the beach. There was no more room. We still didn't own two hundred yards of Iwo.

My toothbrush gunner was firing. I moved back down the line hand-signaling my demolition runner to keep his eyes on me. I got to the gunner. He was hitting everything but the aperture. Jesus, Mary and Joseph! I just about knocked him out of the way and took his gun. Instead I whacked him on the head again and pointed to a spot down the beach thirty feet away. He could get an angle there that would ricochet the bullets into the aperture, a bank shot. He was going to get a second chance. He and his ammo carrier moved out in a split second, hit the deck exactly on the spot I wanted and started pouring fire into the hole. He was a damn good Marine and a lucky son of a bitch to still be alive.

After we sent a few of our steel calling cards through the aperture, they slid a steel door over the slot, just like the slots in the front doors of the old speakeasies. My gunner had his orders to keep that slot closed. The bunker was now blind toward our side. I looked back and my demo man was facedown in his hole. When I got there he was shaking like he was in a blizzard butt naked. He was scared senseless. I gave him his orders again. He wasn't from my unit but he had trained for this like every one of my own. He knew the drill. Get to the steel doors in the bunker and put the charge at the base of them. It was game time. He got up on his knees and got ready to go. I knew he would. I never got a chance to shake his hand.

I gave my gunner the signal and he laid down covering fire. The boy sprinted out of the hole and toward the pillbox. The line of tracers flew by him, about eighteen inches above the boy's right shoulder as he ran. This was close work and not for faint hearts. Ricochets were coming off the steel doors along with everything else the boy had to run through, but he ran strong, like a real champion. Next up was the flamethrower of the demo team. A big fella with seventy pounds of napalm on his back. Again, he got his orders and braced for the dash. He saw me point my forked fingers at my eyes and knew to keep his own eyes on me for the signal. I got back to my machine gunner. I didn't need another mistake that would risk the attack. I slapped him on the back and he ceased fire. There was a moment of quiet then, between all the blasts and screaming, just for a second, when the boy stopped and slipped the explosives off his back, getting ready to toss them against the steel doors. He pulled the fuse cord and lobbed the satchel underhand against the steel doors. He turned and ran before the satchel landed. He made it ten or twenty yards before he hit the deck. We all did. The satchel went off like a five-hundred-pound bomb. Chunks of concrete and reinforcing wire blew one hundred feet into the air and landed all over us.

I looked up and the doors were gone. A gaping hole was in the bunker where the doors once were. So far this was textbook. Next in line, my husky flamethrower peeked from under his helmet at me. I gave him the signal. He struggled up and out of his hole toward the smoking bunker. I slapped my gunner again and he started pouring fire into the hole to cover the lumbering fire starter. The corporal trundled along the line of tracer bullets waddling under the seventy-pound firebomb strapped to his back. He made it to the hole. I slapped the gunner again, cease fire, as the big man shot liquid flame into the hole. By the book, just the way we trained, the bunker was put out of commission.

I'd had enough of the gunner's handiwork and grabbed his weapon by the bail and unlocked it from the tripod. Sometimes you just got to do things yourself. I screamed in his ear over the incoming fire. "Get the belt and follow me!" I knew that any soldiers coming out of the bunker would be coming out firing and I wasn't going to let the corporal be the sacrificial lamb. My gunner kept up as we ran to the bunker and climbed up on the roof. Nine or ten enemy poured out of the back door, some on fire, all of them smoking and burned. I killed them all.

There was no time to set up the gun. I swung it by the bail, all thirty pounds of it shaking in my arms, shell casings flying from the side. The gunner kept the belt from fouling as I mowed them down. I didn't feel sorry for them. There was no time to feel anything. They died like a lot of other men that day. Their number was up.

I gave the gunner back his weapon. The barrel was searing hot. There were lots of men to move forward to the airfield and I had to get them into position. Moving down the line was only a little safer than before we blew the bunker. They hadn't gotten to us yet but we were still well in range of the cannon on Suribachi and the mortars and snipers at the airfield. As if that weren't enough the Navy had redirected the rolling barrage into close support. The shells that flew just over our heads before the advance to the bunker were now landing a few hundred feet in front of us. Way too close for comfort. One small targeting mistake and we all would be joining the enemy in back of the bunker.

★

As I moved down the line with Lou Plain, moving the men forward, mortars kept raining down, taking a few more of us with almost every blast. The air was full of the deadly sounding "whish whish" as they dropped like stones on top of us. For some, I guess, the sound of dropping mortar shells wasn't that bad. If you could hear them, your number wasn't up. At least that was the superstition. They say that the shell you don't hear is the one with your name on it.

★ 5 ★

Civilian Life

Gaburo's Laundry, 1943

Angelo told me about the job at Gaburo's Laundry, driving a delivery truck. It sounded okay, outdoors, on my own and old man Gaburo was a decent guy. He ran half a dozen trucks up and down Route 202 to the bakeries, auto shops and commercial printing outfits—anybody who used uniforms. It was steady work.

I walked in on a Monday morning and next thing I knew I was getting outfitted for my own uniform. They gave me a white shirt, pants and cap. I wasn't going to wear that damn silly cap but I took it and shut up. The best thing about the whole deal was that it made Pop proud. A good job, he said when I walked in the house for lunch in my brown company jacket with "Gaburo Laundry" stitched in red letters over the pocket. I could see the relief on Pop's face and that was worth everything to me. I didn't usually come home for lunch but that day I wanted to get back and show him I'd made some kind of progress, a step in the right direction I hoped. We sat at the table, while Mama served the food. It was the first meal I had where I could relax since the day I came home.

I guess this was the step everybody was waiting for. I looked like I belonged somewhere. Mama was smiling like I'd just been elected president. The truth was I felt pretty good about myself. I couldn't exactly say it was my calling—I heard nothing about it in the quiet time, the whisperings, as I was falling asleep—but I suppose any step looks like a step forward when you've been standing still a while. Almost three months had gone by since I came home from Manila.

I drove my route in the big white Reo. Up to Flemington, Passaic and Orange. It would've made things a lot easier if I'd had real driving lessons. The big square truck came around corners like the big 5 tons we hijacked in Manila and a lamppost or two bit the dust on my watch. Old man Gaburo noticed the dents and scrapes and took me aside to make sure I wasn't drinking on the job. On my own time, I came in and knocked out the dents as best I could with a ball-peen hammer Pop had in the cellar. I painted over the scrapes and pretty much got the truck back into its original shape.

Of course, it was good-bye to the fellas at the country club and this time everybody knew it was for good. I'd see them when I played rounds but I wasn't going to be one of the old gang anymore. It wasn't a big event like when I went off to the Army but in a way it felt more permanent. The Army seemed like an adventure. The job I had now was my first try at putting down roots.

I hardly said a word all day. To most people on the route, it was just, "Hello, how you doing?"—and then back in the truck. It was me and piles of uniforms, all day long. I went back to daydreaming the way I'd done in school and knew this was a bad development. I could feel my mind going away at every chance, going back to Lolita mainly and then sometimes I'd be in the middle of one of my fights back in Manila. I'd see it all again just like I was there, only now I could see what I should have done. It was clearer now—the openings I missed, the counterpunch I should have seen coming. I was lonely. Just about as lonely as I had ever been in my life.

In the service, I had a dozen real buddies. These were the guys in my unit who I lived elbow to elbow with for three years. I knew them better than I knew anyone except my family and sometimes even better than that. I didn't know what most of my sisters and brothers like Dolores or Angie really did with their days, but I knew practically every detail of everyone's day in my unit. I was doing exactly the same guard duty, KP and work details they did. On the patrols, we kept each other sharp and helped each other up the steep mountain paths and through snagging jungle paths.

Even though we were chasing starving, raggedy bandits, rags or not, they could shoot straight. I watched my buddy's back and somebody watched mine. We had casualties, mainly to malaria, jungle rot and dysentery, but snipers took down one of us every few weeks and poisoned bamboo spikes flew from booby traps at our faces and groins. This was our life together. Every insult like stinking food or no soap made us closer, every wound made us a more determined fighting unit. We had our little victories too. We'd turn up a cache of old rifles down a well or rusty grenades in a rice bin. We did our job, and we believed for a while that the job meant something.

Now it was just me and this big white truck. I felt like I was sixty years old. Sometimes I would be daydreaming and I'd forget I'd only been driving for a month. Sometimes I thought I'd been driving and exchanging bins of dirty overalls for clean ones for years, that I'd always done it, that I never had another life. I could see years stretching out ahead of me in little conversations, "Hello, how you doing?" I could see I was going the way I did at school, my mind was turning away from what I did all day long.

The whisperings started up again. From the hidden places in my head where I couldn't get a good fix on them. I couldn't hardly hear them at first but after a while I knew they'd come back, that they never left. All the time they were just waiting in the shadows for me to get off my path. They were back. But all they could tell me was I was doing something wrong. They never told me what I was supposed to do instead and that made me mad. They were like flies buzzing around my head. "Push them bins," they told me sometimes. "Get them dirty ones out and them clean ones in."

So then it started again, the push and pull, trying to draw a bead on a target I couldn't even see. Nothing heated me up like not knowing what I was supposed to be doing. At home, in the Army, in the ring, it didn't matter. I had to be clear in my mind, I had to have a target I could see. It was a little different now because I was older and I had learned how to wait.

The Army taught us how to wait in line, wait for orders, wait for everything. While we waited we continued to do our jobs. We changed into dry socks, cleaned our weapons, and killed bugs. So I kept pushing them dirty bins out and them clean bins in. This was my job, my grown-up job. This was where I came out in life and I sure as hell wasn't going to go around moping about it like I did as a school-boy. I was a grown-up now and whisperings or not, I had grown-up responsibilities. People were counting on me to start getting ahead in life. I was going to buckle down and make this work. I would snap-to and hold the line. I would stay in my position until I was ordered to move out. I didn't know who was going to give that order but I was dug in until further notice. I was a laundryman.

No sooner had I had it out with myself than the complications set in, meaning ladies. Word got around Raritan fast and there were a dozen young, middle and almost old ladies who had eyes for yours truly. I never complained about the attention I got from girls before, but now I could see the strings that came attached to each one and it made me think a little longer than I used to. There were the cream-ery girls, the Reiskopf sisters, one light-haired with freckles who made me laugh and the dark one who had me thinking of her late into the night. This wasn't a healthy setup, I could see that right away. I'd have to hurt one to go with the other and the next time I came to pick up cream and butter I might get the curdled bottle from the one I didn't pick. There was the widow Bates who bent over plants all day at her nursery business, working like a man in her big sun hat. There was a ready-made business there and a big four-poster bed with a down comforter all paid for. All I had to do was say the word and the rest of my life was wrapped up with a neat little bow. There was Alma, the morning short-order cook at the diner down Main Street who whipped up scrambled eggs and always gave me an extra slice of bacon. She reminded me a little of Lolita, sort of a rounded-out version, built wide for having children. There were shopgirls who came by the house, friends of Catherine and Mary, who sent messages through my sisters that they were free for the dance at St. Ann's or needed an escort to the grange fair in Flemington. None of it made my life easier. I'd have to pick one eventually. But I had an appetite like a bear. I wanted all of them.

No matter how much was going on inside me, when the spring of 1940 rolled out like a Persian rug across New Jersey, I was happy just to be alive. From everything I'd seen across the country, in California and in the South Seas, New Jersey was the most beautiful. It even smelled beautiful to me. Driving the big, open truck brought all the smells and sights of the countryside to me. If Carlo was around, I'd pick him up in the truck and he'd make a lounger out of laundry bins piled high with uniforms. He'd ride like a king, stretched out with his head propped up on a pillow while we discussed the various young ladies around town and their charms. We'd stop at the Hire's root beer stand for a hot dog and root beer. When we got tired of dreaming about the local women, we'd talk about maybe starting our own business. We thought about all kinds of ideas for making money, from opening a garage to making clothes for working men. We figured Pop could set us straight on how to make them, and then it would be just a matter of getting customers. It always came to silence when we got to that part. Neither one of us was any kind of salesman and we knew it. It didn't stop us though. We'd spin stories about getting rich in things we'd read about in magazines. We drove my route while the spring mud and rain smell blew into the truck as we chattered on about this business and that business, this girl and the other. When we pulled up to a customer's place, Carlo would always be the first one out of the truck. He'd start right in hauling out the bins. Many times I wished there was enough salary in the job to have Carlo help me all the time. We made a good team and short work of it.

The customers knew me by now. Some of them would remember Carlo from the few times he was along for the ride. It was becoming a regular routine. I could feel the sameness of it all settle on me, giving me the order of things that let me relax. I had an easy target now. Just show up, drive the route and everything would be jake.

Part of the routine was a stop at the nursery after work hours. The widow Bates was named Carla. She cooked chicken in a clay pot for me and her hair was long and wild with strands of silver through the red brown. Her hands were rougher than the shop girls' even though she kept them laved with Cornhusker's Lotion trying to stave off the roughness that her digging in the dirt and carrying pots cost her. She knew enough about men and how the world expected things of us that I didn't have to keep up a conversation. This, more than anything else, made me come back to her time after time. If I had to explain what my intentions were, what my plans were, I couldn't have made more than a poor excuse for my behavior. I'd have to talk sideways until I hit on something that made sense to both of us. That would have been too much effort and I would have slunk away like a dog caught in the cat's milk saucer because in my heart I knew making love to her was some kind of sin or crime against society. I didn't ask Father Amedeo, I didn't want to know the details of my lawbreaking. Between Carla and me it was all right. It was easy as the spring rain and we just let it happen. I came to need her all times of the day. Sometimes I couldn't wait for our after-hours appointment. I made a daring daylight raid. She never refused me. She just put up the closed sign on her front door and the world went away for an hour. We were happy and we were quiet about it.

She'd been married for many years and lost her husband a few years earlier to an infection they never did figure out completely. She had only been with two men in her life. I was the second. It wasn't at all like the courting I might do with a younger lady. We had a way, a natural way, of being together that lonely people fall into when they only have the evening crickets to share their thoughts with. I guess it was just easy. It was something we didn't share with anyone else. I didn't even tell Carlo.

Nothing stays a secret very long in a small town. It wasn't long before the whisperings I heard weren't coming from inside my head. It seemed that I wasn't the only one with a desire for Carla's company. She was a handsome, tall woman who stood out wherever she went. She was fond of the color yellow and drew the eye of anyone who passed her way like the new daffodils on the roadside. No one ever came out directly and told me I was a marked man but there started to be plenty of comments and looks directed at me. I heard that people were quite a bit more direct with Carla. It seemed that housewives around town were concerned that an attractive, unattached woman of experience like herself was now taking suitors. No husband was safe and no amount of encouragement for people to mind their own business stopped the flow of rumors.

I never heard a word about any of it through Carla. She stood on her own and didn't blame me or ask me for protection, not that I could have done a thing anyway. She fought her own fights and because of that ended up protecting me. This small town squabbling was a new kind of guerilla fighting. Instead of raggedy-assed Philippine bandits, New Jersey housewives and schoolteachers were taking pot shots at us. It was warfare just the same and I saw how people formed up ranks, sent out scouts and the rest of it. The weapons were different but the strategy was just the same. Some old friends were now enemies and they wanted to invade our lives. That's how I saw the stuff Carla was made of. She stood and fought. She made a line and said no one will cross on my watch. Damn if it didn't make me take notice right away. Somehow when the rough stuff starts flying I'm all in for it— always have been. I can smell a fight coming in the air. I wanted to salute her just like I did for MacArthur or any real fighting officer back in Manila. She was a natural leader and I knew my flank was covered when she was on duty.

I watched her operate. She didn't know a thing about strategy or tactics. She didn't give a damn about the military. It never came into her mind. But she was a commander just the same. I saw it clearly and the vision sunk in so deep that I felt it in my chest. It was maybe the strangest thing, other than the whisperings that told me the future, that had happened to me yet in my life. I had to come all the way back to Raritan to really understand what a real leader was from a lady who grew flowers for a living. It was like the sun cracked open in the sky and inside was the little coal stove in Pop's living room.

She didn't want anything for being the way she was. She didn't need me to say thank you. She wasn't even doing it for herself as much as she was doing it because she couldn't help it. They attacked, she defended. They hurt her, she took the pain and held her ground. It didn't matter if I knew what was going on or not. She wasn't looking for a medal.

All I know is when it sunk in deep, this idea of what a real commander was, it hit something. How the hell was I going to keep pushing people's dirty laundry around when there was a fight brewing just as sure as the sun came up in the morning? I couldn't forget that the Japanese were eyeing my buddies in the Philippines. Just because I wasn't there anymore didn't mean I could pretend it wasn't going to happen. When the steel started flying where was I going to be? I was goddamned if I knew. I didn't see any way in or out of this problem.

Hardly anybody anywhere around knew what was going on. The papers didn't mention a thing except the occasional dispatch from a city in faraway China that collapsed under a Japanese assault. It didn't mean a thing to anybody I knew or met. To me it meant that a war was a few hundred miles closer to Manila, to Lolita, to Mac and the fellas in my old unit who would be running for a cave as soon as the first shots flew. The only thing to do was put it out of my mind. I wasn't a soldier anymore. I wasn't going to draw a line and say that no one will cross on my watch. I was a laundryman.

Where Carla and I hadn't talked much before, we now got into long talks about what we should do and if we should do anything. The truth was I was spoiling for a fight. Who the hell knows what I was thinking really but I felt like I had to go on some kind of attack. It wasn't like that, of course, for Carla, and like any good commander, when she gave an order she expected it to be obeyed. She was not going to attack anyone and I wasn't going to attack anyone to defend her honor or any other such nonsense. I admired her and probably I was falling in love with her. This was the first time for me. I didn't know if I was falling in love or coming down with a head cold. Everything was all mixed up with everything else. I wanted to fight. I wanted to protect her. I thought maybe I wanted to marry her. Anyway it all came out wrong. She couldn't make heads or tails of what I wanted and neither could I.

The End of the Line

I walked into the garage where my big, white Reo was parked. The guys were all just coming in for the day and Mr. Gaburo was lining up the orders for the route. I stared at the truck and knew that as sure as I was standing there that I would never get in it again.

I walked around it, looked at it, then walked back to the office. I didn't know what to say to Mr. G. He was busy checking that the correct bins were put on the trucks in the right order. I had to admire him. He had everything squared away in his life. Everything was in its right place. He came in, did his job and went home to a happy family. You couldn't ask for anything more. I went to the back and helped the fellas with the bins. I didn't know if words would come out of my mouth when I spoke to Mr. G. but I had to say something. I was not getting into that truck again. Not only that, I was never going to set foot in this place again. It was all, suddenly, definitely, over. I felt my heart jumping around in my chest like I was about to step off a cliff. I was hot. What the hell was I doing? Just like that, out of the blue, I'm going to quit the one job that I could tolerate. I was going to disappoint the hell out of Pop and worry Mama and for what? What did it mean?

I never felt more unsure of myself in my whole life. When I quit high school, I'd had years to think it over. I had a job to go to at the country club. I knew why I was doing it. This time I didn't have the least little clue about what I was doing or why. I thought I'd run to see Father Amedeo before I started out for the day. But that would have just made me late for every stop. The last bins got loaded, double-checked and the wheels chocked so they didn't roll and smash into the sides of the truck. Old man Gaburo turned and gave me the flip of his head that he always did that was a kind of hello and good-bye.

"Mr. G. You got anybody can take my route today?" I said.

He looked me over. "Whatsa matter, Johnny? You sick?"

"Nah." I wasn't going to lie. I'd just have to come in tomorrow and tell him the truth anyway. "I wanna quit. If you want I'll work until you find another driver but I've got to quit."

"You gotta quit? What for?" He wasn't mad. He just couldn't imagine what would make me quit a good job like this one.

"I just gotta quit, I'm real sorry. I can't drive your deliveries anymore." I felt like I was going to float away. Like I'd finally gone completely out of my head and there was nothing left of me to keep me on the ground. Mr. G. was a real gentleman about it. Maybe he was sorry for me, I don't know, but he said, "Don't worry, Johnny. George can take over. You take the rest of the week off, maybe you'll change your mind and come back Monday."

That was it. I walked out. I was going from one thought to the other so fast I thought I might fly apart. I was happy one second and scared the next. I knew exactly what I wanted, and then I had no idea. The only thing I could think to do was go concentrate on hitting a golf ball. That seemed like the one solitary thing that could calm and focus my mind while I sorted through all the different thoughts speeding through me. I wasn't ready to talk to anybody. I needed to be outdoors. I needed to walk a long way and be by myself. I headed across town to the country club.

★

I had always been able to find my quiet time on the fairways. I guess some people found the same thing praying in church but I needed to be moving around, out in the open. The layout of the Raritan Country Club course was the perfect open space for me. I knew it like I knew Pop's living room. I could have walked all eighteen holes blindfolded and that day I practically did. I didn't keep score. I don't even know how many balls I lost. It didn't matter. All that mattered was that I was out in the grass and trees by myself. After four or five holes I gave up trying to figure out where the decision to quit Gaburo's came from. There was no reason for it so I stopped looking for one. It was just a mystery. Maybe Father Amedeo could find a reason but I sure couldn't. Somehow it was a part of the whole mess with Carla but that was as far as I got with it. The next thing was to figure out how to explain it.

That would have been a hell of a lot easier if I had something to replace it with, a plan of some kind, even a notion of where I was headed, but there was no luck there either. Pieces of thoughts popped up but I couldn't piece any of them together into anything that would make sense. All I knew was what I couldn't do. I had no idea what I could or would do. Any thoughts of marriage to Carla flew away like frightened birds. It didn't even seem possible that I had considered marriage seriously. She was ten years older than I was. I was still living with my parents. The only thing I could think of was that maybe it never was serious. Maybe I was just fooling myself or maybe I was losing my marbles. That seemed like the most reasonable explanation so far. I was cracking up. That got me to stop and think. Even walking and swinging a golf club took too much brainpower. I took stock of everything else in my life and it all seemed to add up. It was just these few areas—work and women—where everything was like a bad dream. I don't think I even made it through the front nine holes. Whatever had me, had me walking back into town double time. I needed to talk to someone.

Angie was hunched over his sewing machine up to his elbows in material for someone's new suit. He looked up, surprised to see me. It must have been sometime around ten in the morning, the middle of the important morning work hours for normal people. It was clear I wasn't one of the normal working people anymore.

"I quit Gaburo's."

Angie was used to my occasional odd behavior, hearing voices and such. "Why?"

Damn, there it was right out of the gate, the question I didn't have an answer for. "I guess it just wasn't for me."

"Does Pop know?" he asked.

"Not yet."

"What the hell's going on, Johnny? You got some kind of drinking problem or something?"

"Hell, no. I . . ." The truth was I should have thought a little more about what I was going to say before I came in. ". . . I wanted to talk it over with you, before Pop hears it." That went over like a lead balloon. We talked it over for a while but never really came to anything that sounded too good. It all boiled down to the fact that I didn't know where the hell I was going, but I was going there fast.

Angelo was the second oldest of the children just behind Phyllis. Phyllis was married and had a new baby. Angie followed the old man's footsteps into the tailor trade. He was the oldest son so it figured in the traditional way of thinking that he would take on the family business. At thirty, he was already set in his ways and looked like he was going to be a carbon copy of the old man. For the younger kids like me, way down in the batting order at number six out of the ten, he was the next best thing to Pop. He agreed with Pop on just about everything and even dressed like him—black pants, white shirt and jacket. As he sat there behind his sewing machine you got a real good idea of what Pop was like twenty-five years ago. In our house, if you wanted to know how Pop would take to an idea, it was best to run it by Angie first.

From our discussion, I could tell I wasn't going to be the favorite son at the dinner table tonight. I knew Pop wasn't going to yell and he would try like hell to keep Mama in the dark about it, but I could see his face already in the look Angie was giving me. I was like a puppy who was slow to be housebroken. All I kept thinking was how the hell did I get here again?

Dinner came and I managed to avoid most of the conversation in case it came around to how I was doing down at the laundry. Angie didn't let on about our talk even though I said I would take Pop aside before dinner. He knew it was a tough assignment for me and let me come at it in my own time. Phyllis called after dinner to talk about her new baby so that grabbed all the attention. The Basilones had to be the happiest grandparents in the world at that moment. Pop even broke out the grappa for a toast to the little one. I thought the Mother's Milk I sold in Manila was bad until I had a snort of Pop's homemade grappa. One sip of that stuff and I knew why more Italians weren't alcoholics. It tasted like kerosene and felt like it going down. I wasn't keen to break up the party mood with my little troubles, so I waited until the old man had a few under his belt, and the celebration about the baby turning over on its own died down.

He took it better than I expected. Angie's harsh reaction didn't account for a nose full of homemade liquor in the equation. Pop even seemed like he wanted to help me figure my way out, or into where I was supposed to be.

He sobered up a bit and gave me, his troubled sixth child, his full attention. "Whatta you got in mind?" I had to be honest with him. "I don't know," I said. It seemed like I'd been giving him this same answer since I could remember. He looked at me and didn't say anything for a while. Angie was watching every move like I was. Finally

Pop let out a little sigh and said, "Tell you what. I'll call Phyllis. If they have room, I'm sure they'll let you stay with them for a while."

"Okay." I would have said okay to anything he said since I didn't know what to do. I know he didn't mean to make me feel bad, but I still felt like I was being booted out. I know he meant well. Angie saw the sense of it right away and seconded Pop's decision. I didn't feel too bad until Mama got up and went into the kitchen. There was nothing left to do in the kitchen. The dishes had been washed and put away. The coffee had been served. I heard the broom come out of the hall closet. She was sweeping the floor. That was her way of appearing to be busy while she was hiding her face from me. She wasn't going to go against Pop on this decision. She knew it was right and it hurt her. She hung her head and stared at the spotless floor while she swept her pain around the room. I knew then that my time under my parents' roof had run out. I was a problem that they couldn't solve and a burden they couldn't afford. They still had six or seven children to provide for and Pop was getting tired. At forty-five, he was beginning to look like an old man. My parents both loved me, that was clear, but the time had come for me to move on and find the life I was called for.

Reisterstown, Maryland

I said good-bye to Carla outside in her yard among the clay pots and young trees wrapped in burlap. It was something she had been expecting for a while. I wanted her to know it didn't have anything to do with the rumors and trouble from the people in town. As always, she was way ahead of me. If anything, a decent dust-up with nosey neighbors would have been the one thing that might keep me around and she knew that. But a fight was good for a warrior; it wasn't good for a businessperson who depended on neighbors for a living. That was the beginning of the end for us but I was just too young and inexperienced to see it. Carla knew the seasons of things—that they were born, blossomed and died. We were dying. She just let nature take its course and enjoyed the little time we had left. There was no need to discuss it with me. She knew I didn't see the end coming and it could only have hurt me.

So there was no surprise. We weren't clinging, the way I'd left Lolita. We were an extra branch of her life that she now pruned away gently. Whatever I thought I knew about women, and I thought I knew a lot, went away. She was suddenly more like an older sister. She showed me a kind of love between a man and a woman that I never imagined. It was something strong and clear-eyed. It built me up instead of making me feel like I disappointed her or left her heartbroken. She didn't need me and never wanted anything from me except kindness. She was my hero. She became my guiding light that showed me this way of hers—this quiet way of strength and protection.

★

Reisterstown was a sort of grim little factory town about twenty miles outside of Baltimore. I could see that my days of wandering the dirt country roads taking in the scenery were over. Even if I wanted to clear my mind playing golf I'd have to pay now. Not like the Raritan club where I had a special ex-caddy rate, meaning free. But Pop was right about one thing, the change of scenery got me focused on what I was going to do with my life. Reisterstown was my staging area. It was the point of no return.

Phyllis gave me such a warm welcome that I forgot about being the black sheep of the family for a little while. She and her husband Bill picked me up at the train station in Baltimore. I wasn't ready for the sight of her baby, a little niece of my own. The little girl hit me like a ton of bricks. I completely forgot about Phyllis and Bill as she put her in my arms and I looked into this little girl's face. I can't really say what everything was that I felt but it was something that made me feel small. Like she was giving me the once-over to see if I was the kind of uncle she was interested in. Here I was not ten minutes in Baltimore and already I was being sized up by this pipsqueak.

We got in the car. Phyllis sat up front with Bill and the baby in her arms. The car was a few years old, probably bought used. Right away I saw that Bill Sr. had made his play early in life and took on a big responsibility. He was only a few years older than me but he not only had a job but a family to answer for. I got a little worried for him because I could think of a million things that could go wrong with a game plan like his. Maybe he had the faith in God that Father Amedeo was always going on about. Maybe he had faith in himself. Maybe that was what I was missing. In spite of all my overheated brainwork on the subject, I managed to have a real good conversation with him and Phyllis. He came off like a real decent Joe and I liked him right off.

I knew the fix was in right away. From nowhere Bill started on about the Philgas Company. What a great place it was to work, all the great guys there, how you could be outside, on your own—like he'd been reading my mail. Phyllis chimed in seconding everything Bill said. The way he talked about it you might think he'd be happy to pay them to work. Anyway, it was all for my benefit. They sure didn't waste any time. Of course I was grateful and I said I was interested but it made me feel even worse about being a nobody. That's how I felt. Nobody thought I could make my own way. Everybody was going overboard to help me get on the right track. And a track is exactly what it was—straight and long. I got the message and played along. Before we got back to the house, I agreed to a meeting with Bill's boss that coming week. It looked like I was going to move from delivering laundry to delivering gas. I don't know how many times I said thanks, too many probably. I didn't want Phyllis or Bill to get any idea that I wasn't grateful to them both. I wanted them to think I was excited about the prospect of working for a great company. They tried so hard and just wanted to help me. They didn't have to know what was really going on in my head.

It was as bad as it could get. I couldn't get out of my own way. I felt like I was coming apart at the seams. I couldn't remember things they told me just minutes before. It was like their voices were coming at me from far away.

When we got to the house it was obvious they had gone to a lot of trouble to make me feel at home. Phyllis had a pot of marinara half cooked, ready to be heated up. It took most of a day to make it like Mama taught her, so she must have started early in the day. They had bought a book on golf for me that they placed on a small end table near the couch. The house was small—two small bedrooms upstairs, one was made into a nursery, and their own bedroom. My room was the couch. That's when I really felt it. I felt worse than I ever had in my life. Sitting there on the couch listening to all the cheery talk about the future and their plans for the baby made me want to sink through the floor and never see anyone again. I couldn't even be happy for my own sister.

The voice was coming at me from every angle when I tried to sleep and it wasn't whispering anymore. It was telling me I had messed my life up completely and I'd better do something fast or something even worse would happen. But I was stuck. I was completely dependent on my sister and her husband. I didn't know anyone in the area or any place I could go that might give me a chance to gather my thoughts. I couldn't even afford a round of golf. I walked. First around the block, then around the neighborhood, then from one end of Reisterstown to the other. Sometimes I thought I might just keep walking and never come back. That would be one solution.

On my long walks, the music that played in my father's living room came back to me. It was so hypnotizing to him that us children would gather round and sit quietly listening to words we couldn't understand, but seeing the deep effect they had on him. I sang them from memory, still not understanding the meaning of the words, on my long walks. I kept the tune more or less like the records I heard over and over again. I didn't know what the hell I was singing; I just knew it was sad. That was me—walking around singing nonsense, a stranger in this small town. Some people nodded and waved a little, most just stayed back and stared at me. I didn't care what they thought. Singing was about my only entertainment. That and playing with the baby.

I didn't know where I was headed. It crossed my mind to get a job on a ship at the Port of Baltimore and get out of everyone's hair for a while. Maybe I could get lucky and get a ship going to the Philippines. I was full of wild schemes, anything to change the life I saw coming up for me. When it came down to it, I knew that shipping out or joining the circus or hitchhiking across the country was dodging the question of what the hell I was planning to do for the rest of my life. That same question had been at me since high school, with a three-year break while I was in the Army. Terrible and depressing as it was being a paper tiger in the U.S. military, it was beginning to look like the only way to go. Maybe I'd get lucky and war would break out.

The job at Philgas was everything Bill said about it. I was on my own route repairing and installing gas meters and equipment for companies. The boss was a straight-ahead guy with a serious approach. He didn't sound like the type who would be much fun after work but I liked him well enough. He was a company man and he made it real clear that no shenanigans of any kind were allowed. It could be dangerous if you lost your concentration on an install job. He reminded me a bit of the drill instructors at Fort Jay, but without the filthy mouth and the steady stream of insults they used.

At first, I was put on with Bill to get the feel of the work. We were on his calls together all day, then together again all night at home. For a week this was okay but it wasn't going to last much beyond that. He was as nice to me as you could be and I was doing my best to show how much I appreciated that he vouched for me and was risking his job by recommending me. At the end of that first week I was ready to be on my own and I could tell he had shown me all he could.

On this job I saw even less people than on Gaburo's route. I was the invisible gasman. People would nod or point to where I was sup-

posed to get to work and that was that. I'd never see them again. I got
so lonely I started singing opera, at least what I thought was opera,
letting it all out like a real Caruso while I drove to jobs. With the
truck windows open and me thundering out made-up opera at the
top of my lungs, I had other drivers slowing down and turning to look
at me. People on the street turned their heads to follow the sound. If
I could do that, I thought, get people to turn and listen, maybe I
could be a real singer. The idea had something to it.

Phyllis thought I had a great voice. But then she would have liked
it if I'd taken up soap carving, so I couldn't trust her opinion. Bill
was the acid test. I tried him out one night while we were all around
the dinner table and was showing him how to play poker, giving him
all my tricks, everything I learned from the caddy shack all the way
through the cutthroat twenty-four-hour games in Manila. This way
he could have a little extra income if he worked at it. I had to show
him how to cheat, so he could spot at least the basics of it and protect himself. What I taught was smart playing, that's all—the full
game, the mechanics and the mental part of it. My sister did not ap-
prove, so we moved the lessons out to the garage eventually.

This particular night was before we were shown the door. I let fly
with a few phrases of opera singing, making it a sort of joke to keep
the game fun. He perked right up and said I had a decent voice. I
didn't let on how good that made me feel, but it had a big effect on
me. I finally had a little success at something, even silly opera singing. That night as I'm drifting off, I thought that sometimes you just
get used to the idea that you can't do much right. Not doing things
right becomes a habit, like anything else. Pretty soon nobody expects
you to do anything right, and you get shipped off to a relative like I
did. Then the other side was, like in Army basic, you do something

right, you get used to doing everything right, people expect you to do everything right and that's how you become Manila John, undefeated in nineteen fights. You can do everything right one time and everything wrong the next time. So what made that happen? That's when I felt like I needed to talk to Father Amedeo again. He'd have an idea about this I was sure of it. I made up my mind that as soon as I got my first paycheck from Philgas, I was going to pay for a long-distance call to Raritan and see what Father Amedeo's advice was about this.

The idea wouldn't let me go and I didn't think I could wait for my check. Philgas paid every two weeks. I felt like I was finally wrestling with the real problem that had been digging at me since I could remember. How can one man do everything right one time and everything wrong the next? Bill and Phyllis weren't quite sure what I was angling at when I asked them about it. They knew I was talking about myself and wanted to know if I thought I was doing everything wrong. No, I lied, and told them I thought I was doing everything right. I made up something about doing something wrong back in the Army that sounded pretty stupid because I wasn't ready for this kind of question and so I tipped my cards. They knew I was feeling low. They had done everything they could to make me feel at home. Now they felt it wasn't enough. All of a sudden things were complicated. They got quiet. I wanted to make them think everything was okay, so I tried too hard. Reisterstown was a great little place, I said, and Philgas was a company I could really go to bat for. Things were jumping out of my mouth that sounded like they came from "My Little Margie," a silly radio show that Phyllis and I listened to sometimes. I don't know if they believed my act or not. I think in their hearts they just gave up. They had done their best for me. Maybe they were beginning to think I was a lost cause. And there it was again. I was doing everything wrong.

I still sang like a wild man in the truck now and again, but many times I was working over the idea of how things got going in the right direction or the wrong direction. I remembered that when I put my mind to it, like I put my mind to working a machine gun, the ins and outs of it, every slot, latch and spring, everything about it, that was when everything worked out right. I put it to the test on the job. I started to do each installation or repair job with the care and detail that I had in gunnery school. On every job I looked at every detail before I began, broke down the steps to complete it and organized them so I got in and out in the least amount of time. The change was instant. It was like a big clock had moved into alignment. The boss saw I was completing more jobs per shift and he wanted to know what was going on. When I told him how I approached the work he changed completely. Instead of being like a stone-faced DI, he changed into somebody like one of my poker buddies. Word got back to Bill, who couldn't wait to tell sis and almost overnight I was doing everything right again. This was it then. It was the way you did things, not what you did, that mattered. Now I was up at night seeing this going all the way back to high school. I was a shy kid. Somewhere I got it in my mind that I should stay quiet—I was saying to myself that I couldn't do it right when it came to being with kids my own age. From there it was a straight shot to where I couldn't do anything right in school. To me this was a discovery like penicillin or gunpowder. It still wasn't one hundred percent clear how it all worked, it was still the general principle of the thing. But the path was maybe clearing a little bit. All along I thought my path would be a career, a job or a talent that would come out like boxing or singing or being a soldier but now that was not so clear. It looked like my path was something more slippery, something inside me that no one could see and was even hard to explain. Maybe my path was a way of thinking.

I always liked people so it wasn't hard for me to find ways to practice this new discovery on them. If you look at someone like a machine, you can see they have interlocking parts. Their bodies are one thing but they had feelings and fears and crazy little things they imagined that were all connected somehow. When I saw how Phyllis depended on Bill to speak up about things so that she could speak up too, how they depended on me to be happy at Philgas so they could feel good too, I could see it all clicked. It all fit. It all worked. The way I tightened a nut or wiped the grease from a fitting connected directly to the conversation at dinner that night, and from there the connections went as far and wide as you wanted to think about. Honestly, it wore me the hell out thinking about it after a while. I saw the blueprint for how I was connected to everything else and believed that I was onto something. More than anything I saw that I was the main ingredient in the recipe.

The weeks on the job with Philgas started to go more quickly. The big clockwork wheels, the ratchets and rotors and whatever the hell else made the world go round were now working for me instead of against me. I could see how I would move to a house of my own in a few months and how I could make a life out of delivering gas to people. I knew I could do that. That was a life I could have by just applying the simple principle of concentration that I had discovered. After a while I saw that it would be easy. Then I got a bolt out of the blue to get on a golf course. Somehow all this brainwork had to apply to my golf game; at least I wanted to try it out.

I shanked the ball like a one-armed epileptic. Whatever theory on life I thought I had all worked out went to shit on the golf course. I was back at square one. I had to stop thinking entirely to even keep the ball on the fairway. It was my worst round of eighteen holes since I started playing the game. My neat little blueprint didn't have a diagram on it for golf and I guessed for a lot else besides. But in the world of men and machines, it looked like there was a theory of connection that worked most of the time.

Rumor was that I was due for a promotion. I was a top serviceman for Philgas even though I was a rookie. My path in this part of the world looked pretty clear. Bill was busting with pride about his brother-in-law, the new star of the company. Word went back to Raritan that I had found my way in the world, that I wasn't lost after all. Bill handed me the phone receiver and I could hear the relief in Pop's voice and Mama was crying again, I guess with relief as well. Angie, Mary, Catherine all chimed in with congratulations. They were more excited about me being a successful gas serviceman than they were about me being a light heavyweight champ in the Army. Maybe that's when I remembered. Sometimes things come along, things you should have remembered, and hit you on the side of the head. I remembered why I joined up with the Army in the first place. I wasn't going to make my life in any little town whether it was Raritan or Reisterstown. There was something else for me and no promotion or smile from Pop or claps on the back from everyone in my family could keep me from it. There was something else for me. I remembered Father Amedeo's advice in his drafty, old office in St. Ann's the first time we ever spoke. He talked about having faith and said that I would be shown my path. I had lost my faith but now I had it back again. Even as I was hearing the happiness in everyone's voice I knew I was going to disappoint and worry them again. I was leaving the life they wanted for me. They wanted me to live close to them, to be happy in my life like them. But even as I spoke, I knew I was already gone.

There wasn't anything I could do except walk in and sign up. I was on my way to a job. I passed by the place once and felt the tug. I circled the truck around the block once and there it was, the front door I had been looking for. It was a Marine recruiting office tucked in between a shoe repair place and a laundry. Suddenly life snapped into line again. The past few months seemed like a long weekend bender on Mother's Milk or the smelly Philippino hemp weed cigars. I forgot who I was but now I remembered. I was a soldier. There was no other path for me. It was just that sudden and just that final. I belonged with other soldiers, real soldiers, not garrison rats loafing through their tours.

People might ignore us, send us off to remote islands without uniforms or soap, but one day soon they would need us. That much I knew. They would need us, they would need me and this time, I would be ready. I wasn't going to get into any outfit with standing orders to retreat. I was a fighting man. That was my path. I was a soldier. I was a Marine before I walked through the door.

★ 6 ★

Into the Breech

Quantico was a bug-infested flea pit I wouldn't have wished on a convict. I arrived on July 11, 1940, in a heat wave where the only breeze came from a few million mosquitoes. It was enough to give me second thoughts about the Marines. My first night I was awake all night swatting them. In Manila, the sound of a mosquito buzzing around your head meant you could wake up with a dose of malaria, so I didn't sleep at all. The only solution was to coat my face, neck and arms with GI insect repellent that was sticky as honey and smelled like diesel.

After I was in camp a few days, I realized not many people gave a good goddamn about Marines either. They got about the same rough treatment as the Army gobs I left back in Manila. Maybe a little better, at least we had uniforms and weapons. We got our three hots and a cot, that the DIs informed us was much too good for maggots like us. The hots were mainly shit on a shingle, chipped beef and gravy on white toast. According to our instructors this was the finest food yet created for fighting men. It had the ability to make the weak strong and the timid brave. These were the only type of Marines there ever were, so obviously the stuff worked.

My cot was standard Government Issue but was described by the DIs as the perfect vehicle for exactly the prescribed number of hours the Corps assigned for sleeping. These cots had always produced the world's most feared warriors, so obviously they worked too. That was supposed to take care of any doubts we had about the Corps providing exactly what we needed. It was our DI's job to harden our minds against mistreatment and that was all fine, but it rang a bell in my head when I saw most of the important equipment was the same stuff I trained with in the Army. That didn't bother me but what did bother me was that it was left over from the First World War over twenty years ago. We were using the same old Browning 1917A machine guns and Enfield rifles. That got me thinking that maybe the Marines were the same as the Army except for the fancy striped dress pants. Like I said, it still didn't seem like anybody much gave a cold crap about soldiers and it didn't matter if they were Marines or Army or anything else.

But I made my mind up quick to do things the Marine way. I was going to trust the Corps. This was their spit of land and I was in their outfit now. I had nothing to go back to. If I were to work my life away at Philgas, I could survive, but I wouldn't be much good for anything after a while. My path was clear now and just like Father Amedeo said I would, I knew it.

If this was the way things were going to be as a Marine, then this was the goddamned way things were going to be. If they wanted me to fight a war with an old Browning, that's what I'd do. No matter what, I was going to make something out of this stint. I was going to trust the Corps. To hell with everything else.

Right off I got to like the idea that Marines weren't big on griping about every little thing like some Joes in the Army who made complaining a second career. The bugs and the heat weren't something to waste your breath on. Marines were big on overcoming things and this way of thinking clicked in my mind. I knew enough about being a fighter that if I let things like bugs get my attention, my mind was on the wrong track. In the ring, I would be headed for a big right hand that could turn the lights out. If we were heading into a shooting war I wanted to be with Marines who kept their minds on the right track, and that track was being a warrior. That's what I signed up for. There weren't any sad sacks in the Marines. Sad sacks were strictly Army and I wanted nothing to do with them.

On the other side of the coin, there were a lot of stiff-necked peckerwoods who wanted to be heroes. A lot of them washed out early but there were still plenty left over. I never had a problem with Southern boys before but these peckerwood types started irritating me. They pronounced the "I" in Italian like island. They did it deliberately when I made the mistake of letting them know it got under my skin. "I"talian they'd say in their little groups of Georgia or 'bama boys. And they'd whittle, not carve, just whittle down a stick with their Ka-Bar, like that was doing something useful. I always encouraged them though. I told them if they kept at it, they could learn to carve like grown-ups one day. One thing led to another. It was the fourth week in basic so everybody was ready to fight anyway. I had my twentieth and twenty-first fights unofficially. I remained undefeated. Nobody knew I was "Manila John" and I didn't tell them. After that, the Southern boys were polite as anyone I'd ever met. They were naturally more respectful than most once you were on the right side of them. It was the Southern hospitality. After a few weeks, some of them even turned into decent fellas. They were still pecker-woods, but now they were friends of mine.

★

The Nazis took Paris and everybody was still sitting on their hands. The Nazis had signed a deal with the Italians and the Japs, every-body called them Japs now or Nips since the Rape of Nanjing three years ago in '37. At least most Marines did. We had a dozen more names for them as well. I couldn't help seeing the Japanese business-men who I caddied for as a kid every time someone started in on the Japs this or the Japs that. These were men like other men I thought . . . but then I started to think twice. They spoke English, they seemed regular enough, played golf like gentlemen. So I had to think hard about it. Were they different somehow? Were they cruel or stupid somehow that they could be tricked into doing the things they did? They weren't stupid and I couldn't tell if they were cruel. I couldn't figure it out. They were just the enemy now, even though it wasn't official. They were just the enemy I'd seen a long time ago.

I'd been in Manila just a year when the first word came down about Nanjing. Now everybody knew the details. They had raped and slaughtered three hundred thousand civilians. Most of us Marines

couldn't quite figure out why they did that. It didn't make any sense
in the military way of thinking. It was some kind of sickness I
guessed. A lot of the others didn't care one way or the other. They
just had a natural dislike of murdering bullies and wanted to show
the Japs what a fight was like with someone who was prepared.

The deal between the Japanese and the Nazis was supposed to be
against communism but anybody who believed that never played
poker. Why pick a card like Nazi Germany, which was eating Europe alive, unless you needed that card in your own hand? Their
hand was clear to me and anybody else who thought about it for a
while.

What I heard years before, from my small voice, the whisperings,
was coming true. But that was strictly my business and I wasn't going to go around telling anybody about little voices in my head. Who
the hell cared what I heard and saw in my mind except me? Carlo
knew and Phyllis knew I was right all along. They'd heard my predictions long before Japan ever made a move and thought I was off
my rocker then. But now when I said I heard something, we, my family and I, knew I was hearing the truth.

It was plain as day now that the Japanese meant to have war, but
Washington was still buying into their bluff. The Japanese ambas-
sadors said they weren't going to come after us. Our politicians took
that bait like marks in their first card game. Meanwhile the Japanese Army marched across China. Everybody could see it coming,
but it seemed like nobody in Washington wanted to admit it.

I kept my mouth shut about it. I knew what I knew and kept it to
myself. It was all over camp anyway. Fighting men know war is coming like a farmer can smell rain. It's in the wind. For me, I knew years
ago, even when I was a kid carrying golf bags in New Jersey. But I

left that kind of talk out of it. I didn't need these jarheads looking at me sideways.

A few weeks before I showed up in Quantico in July, Colonel Lemuel Shepard Jr. had started up a special unit to train officer candidates. They were only taking college graduates so I didn't have a chance. That bothered me quite a bit and I wasn't too quiet about it. I knew I could be a Marine as well as any of them but the more I talked, the clearer it got that I wasn't going to get a chance. I knew it was my own fault. It seemed like I was never going to stop paying for leaving high school when I did. This was a kind of griping about myself that I wanted to leave behind. There was no use to it. I was going to be as good a fighter as there was in the Marine Corps. That's what mattered. That's what I was here for.

I took up the same specialty I had in the Army, machine guns. Since the Marines used the same water-cooled Brownings, I had the jump on some of the recruits. I especially took advantage of the peckerwoods. Even though some of them had learned their lesson, others just couldn't help themselves. These ones were just dumb as bricks and it was my duty to relieve them of some of the complicated things of life, like cash. When I wasn't taking their money with cards, I'd take it by doing my blindfolded gun assembly. It wasn't as easy as it was at Fort Jay. During the assembly drills, I'd fumble at the right time so the marks could see me but the DI couldn't. I'd curse and then I'd act like I was all thumbs, like I couldn't find my ass with both hands. That would get the smell of the bait in the water. Then I had to wait for exactly the right moment during a break. I'd wonder out loud if I would ever get the knack for how these darn guns went together. I added some camouflage by looking down the barrel and scratching my head. This was usually all it took. A young peckerwood would see me and make a comment about me shooting myself or hoping he didn't get caught in a foxhole with me. Of course, I'd get hot and act like I had to do him one better. I challenged him or any of his buddies to a race—first to assemble a weapon while blindfolded won. If I did this setup right, it looked like easy money. They saw a chance to teach me, the Yankee, a lesson and make a few bucks to boot. That set the hook. Soon a pile of peckerwood markers and cash would be laid in a pile at my feet. We'd have to get an impartial referee, which wasn't easy because everybody wanted some of the action. I kept the pot small so I could trim these clodhoppers just a few at a time. I didn't want the word to get out too fast. Eventually I'd get to them all.

About ten minutes after the loot was laid up in a pile, it would all be in my pocket. There was just about nothing I liked better than relieving some loudmouth tobacco-chewer of his duty pay. It really passed the time. They still didn't know I was 19-0 Manila John or that I was once the top dog in a top machine gun outfit in the Army, and I wasn't about to tell them. By week six in basic, that jig was up anyway and I had to fall back on poker for my extra money.

★

You could tell the bad news overseas kept coming by the number of recruits that came into camp. Every barracks was full and tents went up a hundred at a time.

By week six in basic I was back close to the fighting shape that I had in Manila. The newspapers were filled with news of England standing alone against the Nazis so I figured there wasn't going to be any long garrison deployment, we were gearing up for a real shooting war and it looked like soon. I thought about getting back into the

ring, since it was hard getting by on duty pay and just poker win-
nings. But it didn't make much sense to get back into the ring now
and risk getting called up with a set of busted ribs.

Guantanamo

The fellas left standing after basic felt like they could eat glass. I
started to understand what all the Semper Fi was about. All through
basic we'd hear about our warrior brothers in Belleau Wood where we
saved France's ass the first time as far as I could tell. Maybe we were
about to do it again. That's what we thought anyway until we got our
orders for Guantanamo Bay in Cuba.

We weren't going to Europe in the footsteps of our brothers of
Belleau Wood, that was for sure. We were training for the Pacific.
From first light to lights out it was amphibious assault exercises. We
started working with different boats until they saw that the things
would swamp in a small swell while we tried to pile overboard in full
gear. Basic training was a walk in the park compared to this duty.
Quantico was humid in July. It took all the energy out of you. All
anybody wanted to do was find a spot with a little breeze and lay
down. But it was September now and Guantanamo was a roasting
oven. All anybody wanted to do now was find a cave, someplace
where the sun never came in, and stay there.

If we made it out of these tipsy boats we spent the next hours
practicing our maneuvers moving inland, setting up beachheads and
digging in. Then we'd simulate a forced retreat back into the pounding surf, into the boats and back to offshore transports. We spent
hours on the water before and after each assault exercise, wallowing

in the surf in these rocking horses. Nobody kept their lunch down. The sun came off the water like steel needles so that you couldn't even look at it straight on. The sun beat down on our heads and necks until everybody had some sort of sunburn or sunstroke and it felt like our steel helmets could cook soup.

News would go up to Topside about all the fouled anchors and drowned recruits. The next week new boats would arrive for us to try our luck on. It got so that we all headed for the Higgins boats when we could because they seemed least likely to kill us. What we needed was a shallow draft boat that could get us over the coral reefs and would squat down flat on the beach so we could get out. The squawk up and down the line was that Brigadier General H. M. (Howling Mad) Smith got his nickname there in Cuba when he took on our first problem, the boats. He was trying to equip us for island fighting and he chewed through junior officers, requisition forms and Congressional budget committees like a rabid dog. If he wasn't before, he was howling mad when he got done getting us our boats.

We eventually did four fleet landing exercises trying to get it right. We earned the name "Baggety Ass Marines" for the sagging wet cotton we lived in. We had sand and dried sea salt in places where sand and salt were never supposed to be. Then we carried seventy pounds for ten miles with the stuff still there. We lost more men to diaper rash than anything else, even more than sunstroke. This went on for seven months.

The heat of late summer had gone off and we had a few days to find shade in the palm trees when orders came down for Culebra, Virgin Islands. The pace we saw of new recruits coming into Quantico, the development of equipment and tactics in Cuba and the orders for Culebra let everybody know we weren't going to be allowed to become barrack rats. We were on the march. Like they shouted down the line when it was time to go, "Drop your cocks and grab your socks. Shipping out!"

Culebra had the nasty bugs of Quantico and the blistering heat of Cuba. I was back in the tropics again. It was like Manila where everything turned green and rotted. Now instead of sand and salt everywhere, fungus kept us busy with powder and soap. I started taking extra dry socks instead of cash from the poker games. It was February 1941. We were now officially a part of the First Marine Division that was formed up on February 1.

February, March and April rolled by while we continued to work on landing exercises. All of General Smith's howling finally started to get us some flat bottom boats. We also started to see an attack version of the old water-cooled Browning machine gun. At ninety-four pounds, the water-cooled 1917A1 could have been used for an anchor. I carried the gun itself at forty-three pounds and one hundred to two hundred and fifty rounds of ammunition at around another forty pounds. The loader carried the tripod, fifty-three pounds, and more ammo. We looked like the old leatherback turtles waddling out of the surf, loaded up with equipment on our backs and in our arms. The new 1919A4s were the same gun but air cooled with a perforated metal jacket around the barrel that allowed air to circulate and replaced the water jacket. This and a redesign of the tripod cut the weight in half to forty-three pounds. They weren't as stable and couldn't handle sustained fire like the old water-cooled guns but they made it a lot easier getting up the beach and back. We started working with a mix of light air-cooled and heavy water-cooled guns. Each machine gun company was equipped with six light and six heavy. The heavies were set up in forward positions to provide covering fire for the assault. The lights went forward with the assault to new ground, then covered while the heavies were brought up. At night, the old heavies were set up guarding perimeter positions. On a battalion front, we had eighteen lights and eighteen heavies cutting a path in front of us. It was an interlocking steel curtain when we were all firing, like the sharp teeth of a dragon.

★

I guess Topside was satisfied we could get the job done and orders for shipping out came down again. We were heading back to Quantico. I was starting to get used to island life and wasn't looking forward to another summer with the mosquitoes. We got back in May and the place was overrun with new recruits. We couldn't even get back into any barracks. We got shoved into tents in a tent city that now stretched for acres in all directions.

Things were starting to move fast now. Within a few days we were reassigned to the Seventh Marines, ordered to repack and shipped out on troop trains headed south for Parris Island, South Carolina. Parris Island didn't have room for us either. After a week, we got marching orders for a troop transport ship that was taking us north to New River, North Carolina.

The word was the Navy had bought us a brand-new training facility where we were to continue to sharpen our skills in amphibious assault. Since we were the most highly trained force the Navy had, we were going to be treated like an elite fighting force, one that had earned its own training camp and the special treatment that came with it. We would get steak and apple pie every night and there was a base theater where we'd get to see a new movie every weekend. The nearby towns were full of healthy young Southern belles who loved soldiers, especially Marines. The new base was the talk of the town and you could hardly walk a hundred yards without some kindly townsperson offering you a home-cooked meal. This was the reward for a year of eating sand and roasting on foreign beaches. It just seemed too good to be true. It was lights out on the transport ship with the gentle southern breezes lulling us to sleep up on deck. Almost nobody slept in the stifling hold of the ship that smelled worse than a hog feedlot and boomed all night with the sound of the diesel engine.

We knew we were toughened up by our hard year of humping steel across the beaches of the Caribbean. The weak links had been knocked out and we were one unbreakable chain of men, weapons and tactics. If we wanted a beach, we were going to take it. We deserved our own base, steak every night and the daughters of a grateful nation. We dozed off on the breezy deck of the transport knowing all our hard work was finally being appreciated.

The sun came up over our new home. New River stretched over one hundred thousand acres of swampland infested with snakes, chiggers, sand flies and reeking of foul swamp gas. There were no gleaming new barracks, just a few plywood command offices, no snug dining hall, no nothing. Just swamp. The tales of comfort had been just that, tales. It seemed like the only thing tired fighting men liked better than making up rumors, was believing them and we believed it all. Word raced through the company that when we found the guy with the big mouth we were going to find him a nice spot in our new home. We were more than disappointed. Somehow all the moving got to us and made us feel like just the opposite of the finest raggedy-assed Marines in the Corps we were told we were. We looked at this swamp and felt like we were being dumped in a spot nobody else wanted. All the months of sucking up the injuries and weariness of constant training and moving were exploding in a storm of fucks, shits, goddamns, thrown equipment and dirt kicked in frustration. It seemed like the Seventh Marines were the shitbird of the Corps to us and the commanding Major General Terrey couldn't carry Howling Mad's canteen when it came to provisioning his troops.

We had two months to pass in this wilderness until a scheduled coordinated assault exercise in August would bring together all the capabilities of the Marine Corps. Our new playground was Onslow Beach.

I was a squad leader now with a twelve-man squad to wrangle. I was a few years older, which helped when it came to settling fights in the squad. They knew how to fight, not much else, but they sure knew how to mix it up. A few times they might have ended up getting each other killed if I didn't step in. That became a big part of my job.

Bob Powell seemed to be one of the chief scrappers in the group, but I generally could see his side of the argument. He was just particular. He wanted things done by the book and didn't take kindly to creative ideas like carrying less ammo on exercises to make it easier. When push came to shove I was going to keep Bob close on my flank. Steve Helstowski reminded me a lot of myself physically because he could run all day with a full pack without getting tired. He was the one who carried the fifty-three-pound legs of a heavy through the pounding surf up to our chests and across a half mile of loose sand. He generally did it at a trot once he hit dry land. He was my other flank. The other nine all fell into line with their strengths and odd ways as we got to know each other, but one thing got real clear as the pace of war picked up around us, it was only us who were going to keep each other alive or get each other killed when the steel started flying. That started to make us look at each other differently. If a man didn't roll his socks regulation, you tended to want to know why. Was he going to do that when the shooting started? Was he an odd duck who was going to zig when he should zag? It tended to make us kind of prickly. I had my work to do sorting out the trouble spots and keeping the fights short.

In time all my stories came out: the fights in Manila, the girls of New York City, busting one of our buddies from jail. That was the main entertainment in New River. If things got really low, like when it rained for a week, I got a rise out of them by singing opera. I only knew a few songs, parts of arias, but that was enough to shut them up and get their minds off of mutiny and homesickness. That was all I could do since I couldn't very well shave my own squad in poker. I wasn't keen to give up all my hard earned card-playing education to such a large group either, so I had to move on to a new pastime. I also couldn't be just one of the guys like I had always been. I gave orders now—some that might soon send these young boys into deadly fire. I was a part of the Marine Corps more than I was a part of them. I left the card games early, got to bed first and was first out of the rack in the morning. My new pastime was being Gunny, the sergeant who might keep them alive if I did my job right. And they might do the same for me. They were Sig, Pete, Jackie Schoenecker, Nash, Foley, Hatfield, Garland and Crumpton. They were all youngsters, all full of piss and vinegar and wanting, like me, to be the best fighting man in the Corps, in the world. We'd already been all over the Caribbean together but New River was the beginning of us as a squad. Whatever we didn't already know about each other, we were going to find out real quick.

★

Of all the places we'd been so far, New River was the worst. As the heat built up through June and July, the mosquitoes, flies and humidity built up right along with them. Carrying a seventy-pound pack through swamp gas and air so thick with water vapor and bugs that you could cut it, got to be our picture of hell. We drilled day and night in amphibious assaults and inland maneuvers through the swamp. It was misery.

A weekend pass was useless since the best you could hope for was a dirt-road town with maybe one roadhouse full of tobacco farmers. Most of the men didn't even bother to leave base. They just found a shady spot and did their best to sleep all day.

When it came to business, my squad could do everything I could do with a machine gun. They could take it apart and put it together blindfolded and almost one-handed. One of the new pastimes of being the Gunny was having the best time for setting up and tearing down the guns. I set the pace with the weapons, physical training and state of mind. If I slacked off, started griping, they would follow right along. If they kept up or beat me at setting up the guns, their reward might sometimes be a lesson in card playing that could improve their income. Other than that they worked for themselves, for the satisfaction of knowing that they were the best. They were the finest men I'd ever met. It was hard to think about losing any of them in battle but that was how I was told to think. I became altogether different in my thinking after getting command of the squad.

The big push, the coordinated beach assault, went ahead as planned in August. We could have walked to our positions in our sleep by this time. We were a force of over twenty thousand men, thousands of machines and hundreds of tons of supplies that moved through the surf and on shore that morning. Air cover from Marine fighter squadrons flew overhead as we made our practice assault over Onslow Beach one more time. We still had boats capsizing and I figured we might have drowned a dozen or so men that day. The boat next to us went over just a hundred and fifty yards offshore. The most important piece of equipment we had when that happened was our Ka-Bar knives to cut us out of our packs that would have taken us right to the bottom. I couldn't see what rescue efforts were attempted but our boat wasn't diverted. We kept right on going and ran right up on the sand as we'd been doing for months. We ran to our positions where we had fighting holes already dug from the last week's exercise. We got our guns set up in seconds, like I trained them to do and I checked for sand fouling the mechanism. If there wasn't any I threw some in. That got them cursing and scrambling for their cleaning kits. While my squad was cleaning up after my mischief, I looked out to the dumped boat. I could see men still in the water and an observer boat picking them up.

It seems Topside was pleased with the whole shebang. The way we knew was we didn't have to do it again. That was it for New River and we were happy to hear the orders come down that we were shipping out again. This time it was off to a place called Camp Lejeune. Like New River, it was going to be a camp one day. When we got there it was still a coastal swamp, just like New River. This was almost more than the boys could take. We believed the rumors the first time that we'd find steaks and young Southern girls at New River. The same rumors came around again as we were on our way to Lejeune.

It almost seemed like we had been run around in a big circle and put into another part of the same damn swamp. It could have been for all we knew. This was almost too much. The Marine way of keeping the griping to a minimum went right out the window when we first laid eyes on our new home—another barren swamp with no buildings, no nothing. We ended up living in tents. If Major General Terrey had suggested that he wanted to review the troops just then, I would have told him it wasn't such a great idea. I couldn't guarantee that a few of my guys wouldn't have said a few things that might have gotten them locked up.

The one thing that did change was the weather. August blew off and September came in cooler. October was even cooler than that. We were stranded here even worse than in New River. There were no train lines anywhere close and bus service was two old busses that most of the men could outrun. As the weather cooled the humidity stayed the same so that the suffocating steam of the swamp turned to a bitter wet chill that got under all the wool you could put on. Sick bay visits from heatstroke and exhaustion turned to men down with colds and flu that took weeks to get over since there was nothing but aspirin to give them. It was more misery. Endless weeks of it. We didn't have any big exercise to look forward to, we were just dumped here in this swamp and expected to stay sharp. That's where I really had to reach down deep for anything to keep the men from turning on each other. All I could come up with was the same routine that had kept me going in Raritan when I couldn't stand another minute there. I managed to get ahold of a few pairs of boxing gloves and started a training camp. I made it mandatory. Everybody in my outfit had to learn how to box and I was going to teach them. Sometimes the training was the only thing that kept them warm.

The other thing that kept us hopping was the goddamndest Marine I ever met. Major Lewis B. "Chesty" Puller called me into his plywood shack command office and looked me up and down like I was meat on the hook.

"At ease, Sergeant," he said. He had a big, square face and dark tanned skin like a farmer who lived outdoors year 'round and from the look on him, I thought he didn't like me much. His barrel chest looked like it was two feet thick, which is where he got the nickname Chesty. He already had two Navy Crosses from the Banana Wars in Nicaragua and a reputation as a fearless frontline commander, so I was a little put back on my heels from hearing the news he was our new CO.

"I hear you're a new Sergeant in my outfit."

"Sir. That's correct, sir."

"And that you have some ability as a knockout artist?"

"Nineteen and zero, sir, in the Army."

"The Army. How long were you in the Army?"

"Three years, sir."

"Where?"

"Mostly the Philippines."

"And that's where you got the name Manila John?"

"Yes, sir."

"Tell me, Sergeant. Why in hell should I let someone spoiled and softened by the U.S. Army command a squad of my magnificent fighting Marines?"

"I joined the Marines to fight, sir. And that's what I aim to do. I believe I can do a fine job."

"I also heard you were involved in some kind of card game."

"I'm sure it's true, sir."

"And this game led to a fight?"

"That's true too, sir."

"And that you whipped the hell out of whoever it was?"

"Yes, sir. Twice."

"Why? Didn't he learn the first time?"

"Two different people, sir."

"Also heard you are a womanizer who takes 'em on two at a time, when you can afford it?"

At that point, it looked like I might be heading for the brig and I wasn't sure how to answer but I went ahead anyway and called his bluff.

"Even when I can't afford it, sir."

"Goddamn, I believe you will be a fine leader and credit to my beloved Corps." He opened a box of cigars on his desk. "You smoke, Basilone?"

"Yes, sir."

"Have a cigar, Sergeant. Tell me about the Philippines."

Major Puller and I saw pretty much eye to eye about things. I knew after that first meeting that he was the kind of fighting man I wanted to be and the kind I wanted making the decisions in battle. With Chesty Puller at the helm, I knew the morale of the men would improve. That was when I thought maybe we really were something special.

We never stopped training for beach landings even as the weather turned bitter. The sick list got longer and longer but we kept right on splashing through the surf and then tramping inland through the swamp day after day. Once we took up a position, we'd sometimes have to lie there for hours waiting for word that the exercise was over and we could return to barracks—or what they called barracks.

Nobody wanted to say the word "tent." The Coast Guard kept us supplied with crews to pilot our small landing boats but the Navy wasn't providing any more large transports since the big powwow in August. The one thing we couldn't practice was going over the side in full gear and climbing down a cargo net into the landing boats. This was one of the trickiest maneuvers we had to do, especially in a heavy sea. There were a dozen ways to get seriously hurt but we'd only done it one time back in August.

We soon enough found ourselves building full-scale ship hulls out of wood. They were the first permanent man-made features in this swamp that soon became Camp Lejeune. We rigged cargo netting on the hulls and that was our transport disembarkment practice. Of course they couldn't provide the up and down and side to side rocking like climbing from one ship into another at sea, but they were all we had. I tied pull ropes to the sides of the nets and let a few lucky Marines have fun by trying to shake their brothers free.

Our tent city began to look more and more like the old Hoovervilles during the Great Depression. October blew out and November blew in off the ocean, bringing freezing rains that turned into freezing mud. Decks of rough-sawn planks were laid down in our tents to keep us out of the mud, but the planks had gaping cracks between them where the wind blew through. Oil stoves were hastily provisioned and set up on the wood decks. We took to stuffing the cracks in our decks with newspapers, magazines or whatever we could find to keep out the cold wind. Between the oil smoke, the mud and the newspaper blowing everywhere, we were as sorry looking an outfit as I'd ever seen. Even Manila started to look good as I remembered it. The stoves smelled terribly and made the entire tent an almost perfect firebomb. The things would just go up, whoosh, in the middle of the night. Sick bay kept getting bigger. Burns joined cold, flu, insect and snake bites as common injuries. Often waking up in the morning, we were covered in black soot from the exhaust. After a few months we were provisioned with tar paper to cover the decks. Life in camp was certainly nothing like what we'd been told in the recruiting offices.

Camp settled into the deadly routine of meaningless exercises and long periods with nothing to occupy the mens' minds. There was a makeshift PX, which was just about the size of a toolshed, that dispensed beer but there was no place to sit out of the wind and drink it.

It came down to boxing matches to pass the time. A traveling circus had donated a worn-out tent to the base and we used it as our Madison Square Garden. That had to be the low point. We were down to accepting the castoffs of a traveling circus. It was hard to imagine, when I lay down to sleep in my squad's cold, dark tent that was full of oil fumes and ready to catch fire, that anybody really cared about what happened to us. Were we really lower than circus performers? That really bothered me. It bothered all of us. The little local newspaper was just about the only contact we had with the outside world. It was published once a week. That paper and our little boxing matches were all we had during that winter. Sometimes I thought we were never going to get out of there.

★

Then came December 7, a sneak attack on a Sunday morning. Three thousand, nine hundred and sixty-seven casualties, just like that, in three and a half hours. Our entire force of Marines at that time was only fifty-four thousand men. There was dead silence in camp for quite a while after we got the news. We just kept repeating the number to each other and then to ourselves.

Pearl Harbor was torn apart. Seven of our largest battleships were sunk, the remaining four were seriously damaged. Seven more cruisers, destroyers and auxiliaries were seriously damaged. Practically the whole Pacific fleet, gone. The Japanese had done a thorough job of it. They were bold. I could only see the faces of the men I had caddied for in Raritan. It didn't fit. Those men were just about as American as me. But they were the only Japanese faces I knew. So I had to wonder for a second, was there something I missed in those faces? But no, they were just friends playing golf together. This was something completely new.

The sound came back to camp slowly, then got louder and louder. They say the Japanese Combined Fleet Commander, Admiral Isoroku Yamamoto, who had designed the attack, said he was afraid they had ". . . awakened the sleeping giant." That must have been the sound we were making. We were the giant and we were waking up bleeding.

There almost wasn't a man or woman in America who didn't want to fight after that day. The word came down the line that our outfit, the Seventh, was going to be the first to see action because we had the longest time in training. Hundreds of men from other companies volunteered and were granted transfer to our Seventh. Somehow all the uncomfortable things about camp faded away even as new men crowded into our tent city. We were taut as bowstrings after months of running through deep sand carrying seventy pounds of steel and supplies. The time had come to move out. Training was over.

We were detached and assigned to the defense of Samoa. Of course, we had never heard of it before and never heard of the Japs attacking it, so we all thought Samoa was just a stopping-off point on the way to the action. It was March by the time orders came through and we shipped out on April 10, 1942, from Norfolk, Virginia.

The ship rolled toward Samoa like a sick whale for almost a month. We started to feel like Columbus sailing toward the edge of the earth but he might have sailed faster. We had rusty merchant ships fitted out with racks of canvas hammocks belowdecks where cargo used to be. The riveted steel sides of the ship shivered and boomed from the pounding ocean and thumping engines. There was almost no ventilation and after a few days the smell was slightly worse than a feedlot.

On May 8, we reached Apia on the western shore of Samoa and set up camp. For the first time in our history, some of the rumors about the luxuries of the new camp were true. The island was thick with friendly women willing to help in any way they could. We were suddenly the honored guests of these kind island people. Proper grass huts were up and ready for us. Our laundry was taken from us and washed for a few cents. We were given fresh eggs every morning and toast with genuine butter, all we wanted. It was a strange kind of paradise. Our training never stopped.

Over the next four months, we studied the local plants, practiced camouflage techniques and adapted to the new climate. We were jungle fighters now where stealth and camouflage were more important than frontal beach assaults, although we expected to need both before it was all over. We learned new survival skills for the jungle, what was edible and what was poisonous, where the paths were, spotting booby traps. Summer passed in this very serious and sometimes pleasant way. We were living the life of carefree beachcombers half the time, the other half we were practicing to be stealthy killers. The first intelligence reports told us that the Japs trained for infiltrating behind enemy lines at night. They also dug caves into solid rock where they would be safe from artillery. We adjusted our training. We were constantly rousted in the middle of the night to practice wiping out infiltrators. Intricate systems of codes, passwords and responses were cooked up so we wouldn't end up shooting each other in the dark. We always used passwords the Japs couldn't pronounce like "clear" and "weather." We had been training for over a year and even though we were shaken up by some of the stories of the unbeatable Japanese, we were spoiling for a fight. We thought we were the best trained and the most motivated outfit in the Marines. Day in and day out, night after night, we drilled and regrouped. Our COs Rodgers and Webb knew our orders would be coming any day. They didn't let up. They didn't want surprises once we got into the shooting war.

Everybody had a hard time packing up. Many of the boys had fallen in love for the first time. Samoans were very open and unashamed about sex. It wasn't all tied up with ideas about marriage or sin the way we were raised to think about it. In Samoa it was something like our social dancing. There was no shame in it, no sneaking around. I don't think many of us wrote home about what we were really doing. Not many back home would understand. They would be upset and worry that our morals were being all corrupted to hell. It made me think about how things can get turned around in your head once you see the other side of a thing. I started to wonder who was being corrupted when nobody really said what was on their minds. I never could when it came to women. Of course, I'd be polite and never say what I was thinking. Then I'd find what I really wanted in bars and backrooms. We all did. That was just part of being a Marine, somebody with no attachments except to your outfit. What we did with the girls of New York City and Manila we thought was normal. It was nothing like that at all in Samoa. It was a forbidden dream to most of us. Lots of the boys swore they were coming back to stay, if they were still alive when it was all over.

That was starting to look less likely by the news we were getting. The Japs had been stopped at the battles of the Coral Sea and Midway where the Navy had fought them to a draw but they hadn't been turned back. We hadn't won a battle on land or sea and I know some started to wonder to themselves if we even could. They had humiliated us in the Philippines like everyone knew they would, they threw the British out of Hong Kong and took the Dutch East Indies. Outside the Corps, I don't know if anybody really thought we could win. They still had practically their whole fleet and we were limping along on the ships we could scrape together. It was looking like Guadalcanal was going to be it. If we didn't win there, we would lose the Pacific, which included Australia. The Japs were already bombing Point Moresby on the southern coast of New Guinea, and Australia's front door was left open. Her troops were with the British in Africa. They had no defense, except us.

The U.S. Navy Task Force with the 1st Marine Division on board sailed from New Zealand on July 26. Since we had been detached from the 3rd Marine Brigade and reassigned to the 1st Division while we were posted in Samoa, we figured to be in on drawing first blood from the Japs. We were the unit that collected all the hard-nosed volunteers from all over the 1st when word came down about Pearl. We were the raggedy-ass Marines with the longest time in training and we were the first deployment after Pearl. Our five thousand got sent to Samoa to keep the Japs from cutting the shipping lanes between the U.S. and Australia. We were the guys who everybody thought would get the job done. But we were the guys who got left behind.

When we heard that Operation Watchtower went off without us, I don't know what the word was for what we felt, but it wasn't good. The 1st landed on Guadalcanal on August 7 and had a cakewalk up to the new airfield that was the big worry for the brass and was the reason for choosing the Canal in the first place. They had some fighting on the other islands close by but the Canal was a pushover, just a couple of engineers they ran off from their lunch when our 1st Division showed up.

That was about the last straw for some of the boys who had been training day and night for over a year. We got shipped to Samoa in May and were still sitting there waiting to see our first action in August. All that time, the feelings toward the Japs had been getting worse and worse. We were as bloodthirsty as pirates now and filled with hate for these people. Just about everything we saw, read or heard was filled with hate for the Japs. We even saw a newsreel with cartoons that made them out to be just like animals. We thought they were just underhanded, lying, murdering apes and we were thinking of nothing else except that we were going to kill them all like a pack of wild dogs—cut their throats and slice their ears off for souvenirs. Some of the boys were quite worked up about it. Killing Japs was our everyday dinner conversation now and to hear a few of the boys talk you might think they had been killers their whole lives. A few, like Sig and Crumpton, were no more killers than any quiet young fella you might know working in your hometown filling station or market, but you wouldn't know that to hear them talk. The change had come over them, over all of us. We were an older type of human now. We'd gone back to the time before countries existed. We were a pack, a hunting tribe. We had the discipline of modern soldiers but in our hearts we were just like the first men who ever hunted other men. To hear we got left out of the fight was more than just tough on our morale, it was like we got punched in the gut. We had three more weeks to sit and stew about it.

In late August we got our orders. We were shipping out. The Higgins boats came for us and took us out to what looked like a ragtag Navy, thrown together from scraps. All together we were maybe a dozen or so ships of every shape and size; some fancy passenger freighters and some rust bucket cargo haulers. We set a course northwest toward Guadalcanal over two thousand miles away.

We'd heard that the 1st had almost no resistance when they got there almost a month ago, but during our briefings on the way we got the picture that things weren't going to be near as easy for us. It seemed like them Japs were as keen to get back their airfield as we were to keep it and it was shaping up to be one hell of a fight. We hadn't missed anything after all. All we knew from what we heard was our Marines were left high and dry. How the hell that happened, we had no idea.

Torpedo Damage to USS Chicago *after*
Battle of Savo Island

IRONBOTTOM SOUND:
THE BATTLE OF SAVO ISLAND

On August 7 at 1030 hours, a Japanese attack force composed of heavy bombers, light bombers, and fighters was headed for Guadalcanal. U.S. carriers retreated one hundred miles to the south out of range of the attacking Japanese aircraft and sent fighters to thwart the attack. Twenty miles northwest of the island the Japanese strike force was intercepted and turned back before they could disrupt the invasion. Alarmed by the defeat, the Japanese command station at Rabaul, New Britain, a small island off the coast of New Guinea, immediately sent a larger attack force of planes and ships to finish the job.

On D-day, the U.S. Marine 1st Division met no resistance from the two thousand Korean laborers and engineers who were building the airfield on Guadalcanal. The workers ran off into the jungle to avoid the naval shelling before the invasion. The Marines quickly established a beachhead to receive the supplies that were being dumped as fast as landing craft could shuttle from ship to shore. Without close air cover from the distant aircraft carriers, the transports and their destroyer escorts were vulnerable to air attack. The piles of ammunition, rations, tents, fuel and vehicles became a disorganized mess.

The second wave of Japanese bombers penetrated the American fighter screen, dropping their bombs from over twenty thousand feet to escape antiaircraft fire. They were wildly inaccurate but by concentrating on the ships in the channel, they damaged a number of them, sinking the destroyer *Jarvis*. In their battles to turn back the attacking planes, the carrier fighter squadrons lost twenty-one Wildcat fighters.

That night the Imperial Japanese Navy dispatched a cruiser-destroyer force to destroy the American battle group protecting the transport supply ships near the island. The strategy was to destroy the supplies and let the Americans starve on Guadalcanal while a land-based counterattack could be mounted. The American battle group, Task Force 61, was composed of three cruiser-destroyer groups commanded by Admiral Kelly Turner. They were stationed in the narrow channel between Guadalcanal and the island of Tulagi to the north. As the eight heavy cruisers and destroyers of the Japanese attack force approached Task Force 61 just after 0100 hours on August 9, a series of tragic communications errors between the Australian and American naval commanders left their southern flank completely exposed. This flaw was boldly exploited by the Japanese and demonstrated their superiority at night warfare tactics. The American battle group was caught completely unaware. Even the last perimeter, the destroyer *Blue*, which was sailing picket duty for the battle group, failed to notice the approaching Japanese ships and turned away as the Japanese force sailed to within a few hundred yards of Task Force 61. At 0143, a lookout on the destroyer *Patterson* sounded the alarm but it was too late. Japanese torpedoes were already in the water. By 0215 the firing stopped and the Japanese slipped away in the darkness before any carrier-based planes could retaliate. The American cruisers *Vincennes*, *Astoria* and *Quincy* went to the bottom, as did the Australian Navy's HMAS *Canberra*, so critically damaged that she had to be sunk by American torpedoes. Both the cruiser *Chicago* and the destroyer *Talbot* were badly damaged. Over thirteen hundred sailors died and another seven hundred were injured that night in one of the worst naval defeats in American history. The disaster further weakened U.S. naval forces in the Pacific that were already severely reduced by the attack on Pearl Harbor. The channel became known as Ironbottom Sound.

The Japanese destroyed the battle group but failed to destroy most of the transports. In the early hours of August 9, Marines who had watched and heard the entire battle from shore, saw the Higgins boats swarm out to rescue survivors. Eleven thousand men were on Guadalcanal but only half of their supplies had been unloaded before the attack. Another fourteen hundred Marines and the other half of their supplies were still on board the transports that stood offshore receiving the Higgins boats full of survivors. On shore, Maj. Gen. Alexander Vandegrift got to work securing the remaining half of his supplies and getting his men dug in until reinforcements arrived, whenever that might be.

The transports hauled anchor, then headed out to sea toward New Caledonia with the scraps of what was left of the battle group. Most of the heavy equipment and weapons left with the transports. The Marines were left completely on their own with seventeen days' rations, after counting captured Japanese food, and only four days' supply of ammunition for all weapons. With the carrier group out of the area, the Japanese sent their destroyers and bombers back to Guadalcanal. They shelled and bombed the Marines at will, starting promptly at noon every day. The Marines called the daily barrage the Tokyo Express. There were no fortifications on the island that could protect the men from it because the heavy equipment to build them left with the battle group in the holds of the unloaded transports.

The Japanese strategy of isolating and then starving the Americans was working. The Marines were forced to subsist on half rations until somehow they could be resupplied. In their weakened state, they began to succumb to various tropical diseases and infections that lurked in the stinking decay of the tropical swamps that were filled with stinging centipedes, poisonous spiders, snakes and swarms of malarial mosquitoes. They were losing men by the dozens.

Imperial General Headquarters in Tokyo ordered Lieutenant General Haruyoshi Hyakutake's Seventeenth Army to attack the Marines and take back the airfield. Hyakutake chose the 35th Infantry Brigade commanded by Major General Kiyotake Kawaguchi. Hyakutake selected the crack 28th Infantry Regiment to land first. Underestimating the Americans at two thousand men, only one battalion of nine hundred men was transported to the Solomons on the only shipping available, six destroyers. The Japanese had easily defeated the Americans in the Philippines, the British in Hong Kong and the Chinese. With their highly trained, experienced army and overwhelming naval superiority, they and many of their enemies believed they were invincible. As a result the Japanese troops carried just small amounts of ordnance and supplies. A follow-on echelon of twelve hundred troops was to join the assault battalion on Guadalcanal.

Marines got their first taste of action against a determined Japanese combat force four days after D-day. The experience reinforced the myth of the invincible Japanese they would soon be facing in large numbers. Captured Japanese sailors, taken in the constant patrolling to the west of the perimeter, indicated that a Japanese group wanted to surrender near the village of Kokumbona, seven miles west of the Matanikau River. This was the area that was thought to hold most of the enemy troops who had fled the airfield. On the night of August 12, a reconnaissance patrol of twenty-five men led by Lt. Frank Goettge left the perimeter by landing craft. The patrol landed near its objective, was ambushed, and virtually wiped out. Only three men survived to swim back to the Marine lines.

One week later, Japanese destroyers delivered the vanguard of the Japanese land attack force at Taivu Point, twenty-five miles east of the Marine perimeter. A long-range patrol of Marines ambushed a sizable Japanese force near Taivu on August 19. The Japanese dead were identified as Army troops. All Japanese encountered to this point had been naval troops.

The starving and sickly Marines dug in along the Ilu River while the Japanese commander, Colonel Kiyono Ichiki, issued explicit orders to his troops to fight "to the last breath of the last man." Continuing to use their successful night fighting tactics, they attacked the Marine lines two days later at 0130 hours. In a screaming frenzy that they had been assured would terrify and route the Americans, the Japanese charged across the sand bar astride the Ilu's mouth. The Marines cut them down. After a mortar preparation, the Japanese tried again to storm past the sand bar. Again, they were mowed down. The 1st Battalion, 1st Marines moved upstream on the Ilu at daybreak, waded across the muddy fifty-foot-wide stream and outflanked the Japanese. Carrier-based Wildcats strafed them as five light tanks blasted the retreating force. By 1700, as the afternoon sun was setting, the battle ended. Colonel Ichiki, disgraced by his defeat, burned his regimental colors and shot himself. Close to eight hundred of his men joined him in death. The few survivors fled eastward back toward Taivu Point. Thirty-four Marines had been killed and seventy-five wounded. The Guadalcanal force finally had a victory, but reinforcements were still weeks away and supplies continued to dwindle.

Air battles over the island continued to intensify as the Japanese committed more resources to retake the airfield that the Americans had now named Henderson Airfield after a Marine pilot, Lofton R. Henderson, killed in the battle of Midway. On August 12, a CBY Flying Boat skidded to a stop on the rutted, muddy runway of Henderson Field. It was the first plane of an air group that would come to be known as the Cactus Air Force, a combination of two carrier squadrons totaling over thirty planes. Cactus was the operation code name for Guadalcanal. The planes were able to extend the seventeen days of rations the Marines had and eventually shuttled over twenty-eight hundred wounded Marines off the island. The constant Japanese bombing raids chipped away at the Cactus Air Force. Even with the planes, the Marines were still in a precarious defensive position with few heavy weapons to defend against the certain Japanese counterattacks.

THE FIRST BATTLE OF BLOODY RIDGE

Henderson Field was now a vital foothold in turning back the Japanese march across the Pacific to Australia. It was to be held at all costs. General Vandegrift called for infantry reinforcements to defend the field against the imminent counteroffensive. Colonel Edson's parachute/raider 1st and 2nd Battalions, 5th Marines made the harrowing crossing over Ironbottom Sound from Tulagi, where they had wiped out Japanese command garrisons on D-day. They filled in the thin perimeter defenses of the airfield and dug in as best they could, fashioning sharpened bamboo breastworks to take the place of the barbed perimeter wire that was still in the evacuated transport ships along with most of their ammunition. A few days after they arrived, intelligence reports indicated that the Japanese had landed in force on the southern coast of the island. Additional reinforcements were called up. Edson's Raiders were stationed along several hundred yards of high ground that rose out of the thick jungle kunai grass just a hundred yards south of the airfield. This ridge would become known as Bloody Ridge.

On Samoa, two thousand miles to the southeast, Lt. Col. Lewis B. "Chesty" Puller and his 1st Battalion, 7th Marines, including Sgt. John Basilone, stowed their gear in preparation to join the fight on the Canal. Their turn on Bloody Ridge was still over two months away.

★

General Kawaguchi, the direct superior of the failed Colonel Ichiki, with his brigade of two thousand battle-hardened veterans, cut a swath through the heart of the thick, inland jungle to avoid detection by Marine patrols along the rivers and coast. They planned to attack Henderson Field from the south, directly through Edson's lines on the ridge. They believed that the southern perimeter would be thinly defended in favor of stronger defenses on the more accessible east and west flanks. To avoid continual aerial bombing, Vandegrift moved his command post to the base of the ridge on the airfield side, directly in the path of Kawaguchi's attack.

By September 10, Kawaguchi had cut his way to within a few hundred yards of the ridge. Beyond the palm and mangrove trees of the jungle lay a fifty-yard field of thick, five-foot-high kunai grass that ran up to the base of the ridge. The following day Japanese planes began the attack, dropping five-hundred-pound bombs on the defenders of the ridge. The Cactus Air Force, with half of its planes damaged, could only slow the attack. The bombardment continued into the next day after dark when offshore battleships lobbed fourteen-inch shells down on the Marine's heads, blasting huge holes in the perimeter defenses. Just after 2100 hours, Kawaguchi launched his attack. The Japanese rushed against Edson's left flank directly into rifle and machine gun fire. They closed to within bayonet distance and hand-to-hand fighting but could not breach Edson's lines. They fell back and regrouped. They attacked the right flank, again closing to fight hand-to-hand and this time penetrated. Edson called up his reserve forces into the breach and repelled the attack. The Japanese fell back again and regrouped. For the third time, Kawaguchi's jungle fighters swarmed fearlessly up the ridge into the teeth of the Marine defenses. Again it was bloody bayonet and hand-to-hand battle but the Marines held the line. Just after 0230 hours, the Japanese retreated to their jungle positions.

After the third attack subsided, Colonel Edson cautioned his men, "They were just testing, just testing. They'll be back." The next night, September 12, they were. The Japanese attacked all positions with a suicidal ferocity. Individual soldiers and small groups broke through and attacked foxholes and gun pits from the rear. They swarmed against every position. Edson calmly moved along the line of defense calling up reserve engineers, pioneer units, anyone who could walk and carry a rifle to reinforce positions where the heaviest fighting was going on. A Japanese infiltrator was shot as he broke into Vandegrift's command post. Wave after wave of attackers stormed the ridge. Marine artillery landed on the Japanese at a range of only 1600 yards. The fighting continued for hours until near dawn, when Kawaguchi's shattered brigade melted back into the jungle. They left behind six hundred dead and six hundred wounded.

The American victory was an enormous morale boost for the troops and civilians at home but it marked the end of Edson's 1st Parachute Battalion as a combat force. The loss of fifty-nine men killed and over two hundred missing and wounded combined with the losses in the fight on Tulagi left only eighty-nine men who could walk away from the battle. The ridge became known as Bloody Ridge. Colonel Edson received the Medal of Honor along with Captain Kenneth Bailey, posthumously, for their actions on Bloody Ridge.

Remnants of Kawaguchi's force, determined to fight to the last man, attacked the flanks of Bloody Ridge again on September 13 and 14. Both times they were repelled, losing an additional three hundred men. Utterly defeated, Kawaguchi retreated with his remaining men back to the tortuous path they had hacked through miles of jungle. Along the way they lost dozens more to disease and starvation.

The Americans, although victorious, were decimated by the weeks of bombardment, fighting, disease and reduced rations. The Cactus Air Force had barely a dozen planes that could fly and supplies, including ammunition, were nearly gone.

By September 16, news of Kawaguchi's defeat reached Tokyo. The Japanese high command realized that their intelligence reports numbering the American force at two thousand men on Guadalcanal was wildly inaccurate. Rather than a diversionary tactic, they also realized that the invasion of Guadalcanal was the main thrust of the American counterattack in the Pacific. Within days, a massive naval task force and two infantry divisions, including the elite Sendai division, were assembled and ordered to wipe out the remaining American forces and take back the airfield.

On to the Canal

After we heard the 1st had started the war without us, we didn't hear much else except, of course, rumors. If they'd beat the hell out of the Japs we would have heard about it, so all we knew was things weren't going well. I knew all the crap about the Japs being unbeatable was going through everybody's mind, but no one would say a word about it. All of these boys were still gung-ho and hell for leather. The only thing they were scared of was being left out of the fight.

When the weather was nice the boys sat out on the deck and filled the green fabric ammo belts from the boxes of cartridges. We had a new gadget that did it automatically when you cranked it like a meat grinder. So they'd sit around and trade big talk about how this particular bullet was going to send honorable Jap to ancestor, so solly, that kind of stuff. We hated the Japs. We were going to get our revenge for Pearl, maybe even for the 1st Division, and we were going to spill Japanese blood. We were going to cut them down because they were cruel murderers of children, because they were underhanded liars and low, sneaking assassins. Death seemed too good for them. Some of the boys were ready to show them the cruelty that they had shown against others. They talked like pirates, boasting about their dark and bloody work. I didn't go in for all that and they knew it. It was just a lot of big talk about taking back a string of Jap ears or scalps. That kind of talk died off when I poked my nose into their discussions.

For the first week or so at sea, we didn't even know for sure where we were heading. For all we knew the 1st could have been wiped out and we were being evacuated. Reckoning by the stars and the setting sun we could tell we were heading northwest. That meant we were either on our way in retreat to Australia or in advance to Guadalcanal.

Once the briefings started on board and we knew we were heading to Guadalcanal, then the question was, how bad a shape was the 1st in. That knocked down the happy chatter about getting into the fight quite a bit.

August was the start of the rainy season. The sky clouded over and the sea turned gray. Just when it looked like we were in for it, it would blow over. A few days out the squalls finally caught up with us and dumped buckets on our heads. Once you got wet on our transport, there weren't too many places to get dry. We weren't on one of the fancy ones with staterooms and a card room. The sick lists started filling out again. There was no sleeping up on decks this time with the cold rains coming down in showers most of the night, so we were all crammed belowdecks. It looked to me like about half the men were sick with the same flu. It raced through the stinking, frigid hold of the ship knocking out one wet, shivering Marine after the other.

We'd started to see Jap spotter planes off in the distance and heard our battleship escorts testing their guns. The carrier *Wasp* was in our escort screen. Sorties were coming and going from her deck, flying air cover for the column as we approached the Solomons. General quarters rang at all times of the day and night after the first week. On August 14, we had the first shots fired at us. Jap dive bombers and fighters swooped in and shot the hell out of us, putting rounds through the deck and superstructure and lining up for dive-bombing runs until the carrier Wildcats shot a few of them up and chased the rest off. Every night the planes attacked and every day we were on the lookout for submarines. Already it was getting to be a bloody business and we were days away from the Canal.

The action reports were coming in about the Japanese holding up in caves and fighting to the last man. We'd heard all about the night fighting tactics and trained for them. Now we were warned that the Japs were fanatics, insane or hopped up on some kind of drug. All we knew was that you could never be sure one was dead unless you shot him yourself; always make sure was the watchword. This news didn't add too much to the mood. With the general quarters going off every half hour and planes flying cover over us constantly, it was getting hard to put two solid hours of sleep together. When the weather was overcast, the planes were grounded. Then all you could hear was the water rushing past the sides of the ship.

In spite of all we heard and everything we imagined might happen, I'd never seen the men as calm as they were then. Mostly they sharpened their Ka-Bars and cleaned their weapons one more time. It was just an excuse to do something with their hands. A couple of the men took to skeet shooting at tin cans thrown off the deck.

It was all going along as usual, air attacks and counterattacks, the whomp-whomp-whomp of the antiaircraft guns, the general quarters alarm when some of the men heard distant explosions. The Japs had penetrated our destroyer screen and put three torpedoes into the aircraft carrier *Wasp*, a few more into the battleship *North Carolina* and hit a destroyer as well. The *Wasp* was our air cover. Without her we were just naked in the breeze. In less than an hour all three were out of the battle. The *Wasp* sank later that afternoon. We were still four days away from Guadalcanal with our two biggest defensive ships out of commission. Anybody keeping score knew that our entire South Pacific fleet now had only one carrier left, the *Hornet*, and one modern battleship, the *Washington*. I know it crossed more than a few minds that we might not get the chance to use all the training we had since we just got reduced from a heavily armed task force to little better than sitting ducks.

Why they didn't come and finish us all off right then and there is one of the mysteries that you just live with. I know a lot of the men didn't think about it much but it didn't sit that way with me. I just kept thinking of Father Amedeo. I could hear him saying over and over that God had a plan. Maybe it was something I couldn't understand right away or maybe even something I'd never understand, but he had a plan. So to me the fact that we didn't all get blown to pieces and go right to the bottom with all the others must be part of the plan. I still prayed. It seemed foolish not to. Why not draw the extra card if you got one coming? I prayed to live, to do my duty and not let my squad down but I knew it didn't mean too much if I wasn't in the plan anyway. I did it to calm my mind, I didn't really think it would do much good.

We fought our way through for the next four days and nights, fight-ing off dive-bombers and torpedo planes that suddenly swooped in out of the sky and flew between us at mast height, close enough to see the Jap writing on them. We lost a few more ships to them and to the sub-marines before we finally got within sight of the island. In all these days, with all the steel flying through the air, we still hadn't fired our own weapons. So far it was the Navy's fight. We were just passengers, praying we'd get to the island in some kind of shape to fight.

Word was things were bad for the men on the Canal. They held on and beat the hell out of a Jap division, but just barely was what we heard. They had been there for over a month under constant incom-ing artillery and infantry attacks. We had no idea how bad it was until we got up close and took a good look at them.

★

After all our training and waiting the day finally came. It was Sep-tember 18, 1942. General quarters sounded around 2:30 A.M. but not many of us were asleep anyway. The Navy gunners took up their positions at their battle stations with eyes peeled for any sign of a plane, ship or submarine in the area.

Breakfast was steak and eggs instead of the usual beans and white bread. Everybody ate without talking. Crates of fruit were opened up and we filled our pockets. Chesty briefed us that the beach land-ing area was secure so if we made it that far, we were home free. It wasn't the best news we ever heard. We weren't looking to get shot but we were sick and tired of getting shot at and we wanted to get into the fight. We thought we would be hauling the 5th Battalion's bacon out of the fire but it looked like we came all this way for just another landing exercise. Chesty didn't like the looks on some faces and tore into us about staying on our toes. We'd get our chance to kill Japs soon enough. Chesty was one of the best cursers any of us ever heard. When he talked it sounded like somebody shaking a coffee can full of nails. He'd yell at us "fucking" this and "sons of bitches" that, but it was just his way of talking. Like a lot of Marines, the word fuck was in almost every sentence when we were talking to each other. In the real world, of course, our language was cleaned up. For a while, I copied everything Chesty did, even for a while, the kind of rough language he used. After a while, I dropped it. It didn't sound like me. I kept thinking about how Pop would react if he heard me.

Chesty would never eat until the last of us had gone through the line. He wouldn't turn in until he saw we were all bedded down. We called him Mother Hen when he wasn't around. After his two Navy Crosses in the Banana Wars in Nicaragua, we knew he'd walk into the thick of any fight. There wasn't a man among us who wouldn't be proud to be right there with him. He meant more to us than a priest, for some of us even more than our own fathers. The boys in my squad followed me because I followed Chesty. He was everything I wanted to be and if he was with us, we knew everything would be all right.

We assembled on deck in the pitch-black. There was no light from any of the dozens of ships around us. For a moment, there was no sound except the slapping of the sea against the side of the ship. This was the time when the Japs liked to attack—the dead of night. It was overcast so not even the stars broke the total blackness. I could hear my squad breathing and sometimes shuffling as they shifted their weight. For that moment, we were all floating in black space. The gentle movement of the ship under our feet made us feel like we weighed nothing, like any breeze could blow us in front of it like dry leaves. The silence was broken by the davits as they creaked under the load of Higgins boats. The donkey engines chuffed to life. The davits were swung over the side and the boats were lowered. We could hear the boat engines starting one hundred feet belowdecks on the water. Roll call was taken as the huge, heavy rope landing nets were flopped over the side. The ship was pitching in the sea swells. I knew this pitching would be multiplied by the swinging of the nets, the weight of our packs and the pitching of the landing craft one hundred feet below. We could hear the nets thumping against the steel hull of the ship. It wasn't going to be the easiest disembarkation we ever had. We were loaded up with full packs, extra ammo, water and bedrolls. Everybody needed help lifting their packs onto their backs. I know a few of the packs with the weapons we carried weighed over a hundred pounds.

Chesty walked the ranks checking our gear like a careful father sending his boys off to school for the first time. He tugged on buckles and shoulder straps, looked us straight in the eye and told us we were too ugly to die today. God didn't want ugly looking killers like us in heaven, that's why he created Chesty's beloved Marine Corps. That's all we needed to hear. A word from Chesty and we were ready to go. Even so, somebody, it might have been Crumpton, puked right in front of him. Probably from nerves. Chesty didn't say a word or take a second glance. He kept right on walking and talking to us until it was time to hit the cargo nets.

I know a couple of men from other outfits didn't make it into the boats in one piece. One fell the last twenty feet into the boat, one missed a rung and got his leg broken when he fell and his leg got twisted in the net.

The sky was getting light. We could see the black outline of Guadalcanal over two miles away across the open sea. The boat was bouncing like a hobby horse, sometimes banging against the side of the ship, while we waited to fill up. My squad made it into the boat with no accidents on the net but a few more lost their breakfast before we got under way. The lighter the sky got the better the chance we had of making the landing without getting attacked. Water splashed over us as our boat bobbed up and down alongside the steel transport, making it a cold ride for a few of the men. The hours of waiting on deck were nothing compared to the time waiting for that boat to fill. Finally we shoved off and the engine sound took over. We headed out to the rally point and started our circling until the signal came to head in. I figured nobody could hear anyway so I started singing an aria from *Don Giovanni.* Nobody seemed to mind.

★

After all we'd fought through to get here, the landing was like sailing up to Miami Beach. Chesty was in the first boat. By the time we got in, he was shaking hands and tugging on "Red Mike" Edson like they were two college boys at a football game. You could hear them bellowing hellos all over the beach.

"So where are they?" Chesty wanted to know. One of Mike's guys gave Chesty a map that he glanced at for a second, trying to square it with the terrain he saw in front of him. "Hell, I can't make head nor tails of this—why don't we have something better than a National Geographic map anyway? Just show me where they are!" Chesty was impatient as hell when it came to business. Mike waved over toward the hills beyond the airfield.

"All right, let's go get 'em," Chesty said.

That had Mike laughing. Chesty was the same hell-for-leather character Mike had soldiered with in Haiti and in Nicaragua. He directed Chesty toward a coconut grove just off the beach where we would bivouac.

A supply convoy somehow had gotten through the submarine killing fields right behind us and had already started off-loading to the beach. Our first detail was going to be hauling supplies. Once we got to the coconut grove we could see why we were picked.

Our new home was a tent city in a swamp, like the other tent cities in swamps we had lived in for most of our training. This was sticky with tropical heat and ankle deep in water except for where the tents stood up on humps of dry ground. We tramped into the place and encountered some of the sorriest-looking Marines I'd ever seen walking upright. They looked like they hadn't eaten, slept or shaved in weeks, and they smelled, bad. Diarrhea had taken the weight off of most of them and a few had stopped trying to stay clean. They hadn't had toilet paper in weeks and had run out of every kind of paper to wipe with so they just lived with wet asses—real baggety-ass Marines.

The field hospital shuttled a steady line of wounded toward the emptying supply boats. The stories started coming in about the Ridge, the Tokyo Express and Washing Machine Charlie. We got a lot of ribbing about us being the first team, Chesty's hand-picked unit, who ended up coming late to the fight. They were sure glad to see us but most of them were too weak and tired to make much of a fuss. A few of them just stared and didn't say a word, almost like they didn't see us, like their minds were on something else. These were some of the men that came off the Ridge.

In some of their tents it looked like a rummage sale. When they first took the island, the Japs left in such a hurry that they left behind all kinds of booty that was now stashed in every corner of the tents: pots and pans, canned fish, Japanese field hats, uniforms, serving bowls, tools. Anything with Japanese writing on it became some kind of collector's item, a souvenir. We started to hear about the battle just two days before where Edson's Raiders held off a Jap division a few hundred yards west of the airfield, on a ridge over an open field of jungle grass. Some guys said a thousand Japs were killed and a hundred Marines, others said different numbers. Edson's battalion took the brunt of the attack and had 80 percent casualties since coming to the island just a month ago. They called it Edson's Ridge now. That answered the question of why we were pretty much alone when we were turned right around after unloading our packs and put on the resupply detail unloading boats. The guys on this island were in no shape to help. Part of the reason they were in no shape was they had been living on Japanese rice with bugs in it, whale fat captured from the Japs and Australian sheep tongues. The sheep tongues were the only meat off-loaded from the original supply convoy. Two meals a day for the last month and half, that was it—rice, whale fat, sheep tongue and coconut milk. It really made you think about home.

Coconut grove bivouac near Henderson Field

First Bivouac

The first day was just a work detail getting the supplies off the boats and hustled off the beach while keeping our eyes peeled for Jap bombers overhead. When the boats were empty we filled them with the wounded from the field hospital. That was our first real look, up close, at the war. Seeing blood and wounds like that hit hard and put pictures in our heads of what combat was really going to be like. You think you can perform when it counts but then you see wounds like that and, for a second, you're not so sure. You start to wonder what you've really got inside.

We got back to our little coconut grove and dug in for the night, cutting through the rubbery roots of the palms that gave us a little cover overhead. After chow, at least we had our own beef stew in cans, we bedded down for the night bone-tired and nobody said a word. It must have been around midnight when a single plane engine came overhead. It was high up, hard to hear. It must have been out of range because our 105s didn't open up at it. A single flare suddenly dropped out of the sky right over our position lighting up our little coconut grove with a pale green light. In the dark I heard a couple of "fucks" and somebody moving fast. In the next second a shell landed right in the middle of the grove. It tore the hell out of us. We scrambled into our holes and held on while the ground heaved and exploded all around us. Our shore guns opened up on the Jap ship that had snuck in close in the dark and drove it off.

Nobody ever got a full night's sleep again after that. Our little coconut grove bivouac was just smoking holes and scattered body parts that used to be our buddies. Chesty saw what happened and went wild like an animal. I thought he was going to tear somebody's head off. Five men got killed that night. We gathered them up as best we could and covered them with ponchos.

The next day at sunup we buried our five boys. It made me think

Coconut grove bivouac, September 12, 1942

Bloody Ridge

about God's plan to take those five, who had trained so hard and long, instead of one of us or one of the vets. Why them? It was one of those mountain-sized thoughts for somebody like Father Amedeo. It was one of those thoughts you just have to put aside or you'll never get anything done. But first blood had been spilled and not the way we had planned it.

On to the Ridge

The first barbed wire for a proper defense perimeter had come ashore the day before with us. Our work detail was to walk the line on Bloody Ridge with some of the guys we were replacing and reinforce the bamboo breastworks and picket lines that remained. The Ridge sat about a hundred feet above a two- or three-acre grass flatland that was ringed by the jungle. The jungle wrapped all the way around the flatland and surrounded the Ridge. Behind the Ridge was about two hundred yards of jungle cut through with supply paths back to the airfield. We knew we were being moved up to these forward positions as Colonel Mike Edson and his raiders were being rotated out. The constant attacks from enemy ships and aircraft let us know that the Japanese weren't giving up on the idea of getting their airfield back. It was clear now to Vandegrift that if they were going to get it, they were going to have to come the same way the others had, over the Ridge. Only this time, they'd be better prepared. Our battlefield was finally in front of us and the time was drawing closer every hour when we would have the chance to test ourselves.

★

We'd already learned about the enemy's night fighting tactics but Vandegrift took a new approach to the defense of the airfield and what we called the Cactus airforce after the first battle of Bloody Ridge. The first attackers had done the heavy work of cutting access through the jungle. The second force would be able to use it to march up to within a few hundred yards of our front line. The General wanted a special group of scouts and snipers to take the fight to the enemy before they got into positions to attack us. He formed up a special training unit under Colonel William J. "Wild Bill" Whaling, one of his most experienced jungle fighters who was a marksman and big-game hunter in civilian life. Wild Bill took a few men from each unit and disappeared into the jungle with them for a few days at a time. When they finished training, they went back to their outfits and others replaced them. Whaling and his scouts were now the spearhead of our offensive operations.

After getting our base of operations at the airfield squared away, orders came down for our first offensive push. Vandegrift felt he had enough manpower with our 4,262 new men to take the offensive. He wasn't going to sit back and wait for another Bloody Ridge to happen. This was finally it. We were going out to find the enemy and find out if all the training and respect we had as the "first team" was deserved. If we were judged by our eagerness to get into the fight, we were certainly the first team now. We had five brothers to avenge.

The entire 7th moved out heading west toward Mount Austen to clear out any advance Japanese reconnaissance patrols and then we were to swing north where a large force of the enemy was thought to be gathered. The jungle canopy blocked any direct sun and made the interior a shadowy place even at noon. Some strange bird kept screaming like someone being strangled. After all we'd heard about invisible Jap snipers and booby traps, we were more than a little jumpy. Firing broke out along our line when a coconut dropped. Everybody hit the deck except for Chesty. It took him a few seconds to figure out nobody was shooting but us. He calmly walked down the line, talking to us while he looked for the targets we were imagining, until he was sure we had jumped the gun. He called off the firing and then personally pulled a few of us out of the bushes. I had never seen a man so fearless in all my life. A few of the guys were embarrassed that they had panicked the way they did. Chesty didn't make a federal case out of it. He dusted a few of the boys off and kicked them in the pants to get them going up the trail again. His courage passed up and down the line to all eight hundred of us like electricity. Suddenly, we weren't afraid anymore. If I had any doubts before this, I didn't have them anymore. Colonel Lewis B. "Chesty" Puller was my personal hero. He already had a chest full of medals including two Navy Crosses for valor in the Nicaragua campaign. He was forty-four years old, more than twice the age of most of us, so we called him the Old Man.

I made up my mind that minute—if I could be half the Marine Chesty was, I would be satisfied with my life. My path, just like Father Amedeo said it would be, was finally clear to me. To live without fear like the Old Man was the only life I could think of that was worth living. On the second day of our patrol we reached a bridge across the Lunga River. We found three dead Japs and then a sniper took a shot at us from across the river. Chesty walked right across the bridge ahead of the point scouts like he was taking a walk in the park. He wanted to get a firsthand look at the other side of the Lunga. After a moment a squad was sent out to find out what had happened. They tiptoed across, ready to jump in the river at the first sound. As they approached the other side, Chesty popped out of the bushes to wave them on. We never heard another shot from that sniper.

We marched until night, at last climbing a steep grade at the base of our first objective, Mount Austen. It was dark and just as we climbed over the rise to a site where we planned to bivouac we were ambushed. Two of platoon leader Bob Haggerty's squad were killed outright and the rest of us scattered into the bush. Chesty walked down the line unconcerned about the machine gun fire directed at us. He yelled, "A Company, machine gun squad!" The squad pulled their faces out of the dirt and ran to Chesty. He placed them in a clearing and directed their fire to cover our advance. Men were getting hit all around them but until gunner Gerald White's skull got creased by a bullet that punched a hole in his helmet, the squad of gunners was unharmed. The fire stopped but no one wanted to move and give away their position. It was dark now and calls went out to locate the wounded. Private Willie Rowe, a rifleman who was wounded and laying concealed in the bush called out, "Leave me alone, I'm going to die where I am." Chesty was having none of that. He sent squads crawling all over until every one of us was pulled back to safety behind our lines. But Chesty wasn't satisfied. He didn't like having enemy gunners close enough to shoot into our lines. He pulled a maneuver that brought him up from our fearless commander to a living legend among us in the 7th. He walked right up to the forward gun emplacement at his full height, chest out and shoulders squared, and told them to keep their eyes peeled. Then in the blackness he struck a match and calmly lit his pipe! He took one puff and then dove for cover. The Jap gun emplacement opened up on him, aiming hot lead directly at where his head had been. The forward gun crew saw the enemy muzzle flashes and returned fire to the spot.

The firing stopped and we heard nothing more from that enemy gun. Chesty laid on the ground completely relaxed for a moment puffing his pipe.

All that night Chesty paced among us men, assuring the wounded and encouraging the rest that we had nothing to worry about. He said the Japs weren't going to attack that night. Later on that night, undisciplined firing broke out from a few trigger happy Marines. For only the second time, I heard that voice that sounded like he was going to cut somebody into fish bait. Chesty had his .45 out and was waving it around. "I don't want another man to fire another round, unless he can point the target out to me!" Three more of us were killed in that ambush and twenty-five were wounded before it was over. So far, we weren't looking like the first team. At this rate, we would be lucky to survive at all. The first five of us that were killed were almost like an accident but those three who died that night weren't an accident. We had walked into the ambush. They were our fault.

The next day we were joined up with Company A of Edson's Raiders who were sent ahead by Vandegrift for reinforcements and to evacuate our wounded. We were ordered to move out, continuing north. Our full force with Edson's A Company reached a river about midday where discipline broke down again. Our canteens had been empty since early the day before and many of the men were so dehydrated their tongues had swollen up twice their normal size. Some just flopped on their bellies and put their faces in the water. They didn't even bother to disinfect the water with the iodine drops we carried. It was another lesson for me on all the ways I could lose control of the men under me. I got to my squad before they saw the water and made sure they had iodine before they got a drink. None of my boys came down with dysentery on my watch.

The day after that, September 23, we moved on, sweeping due north along the eastern bank of the Matanikau toward the sea where we were to meet up with the rest of the 1st Raider Battalion who were marching up the coast. It was a classic pincer maneuver right out of the pages of Caesar's *Gallic Wars*, the book that Chesty carried with him at all times. Our pincer was intended to flank and trap any enemy forces on our side of the river. The 2nd Battalion, 5th Marine Regiment would wait in reserve at the mouth of the Matanikau on the coast. We moved along the river all that day and the next without making contact. Late in the afternoon of the 24th, we were in rough country—up and down the foothills around the base of Mount Austen, when the point of our patrol stumbled on two Japanese eating rice hunkered down around a hidden cook fire at the base of a tree. The scouts killed one and the other ran off but in the wrong direction, right into our lines. There were a few shots, then it was quiet. The Old Man was up at the point as soon as the last shots died. He took the rice pot and started eating. A machine gun opened up, knocking the pot out of the Old Man's hand. A runner behind him got hit in the throat and died instantly. Everybody dove for cover except of course Chesty, who put his little stump of a pipe in his mouth and directed our counterattack just as cool as a cucumber. "B Company! Second Platoon, in the line here!" he yelled down the line just before he hit the deck and rolled away before the Japs could get their sites set on him. He did that continuously, popping up, yelling his orders to get us in proper position, then hitting the ground and rolling away. Captain Chester Cockrell's B Company didn't move fast enough for him and they heard about it along with everybody else around there. "Cockrell! Goddamn it! Get them fucking guns up!" My squad fell into the skirmish line and helped lay down the covering fire for our advance. We soon pushed the enemy back over the next ridge.

A grenade landed eight yards away from the Old Man. Cox's A company scattered but the Old Man took one look at the grenade and yelled, "Oh that damned thing ain't going off." And it didn't, it was a dud. Meanwhile up front, Cockrell's squad was getting cut up by snipers in the trees with light machine guns. The fight was suddenly at close quarters. The Old Man killed three up close, one of them a major, with his .45. Word came back from the point that Cockrell was killed. Firing from his squad's position was faltering. He called to Cox and told him to go forward to get Cockrell's squad back together. "Take over B down there," he said. "They're scattered all over hell's half acre."

Cox found only six men still alive at Cockrell's position. He pulled the men together and with his own A Company led a charge that broke through to a Jap encampment and ended the firefight. That night we ate canned crab and tangerines from the camp supplies. Chesty collected a beautiful samurai sword from one of the three enemies, a major, that he shot earlier. He gave this with a map case and a diary we captured to his exec officer Major Otho Rogers to take back to HQ the next day when A Company arrived along with our twenty-five wounded, eighteen of them on stretchers.

That night a light rain fell. The camp we captured must have had about five hundred men at one point so we all had cover from the rain. The Old Man was troubled by the way he cursed at Cockrell before he died. He said to a few of us, "God I hated that I had to curse at Cockrell out there tonight. He was a good, brave Marine—the fighting kind." It really bothered him and after thinking for a second, he tried to make himself feel better by saying, "It had to be done."

The next day the 2nd Battalion, 5th Regiment, joined up with us. Major Rogers took A and B Companies from the 2/5 as guards and stretcher-bearers and returned to the perimeter with our wounded and the captured map case, diary and Chesty's sword. We reached the muddy Matanikau by late morning and turned north toward its mouth where it emptied into the sea. Around 2:00 in the afternoon we were getting close to the mouth ahead of the Raiders, the other side of the pincers who were still coming up the coast. So far it was quiet, but within sight of the sea we drew machine gun and mortar fire from the far side of the river. Once more, Chesty waded out halfway into the river directly in the line of fire to get a better look, then turned around and came back without a scratch. Some of us still couldn't believe he would expose himself like that, like he thought he was invisible or armor-plated. That may be when the legend started that his big barrel chest was really armor plating because his flesh and blood chest was blown off in Nicaragua. G Company of the 2/5 wasn't armor plated. They took twenty-five casualties. Me and Sig and Crumpton and Hatfield and the rest of the squad had been in real combat now for a few days. We'd seen how it happened. There was no accounting for who lived and died. At least, that's how it looked to me. Some of the squad, like Hatfield, were superstitious. He kept close count of who got it and how, what they were doing, what position in the line they were. He was trying to get a fix on the odds. I didn't see it that way. I know Chesty didn't either, otherwise he would have been shaving the odds somehow. It looked clear enough that you just did your job and left the rest up to God.

HQ radioed a new plan that night while we held the area. When the Raiders arrived, they would backtrack along the river, cross and come around from the enemy's rear. Mike Edson was taking command

John at one year *(seated on chair)*, 1917. *(Left to right)* Mary, Phyllis, Carlo *(seated)*, John, Catherine, and Angelo.

Basilone family, 1946.

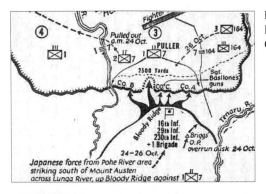

Diagram of the Battle of
Bloody Ridge, Guadalcanal,
October 24–26, 1942.

U.S. Army, 16th
Infantry, Company
D. Winners,
Machine Gun
Competition, Fort
Jay, New York,
September 28,
1936.

(Detail) John hold-
ing flag *(right)*.

U.S. Marine graves on Guadalcanal.

John wearing his trademark sideways "pisscutter."

John receiving
Medal of Honor
in Balcombe,
Australia, May
21, 1943.

Marines dig in on
Bloody Ridge.

Machine gunner,
carrying a
"heavy" water-
cooled Browning
.30 caliber.

Thirty thousand people attended Basilone Day Parade and Bond Rally on the Duke estate.

John attending church before the parade.

John and Lena—wedding day, Oceanside, California, July 10, 1944.

Meeting the mayor, parade day.

Basilone Day Parade, September 19, 1943.

Parade with mother, father, and Steve Helstowski in car.

Iwo Jima, 1945.

First wave of Marines on the black sand terraces of Iwo Jima.

Japanese view of Iwo Jima landing beaches, 1945.

Marines move off beach under fire from Mt. Suribachi.

Illustration of John for the cover of *Collier's* magazine, June 24, 1944. Basilone, who posed for this, is wonderfully depicted in this oil painting as a heroic giant.

SERGT. JOHN BASILONE

The real life Basilone, photographed wearing the Medal of Honor.

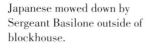

Satchel charge takes out first blockhouse.

Japanese mowed down by Sergeant Basilone outside of blockhouse.

Marines advance to positions near Motoyama One airfield.

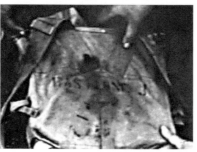

A Marine thought enough of Sergeant Basilone to recover his rucksack after his death.

Statue of Sergeant Basilone, Raritan, New Jersey.

on this one and Chesty would act as his exec. It seemed like a simple plan. I don't know how things got so screwed up but I was about to get the second big lesson in real warfare, besides whether you live or die is pretty much a crapshoot, every plan looks simple on paper.

The Raiders arrived at first light, Lt. Col. Sam Griffith in command. He set off with them down the river. Our air attack pinned the Japs where we thought they were but the artillery support Edson wanted didn't happen. Communication was spotty. No word came until late in the morning, so Edson and Chesty held us where we were, thinking Griffith might drive them up to the river or out to the beach. Finally a garbled message came through that Red Mike thought meant Griffith had crossed the river. He called to base and wanted A and B Companies that had just returned to base with the wounded, to get into Higgins boats, come up the coast right away and close the noose around the enemy from the beach side. Chesty wasn't in on this plan until he saw the boats passing our position. He ran out toward the beach again putting his head in the gunsights of the Japs across the river and tried to flag the boats down. He thought they were coming to reinforce us, but they went right on past. Then another call came in. The Raiders were pinned down. Griffith was wounded and his exec, Maj. Kenneth Bailey, who kept the lines together and threw the Japs back a dozen times on Bloody Ridge, was dead.

Chesty was back at the radio now and got the message first. He read it and gave it to Edson who said, "I guess we'd better call them off. They can't seem to cross the river."

Chesty went at his old buddy, "Christ! You're not going to stop 'em when they've had only two casualties? Most of my battalion will be out there alone, cut off without support. You're not going to throw these men away!" He wasn't sounding too much like an exec. The two of them went at each other and we could hear the tussle all up and down the line. Chesty was loud as hell when he got hot and Red Mike wasn't any wallflower either when it came to getting his way.

The only thing on the Old Man's mind must have been getting A and B Company out of the trap they would be in on the beach. I don't know whether he pretended to follow Edson's orders or not but he marched from the argument, grabbed a signalman and marched him down to the beach where he signaled the old destroyer that was heading up the coast after the Higgins boats. He hailed a skiff from her and got on board. That's the last we saw of him that day.

The story came back that he got the captain to heave in close off of Point Cruz where they saw his men on a hill. They were surrounded and under heavy attack. From the boat they could see roughly where the battle lines were but couldn't get coordinates from the men on the hill who were busy fighting for their lives. The ship opened up, blasting both flanks as best they could. Artillery from far down the coast that was supposed to advance the attack earlier, finally let loose but was now firing into the wrong coordinates and ended up blasting our own men. Major Otho Rogers, the quiet, little reservist and post office employee who had become Chesty's executive officer and sometime whipping boy, was in the wrong place at the wrong time. A mortar shell landed between his legs. There wasn't enough left of him to put on a stretcher. They gathered up what was left and wrapped it in a poncho. Zach Cox, who had led our attack that broke through to the camp the night before, was nearby and had both arms and legs badly torn up. The lines were collapsing and snaked all up and down the hill. Marine mortars were fired at impossibly close range by men laying on their backs and supporting the tubes with their feet.

Offshore, the destroyer's five-inch guns, with Chesty spotting the targets, started blasting a path down the hill to the beach. The men retreated from all parts of the hill as the enemy lines behind them were blown away. Platoon Sergeant Andy Malinowski, who had joined the Corps in Baltimore, like me, picked up a Browning Automatic Rifle from a dead Marine and told Capt. Regan Fuller, "Captain, you take Doc Schuster and the other wounded on down, and I'll handle the rear. I'll be with you in a few minutes." Malinowski set up his gun on a log across the trail and stayed behind. When the men who were left reached the beach, they set up a defense perimeter and waited for the Japanese to catch up while the Higgins boats came to evacuate them. Captain Fuller waited for Malinowski but only heard one burst of fire from the Marine's position, then silence. Malinowski never made it to the beach. Soon the enemy was at the edge of the jungle firing into the perimeter on the beach. B Company had arrived first and was loading their wounded into the boats that had run aground thirty yards offshore under sporadic but accurate fire. Captain Fuller and several brave Coast Guard coxswains returned fire with one hand and helped load the wounded with the other. One coxswain was killed and two others wounded as they worked feverishly to get the men on board.

On board the destroyer, when Chesty saw that his Marines were on the beach, he climbed overboard into the Higgins boats that were going in to evacuate them. As they approached the beach they saw that the first boats were coming under fire. The coxswains nervously swung away and started circling out of range until Chesty unleashed his "colorful" language on them and unholstered his .45. He turned the boats around and led the charge right up to the water's edge where he directed the loading of the rest of our A and B Company along with the Raiders and men of the 2/5.

Our 1/7 Battalion lost another twenty-four dead and twenty-three wounded in the fiasco. The Raiders and the 2/5 took 117 casualties. The only good thing we learned was that there were a hell of a lot more Japanese on the island than we thought. We stayed in position that night and Chesty wasn't talking to anybody about what had happened.

The mouth of the Matanikau River looking north.
The 1/7 was rescued from the hill to the right.

Lt. Col. Chesty Puller (left) in the field

A Lesson from Chesty

The next day we all returned to the perimeter where the Old Man called a few of us together. He took a tough tone as he spoke. "Gentlemen, at least we've all been blooded now. I don't want you to be mooning over our losses and feeling sorry for yourselves or taking all the blame on your shoulders. We've all got to leave this world someday; we're all in the same pickle. And there are worse things than dying for your country. Some things about our action in the last four days I want you to remember forever. There are some we'd all like to forget, but they'll be in your mind's eye for as long as you live. I hope we've all learned something. Now take care of your men, and make yourselves ready. We haven't seen anything yet.

"One other thing. Back there on the hillside at Mount Austen, I had trouble getting company officers up. I hope you saw what that cost us in casualties. Never do I want to see that again in my command. I want to see my officers leading. I want you to know that you're leaders, and not simply commanders. You cannot operate a military force in the field under these conditions with commanders alone. Civilians wouldn't know what I was talking about, but you've found out now that it's true. There are many qualities in a man, but one that is absolutely necessary in an infantry leader is stark courage. Give that idea to your men in your own way.

"Don't worry over things that are done, that we can no longer help. Concentrate on building a better combat unit, because that's the best hope of all of us surviving. None of us could help the fact that I was the only combat-trained man in our outfit when we began. I was lucky enough to get the jolt when I was young. You'll come along fast, and there'll be work for us. Let's be ready when our time comes."

The Old Man went on and was a little bitter when he mentioned ". . . the much vaunted Raiders." I don't think he ever forgave his old buddy Mike Edson for hanging his men out on a limb like that. There was never any talk about Chesty disobeying orders from Edson either. We all knew who had saved our men that day. I knew right then and there that if I followed Chesty I would be on exactly the right path. It was suddenly clear to me, just like Father Amedeo said it would be. If I could live like Chesty, become like him somehow, I could live a life that meant something. I used to follow his orders to the letter, now I followed his every move and word. I was going to become Chesty Puller.

Lessons from Chesty came not just in combat but in everyday life. After a few days back in base, the samurai sword Chesty took from the dead major was stolen out of the command post. One of the officers offered to shake down the entire unit until it was found but the Old Man wouldn't have it. "Hell, no!" he said. "I don't know how he got it, but any one of those boys rated it more than I did. They carried the big load. Let him keep it."

The Old Man didn't miss a single thing when it came to which way the wind was blowing with his men. Captain Fuller, who had maybe seen a little bit too much up close on the hill at Point Cruz and on the beach below, grew a beard and started acting like a bit of an outlaw, like someone who had seen the Devil and spit in his eye. Chesty pulled him aside and gave him a talking-to. "Old man, you're carried away with this war business. You're feeling too self-important about it. That's dangerous. This is just a matter of kill or be killed, and we've got to stay on our toes to have a chance. Clean yourself up.

Here's some shaving gear. And when you're through, you can take a drink from that bottle, if you like." We saw right away that the captain calmed himself down and got back in line with the rest of the unit. Nobody said anything but we were relieved that Fuller wasn't heading off the deep end anymore.

★

General Vandegrift wasn't satisfied to let us just sit behind the perimeter and wait for the Japs to come to us. We hadn't accomplished anything with that first try at the Matanikau. The word came down that we were going up there again. This time in force.

Sergeant Basilone's 1/5 Marines on the trail to Matanikau

We moved out on October 7, due west. Edson's 5th took the coast road toward the mouth of the river where they were to hold that position again. Bill Whaling and his unit of snipers and scouts marched with the 5th and were to move upstream, south, when they hit the river and cross at the Nippon Bridge in the same maneuver that had been executed before. Once across the river, Whaling was supposed to turn around and push north toward the sea, sweeping the west bank of the river. Edson didn't make it all the way to the river before he ran into a fight with an enemy battalion that had crossed the river to the east bank after our retreat. He surrounded this advance force and pushed their backs against the river. It was a tough fight as the Japs tried all through that first night to break out of the noose. It was hand-to-hand combat in the thick jungle in the dead of night because no one could see far enough to shoot anything. They had to practically step on each other to find the enemy.

Chesty and we of the 1/7 took the inland route parallel to the coast. Up at the point we found a slightly wounded Jap soldier who might have fallen out of a tree after we cleared out some snipers. The Old Man took one look at the little man and said, "Don't take chances with him. He may have a grenade ready to go off. We can't slow down to carry him anyway. Kill him." We moved off.

Sniping continued to take down a man at a time and slow us down as we moved along the trail. An occasional shell whistled in from time to time, holding us up even more. The Japs were expecting us. It was getting on toward dark when the Old Man pulled off the trail and gave the order to dig in for the night. He took off his helmet and squatted on it by the side of the trail. As the rear of the column passed him by he saw the little Japanese soldier loaded down with packs and his Marine execution squad walking behind him with lightened loads.

"Say," the colonel asked them, "why didn't you kill that bird? Didn't you hear my order?"

"Sir, we thought he could carry today and we could kill him to-night," the ringleader said. I guess this must have offended the colonel's sense of fairness because the story we heard was that Chesty said, "No you won't. He did your work all day, and you'll sit up and guard him all night." That was his way of making them pay for disobeying his order. At the same time, he wanted to make good use of the help they found. The next morning the prisoner was set to work carrying our wounded back to base.

Colonel A. L. Sims was put in command of this operation to avoid the conflict between Chesty and Edson that had threatened the last one. Communications from Edson indicated he would be able to hold his position and crush the surrounded enemy force on our side of the river. Whaling was moving steadily toward the sea with only light contact with the enemy. The operation was working as planned so far. In the afternoon, we came up to the river and Sims and Chesty had a powwow. Sims made the decision to advance across the river and trail Whaling's advance as a reserve and rear guard. Chesty took a deep breath, ballooning out that big barrel chest and told him, "That's fine. Couldn't be better. My men are prepared to spend the night on the trail. Best place to be if you want to go anywhere."

Sims staked a command post where we were and we moved out, crossing the rough coconut logs that we called the Nippon Bridge over the Matanikau. We turned up the opposite bank and made our way north toward the sea. The rest of the day was a quiet but difficult march up and down the hills through thick brush. Toward nightfall we met up with Whaling's scouts who were holding their position a few kilometers away from the main Japanese force. We were setting up to spring the attack and wipe out what we thought was a force of about two thousand Japanese. We dug in for the night along the river. Just before dawn the storm clouds rolled over and opened up in a monsoon storm that left us mostly blind and paralyzed. We couldn't see a foot in front of us and the trails turned into streams of mud. HQ postponed the attack for the day. We sat in our ponchos like giant green mushrooms covering as much of the equipment as possible, waiting for the order to move out. HQ was flying reconnaissance again from Henderson Field as soon as the storm broke. They didn't like what they saw in front of us.

We formed up our lines with Whaling's unit closest to the river, next in the line was Colonel Hanneken with the 2nd Battalion of the 7th and then us with Chesty in the 1/7 extending the left flank. The Old Man was not happy that Sims hadn't come up from his command post on the other side of the river. It was against the hard-won principles of jungle warfare he'd drilled into us just a few days earlier back in base that in this terrain commanders have to lead too. They can't sit back and hope to know what the hell is going on where the fighting is. But Sims wasn't in on Chesty's speech and he wasn't under Chesty's command; Chesty was under his.

We moved down the river in sort of a rough horseshoe shape three battalions wide. It wasn't too long before we found what we were looking for. Snipers and company-sized outposts held up part of our line as we got near to Point Cruz, the location of our last near disaster. Hanneken fell into a blazing firefight in our middle with his battalion scattered across several ridges. In the middle of the fight, Sims called him from the Nippon Bridge and ordered him to break off and return to base perimeter—plans had changed. Hanneken did as he was told and pulled out, leaving a gaping hole in the middle of our line. That left us, Company C, to fill the gap alone. Our immediate CO was Capt. Marshall Moore, who deployed us on the central ridge. We were suddenly in the direct path of a full scale counterattack, shit was flying everywhere. Chesty pulled A Company out of position and sent them up the ridge to reinforce us but it was a tight fit and we ended up stepping over each other. B Company took the next ridge and laid mortar fire to our front. They were firing blind so we had to call targets to them but it did the trick, we were punching holes in the wave that was coming at us. In the middle of this shit storm, the Old Man gets a call from Sims in the rear. "Puller, we've got a change in orders. Execute a reconnaissance in force with your battalion along the coast road toward Kokumbona. Do not become involved in a large action. Be prepared to withdraw, to maintain communications."

The Old Man blew. "How the fuck can I make a reconnaissance when we're engaged down to the last man?! We're fighting tooth and nail, man. If you'd get off your ass and come up here where the fighting is, you could see the situation!" Chesty slammed down the field phone. I don't think the colonel was used to being spoken to like that and he didn't call back. The Old Man called a conference with Captain Fuller and a few others. He gave his version of Sims's order. "All right gentlemen. There are enemy over there in those ravines. And here we are. Now go get 'em. Drive 'em into the sea."

We went at it full force, firing from all positions and moving up our lines, moving from ridge to ridge. Just after noon, we hit what must have been the main corps of the enemy and it was a pitched battle for over an hour until they wavered and broke, scattering across the broken land in front of us. We spotted them retreating into a circular ravine that must have been an old volcano crater that was overgrown with jungle vines. They were trapped now. We called in artillery on the crater and added our mortars to the fire. It was a massacre. They were driven out of the crater right into our guns. When they retreated back into the crater, we dropped in the big artillery shells and mortars. We killed them all. Six hundred and ninety men.

The phone rang again. Sims said the reconnaissance wasn't necessary. We were to return to base. We carried back 65 dead and 125 wounded of our own. Letters found on the Japanese dead in the crater described us as monsters. "The Americans on this island are not ordinary troops, but Marines, a special force recruited from jails and insane asylums for bloodlust. There is no honorable death to prisoners, their arms are cut off, they are staked on the airfield, and run over by steamrollers."

When we got back to the perimeter, the Old Man was hopping mad. He let the brass have it with both barrels. As we heard it, he lit into them saying the whole damned operation was a cluster fuck of poor command and worse communications. It was only by sheer luck that we survived at all and he was goddamned if he would head out into the jungle again until Topside got themselves organized. This story got passed around among us like the last cigarette but kept getting bigger with each telling. Marine after Marine took his turn with it turning the air blue with his own version of the choicest cursing Chesty was supposed to have used on the officers who commanded the mess that almost got us all killed again. I don't know if that particular discussion made the difference but new orders came down. We were to take up defensive positions on our own territory. We were deployed on Bloody Ridge and told to dig in.

★ 8 ★

Bloody Ridge

Marines in fighting hole on Guadalcanal

We moved into the fighting holes we had started reinforcing before the two offensives on the Matanikau. The Old Man was hovering over us like a mother hen now, getting into every detail of our business, down to how often we washed. Jungle rot had set in on a lot of the boys and we all had some kind of rash somewhere. Maybe he just didn't get along with Topside anymore and felt more comfortable with us. It sure seemed that way. He took to stripping off with us enlisted men and taking a bath once a day in the Lunga River that ran off the right flank of the Ridge. The Lunga and just about all the rivers on the islands weren't rivers like we knew them. They were like muddy streams. Often they were half seawater if the tide was up. The other officers stood on the banks watching as we all washed up together and were probably thinking, like they'd been told to do, that officers shouldn't get too close to the men they commanded. It wasn't professional. They might have to send us to our deaths one day and they shouldn't get personal with us. The Old Man just thought of himself as one of us. If we were going to our deaths, he'd probably be leading the way.

Captain Fuller wasn't the only one headed toward the deep end after Matanikau. The Old Man saw it in Fuller but not in himself. The washing was one thing but more than that, when a few of our boys' bodies weren't accounted for from the Matanikau, he badgered the brass until they sent a special patrol to look for them. Burials became a duty as important as caring for your weapon. We all had to show up and look smart whether we knew the Joe or not. Then he'd grumble about the chaplain's speech, saying he could do better. We weren't really worried but we did notice he was different. He made sure the chaplains were up on the front lines doing what they could for us. He didn't take much stock in what they had to say but he wanted them around for us.

My boys were quieter. They acted like nothing bothered them and went about their usual shenanigans of card playing, craps shooting and lying about women, but alone they spent more time writing letters or cleaning already spotless weapons so they wouldn't have to talk. Many of them were getting sick with malaria and dysentery, some with dengue fever and a type of typhus. That accounted for some of the silence but not all. Hatfield didn't take much notice anymore of who got it and how. Like the rest of us, he knew it didn't really matter what you were doing or where you were. If you were in a frontline combat outfit like ours, the only things that mattered were the guys next to you. If they were alive, your chances were a little better than if they were dead. That was about it. So we didn't care much for anything except each other anymore. Some of the boys like Crumpton and Sig were starting to have that look we saw on the Raiders who came off Bloody Ridge when we first got on the island. They seemed to look right through other people, at something in the distance. Nash slept with his Ka-Bar knife out of its sheath and just under the edge of his poncho. Foley developed a nervous tic that had him flinching like he was protecting himself from a punch. All the talk about how we were going to punish the Japs was gone. We'd already punished them plenty. In the crater, we saw their guts hanging on bushes like confetti. And like the Old Man said, we hadn't seen anything yet.

Our socks and underwear were rotting off us. I kept my socks and boots off and worked barefoot whenever I could since the socks only served to keep my feet wet anyway. With the sun and air on my feet, I managed to avoid jungle rot between my toes that tormented a lot of the boys. A couple of the local bearers taught me this trick. These were big, black-skinned fellas with wiry twists of red hair hanging down their heads who had worked in the coconut plantations on the island, making copra for an Australian company. They carried for us. Their hair was naturally black but was turned red because they rubbed raw limes in it, then worked out in the sun all day. They were good workers and brave fighters when it came down to it, but they usually didn't mix with the troops. It was mutual. Most of our boys didn't know what the hell to make of them. Rumors were that they were cannibals. They knew how to keep their feet from rotting off though. Part of the trick was pissing on your feet. That seemed to work just fine.

Malaria took down over a thousand troops by mid-October and Topside ordered all men to take the Atabrine tablets they provided. Nobody wanted to take them because it was said that they made you impotent. Chesty fought to use quinine injections on us, a remedy he learned in the campaign in Haiti back in the 30s, but was overruled again. It got so bad that they had command staff at the head of the chow line with the Atabrine. If you didn't take the pill, you didn't eat.

About this time the Army showed up with some advance units of a division that was supposed to reinforce us. It was becoming a real tug-of-war with the Japs over this little airfield of ours. They kept up the bombardments at night from the air and sea and were chased off by our ships during the day. The Army gobs were off-loading a warehouse full of supplies on the beach before the rest of them arrived, while a long-range Jap artillery piece that we called "Pistol Pete" dropped harassing fire all across the beach. The Army MPs who were supposed to be guarding all this stuff had their heads buried deep in a foxhole to dodge Pistol Pete. To us this was early Christmas. We stole everything we could carry and when we got tired, we stole a jeep to carry it with. Chesty pulled Sergeant Pennington off his stack of typing at HQ and used him to commandeer the jeep. We loaded that thing up with crates until it sunk up to its axles in the sand. An MP poked his head out of the sand and yelled at us, "Leave that fuckin' stuff alone, damn you! That's Army gear!" Chesty laughed. "If you're guarding this stuff, get the hell out here and guard it." He gunned the engine and took off. We had one hell of a party opening up those crates filled with new socks, underwear, canned fruit, bacon, coffee and a big, iron battalion arms chest that Chesty was hoping was filled with spare weapons parts. We had to cut the heavy lock off of it with a torch, also commandeered from the airfield, but instead of weapons parts, it was filled with hundreds of cans of sardines. Nobody but the Old Man was disappointed on that one.

JAPAN DRAWS THE BATTLE LINES

The stinging defeats at Bloody Ridge and the second Matanikau operation at the hands of U.S. Marines alerted the Japanese high command that Guadalcanal was, in fact, the spearhead of American resistance in the Pacific. If Japan were to continue its conquest of the Pacific and then Australia, Guadalcanal would have to be taken first.

General Haruyoshi Hyakutake was convinced of the need to clear Guadalcanal of American forces but the Imperial Navy resisted providing him with sufficient transport for his forces. They were concerned with the increasing strength of the U.S. naval forces that controlled the straights between Guadalcanal and Savo Island, known as "the Slot," during the day. They had been restricted to harassment tactics during night raids in the area when the U.S. airpower operating from Henderson Field was at a disadvantage. A special envoy from General Hyakutake was sent to plead his case with the supreme commander in the Pacific, Admiral Yamamoto. Yamamoto listened patiently to the officer and eventually agreed that the Navy's reticence had been partly responsible for the two recent defeats on the island, the first in over two thousand years of Japanese warfare. He committed the full might of the Navy to support the landing of Hyakutake's forces and finally engage the U.S. Navy in the "decisive battle" that would settle the question of dominance in the South Pacific.

General Kawaguchi, who had suffered the recent defeat on the island, returned to report to General Hyakutake on Rabaul, the provisional command center in the region. His eloquent description of the brave but doomed men of his command convinced commanders that he was still the best commander for the new operation in spite of his failure. He was ordered back to Guadalcanal, this time accompanied by General Hyakutake, to annihilate the Americans and regain the airfield.

During the weeks since defeat at the second Matanikau, approximately nine hundred Japanese reinforcement troops were being landed on the island each night. On the night of October 12, under the cover of a heavy naval bombardment, four thousand more troops landed at Tassafaronga just west of Point Cruz. Over twenty thousand Japanese troops were now on the island, about equal to the number of Americans.

General Hyakutake had planned to simply march up the coast to attack the Americans from the west but the desperate condition of the existing Japanese garrison, half of whom were wounded or too ill to be effective, caused him to rethink his strategy. He instead sent a regiment up the coast as a diversion, while taking the same tortuous path hacking through the jungle by hand that had contributed to the defeat of General Kawaguchi previously. Kawaguchi did not protest too strongly because of his weak standing in Hyakutake's eyes, having suffered two previous defeats. Hyakutake led 5,600 men into the unforgiving jungle, hacking their way through dense growth and pulling artillery behind them. Each man carried an artillery shell or a mortar (round) on his back.

Hyakutake's route toward Bloody Ridge,
Henderson Field is at the top beyond the ridge

Digging In

We found out that the Army unit that had been thoughtful enough to cater our party was the 164th Army Infantry Regiment, mainly National

Guard reservists from North Dakota. When these farmers turned up in their bright green uniforms, we must have stared at them the way the Raiders stared at us when we arrived. These boys were an awful long way from North Dakota so we took pity on a few. We were happy to trade stuff we had already stolen from them, for other stuff we hadn't gotten around to stealing from them yet. But the exchange rate was terrible for them—we would trade a can of their own stolen sardines for other items of theirs, like chocolate bars, that were five times the value of the sardines. For a while, there was quite a market for their M-1 Garand rifles. These were semiautomatic and could put five times more steel on target than our bolt-action Springfields, that were more accurate but slower. When it came to these weapons though, many of the new men refused to trade. We were forced to keep stealing so our front line men had proper equipment. This was partly because we did not consider these National Guardsmen to be lucky for us.

The day they arrived, the 164th got a warm reception from the Japs. Twenty-four bombers came over and unloaded dozens of five-hundred–pounders on us, then about fifteen planes came in the afternoon blasting more huge craters in the airfield. That night, Japanese battleships moved in and, just like the first night we arrived, they dropped flares overhead and started lobbing in shells. But this time they were the big fourteen-inch shells. There was nothing we could do. The deepest bunker on the island was like an anthole against them. Fifty-foot palm trees that were two-feet thick exploded into matchsticks all around us. All we could do was hold our helmets on, bounce around in our holes and hope our number wasn't up. But instead of the fifteen minutes of bombardment we got when we arrived, this went on for an hour and a half. They dropped over nine hundred shells and for forty-one of us, our numbers were up. The next day fires were still burning all over the airfield, most of the planes were destroyed and all the fuel was burned up. Our air cover was gone.

That was when we knew for sure that the Japs were on their way. Vandegrift reorganized the perimeter. Facing south, the expected route of attack, to his left Sector One started on the beach off of Lunga Point, then curved inland toward the jungle. A battalion and Whaling's special troops held that sector. Then Sector Two, curving out into the jungle south of our position, was covered by the new boys of the 164th. Sector Three was our neighborhood, facing directly south. It was twenty-five hundred yards long, covering all of Bloody Ridge, but only two battalions—ours under Chesty and another under Hanneken—handled this real estate. Then Sectors Four and Five, manned by the rest of our 1st Division, completed the semicircle curving around back to the beach on the north side of Lunga Point near the mouth of the Matanikau. Most of our strength was placed in this area since Vandegrift thought the enemy wouldn't be likely to try another jungle assault like last time.

Heavy rain filled our holes with a nasty soup of mud, piss and floating trash. When we weren't standing in this muck we were out stringing a second and third apron of perimeter wire. Since we didn't have any trip flares to let us know when our Japanese guests might arrive, we hung tin cans full of pebbles and grenades with the pins half pulled on the wires. A week went by while we filled more sandbags with mud and the enemy marched closer each day.

On October 23, a light tank and infantry attack across the mouth of the Matanikau ran right into the teeth of Vandegrift's defenses. It was chewed up in short order with over six hundred Japs killed, many of them trapped in a jungle clearing where U.S. tanks just drove over them instead of wasting ammunition. They ground the poor bastards up like sausage under the tank treads until the entire clearing was covered in gore and left to rot in the sun.

During the attack Hanneken's battalion, to our right, was pulled out of position and sent against the attack along the river. That left a huge twenty-five-hundred-yard front that we had to cover ourselves. Chesty pulled me and other squad leaders out of our holes to pump Hanneken's men for information before they left. We went over the defensive positions and firing lanes in a hurry as they pulled out. The Old Man brought up more machine guns from the rear and personally inspected all our new firing lanes, making sure that our fields of fire interlocked. We were strung out now like a picket fence with too few pickets. Most of us couldn't see the next hole down the line. We were isolated except for the communication wire between us. My squad of twelve men was now spread over about one hundred and fifty yards between our two machine gun emplacements. Each machine gun hole had two heavies—water-cooled Browning .30 cals. We stretched across a point in the ridge a little in front and below the others, the weak point in a high wall of men and weapons. It was the natural pathway over the ridge. A sharp-eyed commander would see this as the obvious avenue of attack. I saw our position compared to the others and knew right away that we got dealt a bum hand.

We dug the holes deeper so we could stockpile ammunition and supplies inside with us. The Old Man remembered a strand of wire along a jeep road to the rear so we sent Bob Powell and a few others back to get it. They brought it up and strung it through the trees, making a fourth line of wire to our front. Chesty came down the line and sighted along every gun, making sure the fields of fire interlocked and the firing lanes were clear. He moved just about every gun to his own satisfaction, checked the communication wire to each hole. Orders were to leave the line open. He wanted everybody to hear every order. He checked and double-checked everything including the depth of our fighting holes, the height and placement of sandbags, trenches, all of it.

Captain Fuller commanded A Company to our left. General Sims had pulled a platoon from A Company and placed it three thousand yards to our front in an outpost just inside the line of jungle. Sgt. Ralph Briggs was a buddy of mine and even though I didn't like my spot in the line, I had to admit his was a whole lot worse. The Old Man was on the phone while we dug in, giving Sims hell again just like he did up on the Matanikau for not coming forward with us into the fight. "You're going to sacrifice those men—that's all," Chesty argued. The open lines let us all hear Chesty's side of the discussion. "We don't need any bait on the hook, as you say. If they're coming, they're coming. It's foolishness to throw away that platoon." The line went quiet. It seemed like Sims might be thinking it over. Then Chesty roared back into the phone, "All right, then, if you think so, why don't you waltz your ass down to Division and get 'em back in here?" Poor General Sims. Chesty laid him out again. It didn't help Ralph though. He stayed out there with his squad just like Chesty said, bait on the hook.

Now we just waited in the rain. We knew they were coming. In the afternoon, we spotted smoke from cook fires and someone said they saw a Jap officer looking us over with a pair of field glasses. Our hole had inches of water in it and the bottom was slick with mud. I could feel my boots slipping on it so I just took them off. I got a better grip with my bare toes. The chaplain came down the line and asked if we wanted to pray. I figured we might as well take a few minutes to set accounts in order. Bob Powell and Garland, in the hole with me, took the time too. We knew it wouldn't be long now.

Dusk fell and a light bombardment raked the line from the PaK howitzers the Japs had dragged miles through the jungle. Chesty walked the line once more as the light faded, making his last check on everyone, then walked back to his command post just down the ridge from us. The rain poured down, the clouds covered any light from the moon. We couldn't really hear very much so we depended on what we could see in the shadows of the jungle in front of us. At around 9:30 P.M., Briggs came over the line whispering to the Old Man from his forward outpost. "Colonel, there's about three thousand Japs between you and me."

"Are you sure?" The Old Man probably guessed that a platoon leader who was hung out like Briggs might be jumpy and exaggerate things.

"Positive. They've been all around us, singing and smoking cigarettes, heading your way."

"All right, Briggs, but make damned sure. Take your men to your left—understand me? Go down and pass through the lines near the sea. I'll call 'em to let you in. Don't fail, and don't go in any other direction. I'll hold my fire as long as I can."

"Yes, sir."

Briggs was off the line a few seconds when Powell spotted movement on the wire. "I see 'em. They're at the wire."

"They're cutting the wire, sir." I spoke into the open phone to Chesty.

"All right," he answered. Everybody down the line was listening in as he gave his orders. "Let's get this straight. Hold fire until you get an order from me. The outpost must get clear before we open up. If the bastards break through, use the bayonet. And keep someone at every phone, wait."

They were through the wire on our right and they were yelling, "Blood for the Emperor! Marine! You die!"

From Hatfield's direction came the reply of a few jumpy, pissed-off Marines. "To hell with your goddamned Emperor!" The others joined in, "Blood for Franklin and Eleanor!"

"Come on you fuckin' bastards, come on and die for the Emperor!"

"Son of bitch, I got something for ya, ya fucking Nip!"

Over the phone, everybody got the order at the same time. "Commence firing!" All the guns down the line opened up at once knocking the first rank of Japs back into the wire. Marine artillery came overhead and punched big holes in the attacking lines of what looked like walking bushes. They were covered head to toe in camouflage leaves. The rows of wire and rain-slick grass slowed them down enough so that we cut them to pieces. In A Company's sector, they had plowed the flat ground in front of their holes that sat on a low part of the ridge. This turned the battlefield into thick mud and slowed the attack even more. But they kept coming, stumbling over each other in the dark. A few got close enough to lob grenades, and fire a few rounds before we got to them.

The first waves retreated back into the black shadows. They had sighted our exact positions and now concentrated mortar and artillery fire on us from the safety of the jungle. Our artillery moved back with them, exploding tree bursts over their heads about fifty yards back into the jungle. They weren't waiting under this hailstorm of steel for long. They came at us again. This time they found the edge of the firing lanes and came up each side instead directly in front of us. We had to split our fire between the guns—right covering the right, left covering the left. The mortars were beginning to find their marks. Men down the line were hit and screaming. Wounded Japs in front of us were screaming. They came now in a rush, climbing over the dead. They closed with Crumpton and Hatfield on the right, it looked like hand-to-hand now. It seemed like a whole division was headed up the hill right at us. Both guns were firing as fast as we fed them ammo. We couldn't even fire in bursts to let the barrels cool. Calls for help were coming over the wire from every sector. The whole front was completely engaged—two 37-millimeter antitank guns firing canister shot, six .30 caliber machine guns, four .50 caliber machine guns, a full rifle platoon, six old Lewis machine guns, most of which jammed early on, eighteen Browning Automatic Rifles and a 60 millimeter mortar.

The Japs kept coming, yelling all kinds of things in Japanese. Grenades and mortars were starting to zero in on our positions that we gave away with each muzzle flash. The water jackets were steaming from the constant firing, so I knew the water would soon be gone and we'd be in trouble with the barrels starting to overheat. We could hear the bullets smacking into the Japs in front of us as the dying fell on top of the dead. The second wave retreated. We were low on ammo and I knew I had a few minutes to resupply so I took off running to Chesty's CP. On the way, I ran into a few infiltrators and ended them with my .45. The Old Man was out of the CP pulling up the North Dakotan "Doggies" of the 164th to reinforce the hardest hit parts of our line. I loaded up with as many ammo belts as I could carry and headed back with them draped around my neck. I had to keep my hands free since Japs were all over the place behind our lines now. The third wave had started against parts of the line before I got back.

Back in the hole, Powell was pissing into the water jacket to refill it. I dropped the belts on a poncho trying to keep them out of the mud and went up front alongside Powell to see what was happening. They were coming again. A barrage of mortar shells, grenades and TNT came at us, landing all around us. The ground was shaking, dirt and shrapnel flew past our heads and fell down on us in a constant rain of debris and hot metal.

In the middle of all this shit, Private La Pointe from Crumpton's hole on my right flank fell into our hole jabbering, "They're gone, both guns gone, they're coming through." The boy was shaking so bad, I thought he might come apart at the seams.

"Son, do you have people back at home?" I asked. He looked at me like I was looney.

"Yes, sir," he said.

"Do you think they'd want to see you like this?"

"No, sir."

"Get into the fight, son." I jumped out of our hole and ran down the trail 150 yards over to Crumpton's position. I ran into a few Jap infiltrators and skirted them since I couldn't tell how many there were in the rain and darkness. I got to Crumpton's hole and all around it were dead Japs. It looked like one hell of a fight had happened and then I hear these two wild men cursing blue streaks at the Japs. In the hole, little eighteen-year-old Evans and big Billy Crumpton were screaming at the top of their lungs, daring them to try it again. All they had were .45s and one of our pilfered Garand rifles. The Brownings were smashed and Crumpton was bleeding pretty badly. Along with the two survivors, three of our boys were dead in the hole, two were lying badly wounded. The Japs had used bayonets in the bloody hand-to-hand combat. Evans and Crumpton were the only ones left standing. Then the terrible silence came and for the first time we turned to see our dead brothers. They looked like they were sleeping off a bender, slumped like sacks of potatoes against each other. But the blood was everywhere, pouring down their necks, soaking their chests. It was the shock of it after the screaming stopped that hit the hardest. I could tell when the two survivors turned and saw their buddies lying dead inches away from them, they probably hadn't thought about it until that moment. I grabbed one and started to drag him out of the hole. Evans pitched in to help me. We dragged our boys, with gaping holes in them, across the mud and laid them out there in the rain. We had nothing to cover them with so we turned them facedown. It didn't seem right to have the rain falling on their faces. Navy Corpsmen would be by soon enough and take them behind the lines. I ordered Nash, who had lost most of his hand, and Foley to fall back to the aid station and get patched up. Between the two of them they had enough working arms and legs to lean on each other and get behind the lines. I went back and checked the guns. One was smashed and couldn't be fixed, the other I might be able to get firing again.

"Strip them guns down," I ordered and left for my hole. I picked my way back, avoiding Japs who might be along the trail, and dodged sniper fire. I was moving fast and low and stubbed my toe pretty bad along the way. I wished I had a pair of boots that didn't make me slip and make my feet rot but I didn't have them that night. I heard firing in the rear as the infiltrators ran into our reserve units coming up to reinforce us. One even broke into Chesty's CP where Pennington shot him down.

Back in the hole, I grabbed the Browning on the right and took the crew with me, yelling, "Powell, Garland." I left Bullard on the left gun and moved out to plug the breech to our right. They don't call these guns heavies for nothing but I didn't even feel it in my arms as we double-timed it along the trail. On the way we ran straight into six Japs coming through the line. I cradled the heavy in my arms and turned a wide arc of fire loose on them. Powell and Garland used bayonets and rifle butts on the rest. We didn't quite get to Crumpton and Evans's hole when the Japs came up the ridge again. This time crawling on their bellies, lobbing more TNT and grenades. We hit the deck and I got that gun firing in less than a second. The belt was lying in the mud so I knew it was going to jam soon. I yelled to the boys to cover me because I had to get up off my belly and sit upright to get an angle down on the Japs who were staying low to the ground. I mowed the grass in front of us and shifted a few feet to my right as a shower of grenades exploded on the spot where I had just been. I kept mowing the grass down the ridge as the boys shot at what targets they could see. Suddenly I saw that the movement had stopped in that area. I picked up the gun and the belts and started running again. The boys were right on my heels.

When we got to Crumpton and Evans they had torn down the smashed guns and were trying to salvage parts from one to fix the other. I pushed them aside and went to work. There was still nobody in the world that could beat me in tearing down and reassembling a heavy. I was flat on my back fumbling with the mechanism in the dark while swarms of bullets buzzed through the rain and smacked into our sandbags. Powell set up his gun and was having trouble finding targets for the first few minutes. Then he opened up. The next wave was on the way up the hill. By his rate of fire, there had to be a lot of them this time. We would need this second gun and fast.

"The head spacing is out of line," I yelled to Powell.

"Tough," he said. "That gun's finished."

I kept working on the mechanism and felt it click into place. I scraped mud out of the receiver and slapped a belt into place. Crumpton had the legs set and the second I laid the body on them, Japs were ten feet in front of us. I opened up knocking back a half dozen down the hill. At the same time a grenade landed near us and went off, tearing a hole in Crumpton's leg.

"Billy, can you move?" I asked him.

"I think so, yeah, a little." He didn't sound good. He was finished.

"Get the hell out of here, go on back." He started to give me trouble about it and I cut him off. "Crumpton! Get the hell out of here. I'm the boss, now go on back and get fixed up. If anybody asks you, tell 'em we're holding the right flank and I think we're slightly outnumbered." Billy dragged himself out of the hole and slithered away as fast as he could. He made it almost the whole half-mile trip to the aid station on his belly before the enemy behind our lines found him.

Evans fed the ammo and tried to keep mud off the belts. He also kept his eye on the rear of our position where we turned our .45s on Japs coming up behind us. A hail of TNT and grenades fell all around us again. Our ears rang from the explosions so that we couldn't hear each other yelling from inches away. The concussion was like getting punched in the side of the head by a heavyweight and made it hard to keep your vision clear. We were seeing double and things were moving around so that we couldn't draw a clear bead on a target. The dead piled up in front of us, obscuring the firing lanes. Both guns jammed. I tore mine open and cleared the receiver of mud. Powell did the same. In the process, Evans yelled just in time and we shot two more Japs coming at us from behind. Garland was frantically trying to clean the mud off the belts but it was tough work. We were getting low again on ammo and were out of water completely. The water jackets were smoking again, which meant they were low or out of water too. If we didn't get water for the guns, the barrels would burn out and never last the night. I got mine firing again but I was hitting only corpses piled high in front of us and others hanging on the wire farther back. I ordered Garland to go down and clear the firing lanes. He looked at me and I looked back at him. It could easily be a suicide mission. The latest assault backed off. I didn't have to tell Garland twice. He was up and out of the hole. Evans and I covered him in bursts of gunfire that kept the field clear on either side of him. He slid down the hill on his butt and pushed the piles of bodies over with his feet, keeping his head below the pile. That did the trick. He slid over to another pile and did the same maneuver. We had a clear field of fire again. He slithered back up the hill while we sent streams of bullets a few inches over his head. A stream of bullets answered back from the jungle below and in front of us. For the life of me, I don't know why we hadn't been cross-haired by artillery and concentrated mortar fire by now but I guess that's where luck comes into it.

Garland got back in the hole. I was out of ammo. The boys all needed water as well as the guns. Powell had a few belts left. He got his receiver cleaned out and was back on duty sighting down the ridge for any movement. The latest wave had retreated. I had to make another run for ammo and, this time, for water too. Down the ridge there was movement. The Japs had almost the same idea I did. They crept up to the piles of their dead comrades and pulled them on top of each other like sandbags. They had a machine gun up behind the human barricade.

"Move out," I ordered. We scraped our weapons out of the mud and hopped out to our left to get an angle on the new advance position of the enemy. Within a few minutes, they had our hole cross-haired and landed mortars on the bull's-eye, but we weren't there anymore. We concentrated fire on the new position and wiped out the gunners. There was no fire coming from Bullard's hole to the left and I led what was left of my squad for cover over there. When we got there, all my boys were dead. We pulled Bullard and the rest out and took up firing positions in the new hole. The phone was still open to CP and I called in our situation—no water, no ammo, the position to our right flank was now out of the fight. We were all that remained of C Company. I told Powell, "If I ain't back in ten minutes, put an ad in the paper for me." I left the three in the new hole and took off again toward the rear.

Sniper and mortar fire was constant now and half the time I couldn't tell if the shadows running across my path were enemy or not. I just kept running. A grenade or mortar went off and knocked me to the ground but didn't open any more holes in me that I could tell. I was bleeding from several places but none seemed too serious. I got up again and kept moving.

At the ammo dump I pried open ammo boxes and draped six of the fourteen-pound ammo belts over my shoulders. I picked up another box and started moving out, then I remembered the water. I was a fully loaded mule and couldn't do much better than a fast walk with all the weight hanging on me. I passed the CP and called in for water. Somebody came out and draped a few canteens on belts around my neck. Chesty was giving hell to someone over the phone. I figured it must have been Sims again. Why that man, our commanding officer, didn't bust Chesty for his back talk, I'll never know.

"What d'ya mean 'What's going on?'!" The Old Man was hot as a pistol. "We're neck deep in a firefight, and I've no time to stand here bullshitting! If you want to find out what's going on, come up and see!" He exploded to Pennington and another aide, "Regiment is not convinced we are facing a major attack!"

I was back onto the trail in the blackness with my heavy coat of bullets banging against my knees, my hands full with the ammo box. I shuffled along as fast as I could. If I ran into Tojo in the dark, I'd have to drop the ammo box to reach my .45 on my hip. I ran behind the ridge crest but that didn't stop sniper fire from whining past my head. They were behind our lines and by the amount of fire, there must have been quite a few of them. I thought, if they can't hit a slow-moving target like me, that must mean that my number isn't up, at least not tonight. I soon couldn't think about anything except making it another few feet. The whole trip was somewhere around six hundred yards and I didn't stop once for a breather. Every thought and scrap of strength I had was focused on just making it a few more feet down the trail. I slipped under the weight several times, covering the belts with mud.

I made it to the hole and gave the call sign, "Yankee Clipper," as I came up from the rear so they wouldn't shoot me thinking I was a Jap infiltrator. I dropped what I had, fifteen hundred rounds, in the hole and jumped in behind it. Powell was out of ammo on his gun. He grabbed a belt and I took over his trigger just in time. The next wave was on the way up the ridge. With Garland and Evans covering our flanks with their rifles, Powell and I leapfrogged from one gun to the other. The water wasn't nearly enough to fill the water jackets of even one of the guns, so I had to fire one while the second gun cooled and while Powell cleaned the next ammo belt and reloaded, then roll over to the second while Powell cleaned and reloaded the first. We were able to keep a fairly constant rate of fire doing this and also make the Japs shift their targeting from our right gun to our left. It was hours after the first attack and they were still coming, wave after wave screaming, "Banzai!" and "Marine, you die!" and we kept killing them. Evans and Garland threw grenades down the hill until they could barely lift their arms. The boys drank all the water in the canteens and when they could, pissed into the water jackets.

Another wave of men ran up the ridge, broke and died in front of us. Some had gotten through. We could hear the firing to the rear. I wasn't sure if our guns would hold up under another attack. We needed more water and still more ammunition. From the amount of fighting in the rear, I decided it would be safer to try for A Company to our right instead of a third run toward the CP. While the boys caught their breath after the last attack, I was out of the hole and on the run again, this time to our right flank. I kept moving fast and low with a rough bearing in the pouring rain on where the first A Company position would be. I found it and laid flat in the grass outside the hole while I yelled, "Yankee Clipper!" The countersign came back, "Joe DiMaggio," then, ". . . who the fuck are you?!"

"Basilone, C Company." I scrambled into the hole. I told them about my guns and scrounged a canteen of water they had. I needed more than that and they called down the line on the phone that was quieter now between attacks. I was off for the next position.

I got back to our position with a few canteens before the next wave was on its way up the hill. Garland was dead. He was a big boy, a quiet type and brave. That night, when I told him to go down the hill to clear the firing lanes of dead Japs, he hesitated just long enough to read my face. He looked at me just long enough to make sure I wasn't kidding, then he went. He was a brave kid, and not a hard case like some of the others. He wanted to show he could be tough and he was. It was just us three now.

It was just after 4:00 A.M. when the Japs found the break in our lines on our right flank. Even though the North Dakota farm boys of the 164th were being fed into our lines from reserve positions, they went to positions where someone was in command and missed our unmanned hole on our right, leaving a 150-yard opening between A Company and us. The Japs overran the position in force and set up a wedge-shaped firing line inside our perimeter seventy-five yards deep and fifty yards wide. We now had enemy positions on our right and front as well as occasional attacks from our rear. We were surrounded and firing in all directions. It didn't look like we had too long before a grenade or mortar would find its mark. Or we would be overrun.

We called in our report on the breech to the CP. The sun was just starting to lighten the sky on the horizon and it looked like this was do or die for the Japs. They were throwing everything they had left into wiping us out and cutting deeper into our guts with the wedge. Our left gun got smashed by shrapnel. Whatever little bit of pisswater that was left in the jacket leaked out into the mud. There was nothing left to do but keep firing until it burned out completely. I fired the rest of the belt and rolled to the one on the right as Powell cleaned the mud-caked ammunition and reloaded. Mortar fire started landing on the wedge. Then more came in. Soon that whole area, that I had just run through to get our water, was covered with exploding shells. A squad of the 164th had taken the position in the empty hole on our flank, on the far side of the wedge. They held on, throwing fire back at the hundreds of attackers running at them and at the ones in the wedge between us. The 11th Marines artillery back by the airfield laid a curtain of fire in the jungle, cutting off retreat and reinforcements behind the attackers. In a half hour of concentrated mortar fire and crossfire, the wedge was wiped out and our lines straightened again. The last great wave of attack broke into pieces under our mortar and machine gun fire and died in groups and then one by one. The ones who could, slipped back into the jungle to face our artillery fire.

Sporadic fire from our perimeter chased what was left of the enemy back down the ridge. The rate of fire slackened, then stopped. The wind picked up and the rain lightened a bit. Then, to our left, the rising sun turned the storm clouds on the horizon deep red. The shadowy lumps all over the ridge became piles of dead men stacked up like cordwood and everything was suddenly quiet again except for the groans of the dying and the mud sucking at our feet.

★

The Old Man was walking the line. He poked his head over the sandbags with Captain Rogers, the CO in our sector, and offered me his hand. He pulled me out of the hole and said, "I hear you came back for ammunition, good work." He was off, on his way to survey what shape the rest of the outfit was in. I don't think anybody even attempted to salute. Nobody moved. They were just dead-eyed, worn-out boys. We all thought we were dead at least a half dozen times in the last few hours. Everybody was still getting used to the idea that we might stay alive for a while yet. I was hungry as hell all of a sudden. I told them I was going to scout up some chow and headed back to the CP. When I got there all they had was crackers and jam. I managed to pick up a few more canteens of water and loaded my pockets with crackers for the boys.

I got back to the hole with the crackers and water. It wasn't much after the night we spent but nobody said a thing. They just ate the crackers. Somebody mentioned that it was Sunday. I sent Powell and Evans to the rear to get some chow and check in at the aid station. We were all wounded. I started digging out the hole, hauling out about a foot of mud and water and the empty cotton ammunition belts. We'd gone through twenty-six thousand rounds. Both guns were burned out. I picked up a few of the Dakota farmboys of the 164th who had been fed into frontline positions during the night and got them to do the digging and repairs to the sandbags. I kept my eyes on the jungle, looking for movement. I studied every tree and each leaf. Death was in there.

In the sky, the fighting was still going on. A few squadrons of Zeros were headed into Henderson Field when they found out that we hadn't been wiped out as reported. Our Cactus Air Force worked them over while we watched. It was clear from seeing how many planes they intended to land at Henderson that the Japs still had big plans for the island and we were in the way. We worked through the day expecting that we'd see the same level of attack during the coming night. Nobody thought it was over. We were all shifted down toward the right flank and the 164th was put in the line to the left. Hanneken's B Company stayed out reinforcing the far right beach approach. We were now back to something closer to a real perimeter line instead of a picket fence. There was still firing to the rear through most of the day as more infiltrators were found hiding in the trees or the grass.

Twelve of my boys were dragged out of the mud that day, some of them in pieces. They were just about everybody I knew on the island. I knew guys from other outfits just to say hello or play a few hands of cards, but these twelve were the only ones I really knew. They were the ones I trained with, some went all the way back to New River like Crumpton and Hatfield who used to hitchhike with me to the one sad roadhouse on some hillbilly back road. We'd get there after riding in the backs of trucks and walking for hours in the dust and heat. We'd land in front of this shack and just look at each other wondering why the hell we even bothered to make the trip. All we could do was laugh and then chug-a-lug the god-awful whiskey they must've made out back, trying to get drunk on a few dollars' worth. I couldn't understand just yet that they were dead even though I saw them. I promised them all they would be okay.

Maybe it was the malaria but I could hardly lift another handful of mud by noon. I got our new hole policed up with the help of the 164th boys who were a damn good group even though they were Army. Then I just stayed in the hole and worked over the new guns making sure they were working the way they should. I didn't want to meet any of the Army boys.

In the whole 1/7 we lost 19 boys that night. Another 30 were wounded and 12 were missing. By the end of the day, I heard we found 250 Japanese dead inside our lines. Outside, laying down the front of the ridge and into the jungle, there were too many to count. Rows on rows of them, some almost like they were laid out by a machine. Nobody had the energy to do anything about them. We had too much to do before nightfall. By the late afternoon, the corpses started to bloat. They made sickening groans as the built-up gases burst and hissed from them. Black island rats and green lizards crawled over and around them.

We all heard a lot about the bravery of the Japanese soldier before we got on the island. They were supposed to be the most fearless

warriors ever to fight. But I kept thinking what kind of bravery it was
that sent them, one after the other, right into the same guns that
mowed down dozens before them. I don't know if that was bravery. I
don't know what it was. Either they were crazy or they just didn't
care. So I didn't care either. They weren't even men anymore. They
were dumb animals who wanted me dead and had killed all my
friends.

We called the day Dugout Sunday. Everybody worked hard, some
like me, with no sleep at all, to get the perimeter back in some kind
of shape. Sniper fire and Pistol Pete kept up sporadic firing of large
and small ordnance into our lines to keep us from ever completely
relaxing. The few planes that could still fly out of Henderson strafed
the jungle in front of us going back a mile or two. This fight wasn't
over by a long shot. Entrenching tools were in short supply so we dug
holes using bayonets and bare hands. I felt the worst for the guys out
restringing wire. They were just sniper bait. It came down the line
that Briggs and most of his men made it safely back through our
lines last night from the outpost. One that didn't was Pvt. Robert
Potter. When the men were on their way back, crawling through the
kunai grass, Jap machine gunners saw them and opened up. Potter
leapt up and ran back and forth yelling to his buddies to run for our
lines. They did. Potter drew the fire meant for the others. The others
made it to a Bren gun carrier that had been sent out by Captain
Fuller. They clambered onto the carrier and made their escape.
Only four of the forty-six men in the outpost didn't make it back. Potter
was one of the four. The news about the men at Sgt. Briggs's outpost
and Potter came down the line. Everybody seemed to look out toward
the outpost position when they heard the story, like maybe they
might spot Potter still alive out there.

The night came down quietly and the rain stopped. Up on the ridge there was total silence. Our ships had stopped the nightly raids by the Japanese fleet. Out on the nose of the ridge you could hear the Japs talking. They were about a hundred yards out and moving in. We heard the bushes rustling. It was just before midnight. Then they rushed us, screaming. It didn't mean a thing anymore. The screams of "Banzai!" got blasted away as we went to work on them again with the Brownings. The whole line lit up. Grenades, TNT and mortars rained down all around us, rocking the ground. We blew holes in the waves of men coming at us and then took down the stragglers in short bursts, taking them apart like working men—pieces of human meat and whole limbs coming off. We were packed snug into our new, shallow holes stacked with ammunition and water. I wasn't going out to skip through bullets this time. Bullets and shrapnel slapped into our wet sandbags and sang past our ears like angry bees. We hadn't slept or eaten anything but crackers in over a day. The shadows rushed out of the jungle, came screaming up the hill and fell, over and over. Nobody got through our lines this time.

On the field phone reports of a breakthrough on the left came through. The Japs had two heavy machine guns on top of the ridge. We kept a keen ear out for noise of fighting getting louder from that direction. A final, hopeless wave came at us. The screams of men and weaponry firing got as bad as the night before, all crashing in on us, all around us. We screamed back at the storm, out of our heads, fucks and shits and crazy things that made no sense. Then the attack faded, broken again.

At dawn, a ragtag group of seventeen soldiers led by Lt. Col. Tex Conoley charged the two Japanese machine guns on the ridge and wiped them out with a shower of grenades. It was over. The sun came up again and the scene was the same as the day before except with some spots of bright red, fresh blood on top of the dried black and brown. The sun was in our eyes, hot and clear. The birds started up with their odd jungle calls. One big, white one that had a sharp scream must have been like the jungle rooster waking up all the others. Marines crawled from their holes filthy and red-eyed. Some of them were shaking. I sent Powell and Evans back to rest. I didn't want to sleep. I didn't want to eat. I didn't want to talk to anybody. I just wanted to stay with my guns. I stayed all through that day watching the perimeter for movement, watching the crows pick at all the dead Japanese eyes. I stayed and watched the jungle and saw each of the twelve boys who were here just yesterday, or was it two days ago? They were in the river, washing and dunking each other. Some were writing letters in the shade of a palm tree. Garland kept looking at me in that way of his, trying to figure out if I was kidding, before he went down the ridge and cleared the bodies. I stayed in my hole until the sun went down again and somebody, I don't know who, came and ordered me to get the hell out of the hole and go to sleep.

★

The next few days drifted by almost like we were all drunk. Most of us were sick as hell by the afternoon with malaria in our joints like arthritis and too weak to do anything but sit up. Days passed, nothing happened, not even card games and there was always a card game. But these days were just different, odd, like a dream. I remember the Army made a stink about getting their Garand rifles back but we weren't about to give them up now and there were quite a few fights about that. The Old Man was hanging around the sick bay a lot, talking to the wounded. Fuller saw him puddle up, crying when no one was looking. He had been acting strangely since Matanikau and since he made the stink about burials. Since he started washing up with us in the river, officers close to him like Fuller kept an eye on him. This was the first time anyone had noticed him crying. But a lot of the guys were acting strangely now. A second lieutenant showed up at the division post office in his starched khakis. He set his sea bag down outside the door and just waited there leaning on a swagger stick like he was waiting for a bus. This was odd even for the island full of oddballs we were living with so he drew a bit of attention. The other boys asked him what he was doing and he told them he was going home.

"Home? How're you goin'?" they asked.

"Why, by the Poughkeepsie bus," he told them, surprised that they didn't know.

"Oh," they'd say, not sure if he was nuts or maybe they were.

Then this looney bird would say, "Oughta be here any minute," and he'd look up the beach as if he expected the bus to drive up. The men would follow his gaze, looking up the beach for the bus, too.

He stood there in his pressed uniform in the sun most of the afternoon. After a few hours, men came up to him with notes of phone numbers and names. They gave these to him and asked him to call their people when he got home and he promised he would. By the time it was getting dark he had a pocketful of notes. That night he slept in his sharp-creased khakis. It wasn't until the next day when he woke up that he understood that he really wasn't going home. It wasn't too funny right then but later on, after the story got passed around, it seemed almost funny. It wasn't really the kind of funny where guys would laugh but a different kind where they would start to laugh and then stop.

Another fella started talking to an invisible dog. It annoyed the hell out of his buddies and they ran the matter up to the captain. The captain called a doctor and they both talked to the man. They were about to send him off the island to have his head examined when his first sergeant got wind of him. He ordered the man to report to his dugout up near the line. When the pet lover got to the sergeant's dugout the sarge screamed at him, "Now don't bring that flea hound of yours in here or my bulldog will chew his damned head off!"

The man stopped dead at the entrance, looked down, and suddenly didn't see his dog. He broke down sobbing and laughing at the same time. After a few minutes he pulled himself together. He never saw his dog again.

A corporal in our outfit, the 7th, put the word out that he'd lost his wallet during the battle. He offered a reward to anybody who found it. In a day or two, a tall ragged soldier turned up by his foxhole and handed him the wallet. He stood there a minute before the corporal remembered the reward. He quickly opened up the wallet and found his 136 bucks in it, untouched.

"Here," he said, trying to hand the money to the ragged soldier. "Take this stuff. It's found money." The soldier took the bills, looked them over and leafed through them like they were something new. He handed them back and told the corporal like he was tired, very slowly, "I ain't got no use for that," then turned and walked away. That was how it was. Nothing seemed real, like things used to be.

After a few days, the stink of the dead was over the whole island. We left them lying out there in the sun where they turned black. At night the smell of them crept over the ridge and flowed down into our huts, sometimes waking us up, making us sick. The guys up on the ridge next to them tried to cover their noses but vomited anyway. I didn't go up there on the ridge anymore. I just stayed in my hut. My

Bloody Ridge, October 26, 1942
Note: Japanese flag, center

skin turned yellow from the Atabrine but it didn't seem to knock out
the malaria. Sometimes I played cards with Powell, just him and me.
Evans wandered off somewhere most times, maybe to get away from
the horrible smell. It didn't matter where he went, it was everywhere.
It clung to you, stuck in your nose. The Old Man couldn't walk the
line anymore without retching. He made Division take bulldozers from
repairing the airstrip to gouge trenches for the black stinkers. That's
when we got the final body count—1,462. They found papers on the
bodies that said another five hundred were carried away. We wiped
out a regiment, the boys did.

★ 9 ★

On the Attack

Marines on patrol on Guadalcanal

Malaria was starting to take us all down. The first week of October we had one hundred or so in sick bay; by the end of the month close to two thousand of us were on our backs and the fighting wasn't half done. More of the Army's Americal Division arrived almost every day and the 8th Marines were on their way. We watched these fresh boys walk up the beach, full of fight and thoughts of glory. I'm sure to them, we all looked like the dead-eyed vets we met when we arrived a month ago—maybe a little worse because our skin was slightly yellow from Atabrine. We stared at them from our shacks made out of scrounged airplane parts, rice sacks, palm fronds, ponchos and packing crates. Some of us who were afraid of the snakes stared down at them from tree houses. Many of us were barefoot and wild haired like island castaways. They stared back at us and I could tell they didn't much like what they saw. But here they were, more boys setting up their bivouac in the shade that was left, that wasn't blasted away, in the coconut groves—just like we did. They looked like they just walked off the streets of their hometowns where they fixed cars and played touch football on Sundays. They walked and talked like big, tough Marines just like we did. Some thought they were killers but they weren't really, not yet. They were just boys doing their bit to help out. They were my boys all over again and I wanted to say something to them, but what? Soon enough they'd see everything and know everything I knew. All their thoughts of glory would go and only duty and survival would be left. Then everything seemed to hit me all at once, from way out in left field. All the boys I left up on the ridge came flooding back into my mind. Some of them were laughing, snapping wet towels at each other by the river and some were dying in agony and it was all mixed up together. I tasted salt. Salt water was dribbling over my lips. I touched with my fingers and felt that my face was wet. I was crying. This really threw me—I thought maybe I was cracking up. Before I started sobbing, I had to turn away and get back to my hut where I stayed until it got dark.

The nights were bad. As the sun faded, without thinking about it, we prepared for another attack. Even lying on our piles of palm fronds or whatever else we scrounged up for beds, we were on watch, our weapons close by, even though we were a mile behind the perimeter. When it got dark, the guys who had been on the ridge tried to sleep. Animals, night hunters, would start moving in the trees making strange squawking or chirping noises. Around midnight, the time when the Japanese liked to launch their attacks, men whimpered and cried out in their sleep. They woke up screaming, waking everybody else up and sending some scrambling for their weapons. Some cried in their sleep. Many never got to sleep at all. Only after the sun came up did some of us close our eyes and rest.

We were thin, most had lost around twenty pounds. We were dehydrated from nearly constant diarrhea and weak from one tropical disease or another. Those of us who had been on the ridge were left out of most work details, the Old Man saw to that. We stayed around our huts during the day or found shady spots and rested. We went to the river and washed. It was the Life of Riley for a few days but it wasn't going to last. Ships were blasting each other offshore and planes shot each other to pieces overhead. Our fight wasn't close to being over. New orders would come. That was for sure.

Two regiments of big guns, 105s and 155s, arrived and more aircraft landed every day. We now had five squadrons of planes. The Cactus Air Force was a real air force again. After a week, Topside felt we were strong enough to try to nail the coffin shut on the Japs left on the island. They had to be at least as sick as we were and probably worse since they spent all their energy hacking through ten miles of jungle and retreating with their wounded back through it. Topside wanted to send a message all the way to Tokyo—Guadalcanal was ours. They wanted to put Pistol Pete out of business. He was still dropping shells on us whenever he felt like it. Some of the boys who came off the ridge only had to hear one of Pete's shells go off to make them dive in the dirt and then spend the next hour shaking so bad they couldn't drink from a canteen without taking a shower.

Instead of heading west again, up the beach toward Point Cruz to mop up the rest of the famous Sendai Division that was now broken and in retreat, Hanneken and his 2/7 moved out in the opposite direction toward Koli Point about six miles to the east of the perimeter. Intelligence spotted an enemy convoy making for that location. It was November 2—just a week after our Bloody Ridge. The 2/7 got across the Metapona River, not long after a Jap patrol had covered the same territory. They made the crossing after dark and made camp about two thousand yards east along the beach. Just east of their positions an enemy convoy, including destroyers and transports, were off-loading. They tried to radio back to HQ but rain had fouled up the radios and all they could do was stay quiet and watch.

At dawn a Jap patrol walked into their lines. Four got away and warned the newly landed force. Hoping to get the jump on them, Hanneken attacked with concentrated mortar fire on their beachhead. Japanese artillery answered immediately followed by a counterattack force of a few hundred men. Hanneken and his men were beaten back to Koli Point and cut off within a few hours. The call for help got through to HQ in the afternoon and we were called up.

Topside might have decided Sims and the Old Man weren't such a good match so they put in Brigadier General Rupertus to command the operation, which included us of the 1/7, the 3/7, and the North Dakota boys of the Army's 164th, Whaling scouts to cover our inland flank, a battalion of the just landed 10th Marines and the left-behind artillery of Hanneken's 2/7 including tanks. It was slow going with a parade of our size. The country up that way was all rugged hills of decomposed coral and thick jungle. Hanneken held on for three days fighting a retreating action back toward our perimeter. His back was against the sea about a mile east of the Metapona when we finally made contact. We loaded into boats and sailed farther east toward the Jap beachhead and landed just beyond the Metapona. We were going to outflank and come up behind the attackers from the west, the Dakota boys struck out south and were going to turn around and come at them from the south on their left flank while Hanneken would continue to push against them from the east. The sea was on their right flank to the north.

Just after dawn the next day, we struck out from the beach near the mouth of the river in a front stretching about six hundred yards inland, sweeping west toward a creek fifteen hundred yards ahead. Marching up and down those ravines and through the tangling vines made me rethink my decision to man the heavy machine guns. Guys like me who used to be able to carry a heavy uphill all day were fighting for breath after an hour. Right away we ran into small arms fire skirmishes. Mortars were difficult to use because of the jungle canopy overhead. This slowed us down enough so that by the afternoon we still hadn't covered the fifteen hundred yards. It also gave them enough time to call up their artillery and machine gun companies. The big stuff started coming at us just after 2:00 in the afternoon. It was a bad day for the Old Man. He was about three hundred yards back from the point. The first salvo from the artillery landed just in front of him and blew him into the air in a wave of flying shrapnel. He had holes in him from his knees to his rib cage and was bleeding badly. He called up the field telephone man. "Call headquarters," he said.

"I can't, sir, the wire's been cut."

He got up to help the telephone man repair the wire and was hit twice by sniper fire through his arm. He fell back down and stayed there. They were in a clearing in the jungle. Bunky Davis, a corpsman, was all over the place with artillery and sniper fire raining in, rigging plasma bottles and tending to the rest of the fallen. Chesty watched Davis working while he was bleeding pints into the ground and told Frank Sheppard, "I want that man recommended for a Silver Star."

Pennington and Sheppard lifted Chesty onto a poncho to keep him off the ground. Sheppard asked, "Are you able to stay here in command, sir?"

"Yes, of course I am. I'll be okay. I can't leave these men."

"May I call for artillery fire if I can get the radio or telephone working?" Sheppard asked.

"Yes, if you know how."

Sheppard and Pennington dug a shallow hole and put Chesty in it with a telephone. He waited for the line to be repaired while Bunky worked on him to stop the bleeding. As soon as the line was up, he was on with HQ lining up a mortar barrage and a dawn attack for the next day.

We were stopped in our tracks and fighting in small groups. Until the Jap artillery was knocked out we weren't moving anywhere. It was getting dark, firing let up a bit. Nobody could see what they were shooting at and nobody wanted to give away their position with a muzzle flash. Sheppard managed to call in coordinates to the 2/7 artillery battery and they found the Jap artillery in the dark jungle. That shut the Japs up for the night.

We were on 100 percent watch, expecting some kind of attack now that they knew we were coming toward their rear. The Old Man called HQ after midnight. He told them he couldn't walk and would surrender his command. He only cared about what was best for us. If he couldn't be up in the thick of it with us, he wanted somebody who would be. Even on the ridge, when they were running through our lines and it looked like we were going to get swept away, he was right there with us. That was why he was closer to some of us than our own fathers. Every man in the outfit knew that if we got out of this war alive, it would be because of Chesty.

HQ called back just after midnight and told him Maj. John Weber would assume command and would leave the perimeter immediately. Weber arrived just after 3:00 in the morning. They didn't come at us that night. Most of us had no trouble staying on watch all night, we were geared for it now, but when daylight broke fatigue started to set in. We were supposed to get our energy from breakfast, a couple of slices of cold Spam with cold coffee. Small boats came up the coast and into the mouth of the Malimbiu River a thousand yards to our rear to evacuate the dead and wounded. They tried to put Chesty on the boat first but he wouldn't go until all the others had been loaded. Bucky tried to tag him with an evacuation tag and the Old Man snapped at him, "Take that and tag a fucking bottle with it. I can go under my own power. Go help the men who need it." When Pennington told him the others were all loaded, he tried to help the Old Man to his feet but Chesty pulled his arm away and would have none of that.

"Let me be," he said, "I can go." He limped and shuffled the full thousand yards down the trail to the boats with more holes in him than a Swiss cheese. They never did get all the shrapnel out of his legs.

We closed the noose on the Japs that day and the next. They ended up surrounded in a small grove. A few dozen survivors made a break south directly into the lines of the 164th who were waiting for them. A few got through but got hunted down later. We lost twelve more killed and twenty-seven wounded including the Old Man. In our two months on the island we lost 50 percent of our officers and 23 percent of all enlisted men. The rest of us were pretty much hollowed out with disease or parasites and could hardly make a full day's march. The 1/7 was at the point where Topside didn't think we were fit for combat anymore.

We were put into the last line of defense, inside the perimeter, around the airfield. By the last week in November, another 3,200 Marines were downed by malaria, making over 5,000 who were out of action. By now just about everybody had it and it made the days into a new kind of torture. By afternoon, our joints ached like we had arthritis and a lot of us couldn't have lifted our weapons even if we were attacked. We had kicked the living shit out of the Japs to the west at the Matanikau, to the east at the Malimbiu and to the south at our own Bloody Ridge but we were just about out of gas. They started pulling some of us even off this last line and filling in with the newer guys from the 8th Marines and Army units. After that, the only raids we did were against the Army supply depots. What we didn't win fair and square in card games, we felt obligated to steal. It just didn't seem right that these Army boots were nowhere around when the shit hit the fan outside the perimeter, but got all the good stuff inside it. It was our duty, as we saw it, to liberate certain items (meaning anything we wanted) for our brave fighting brothers (meaning us). Blankets and socks were hot items since they warded off the malaria chills at night. They started giving us twenty grains of quinine a day but it only helped a little.

I visited the cemetery most days and policed up the plots where my boys were. Me and Powell sat in the shade carving their names on little wooden crosses we scrounged up for them, telling each other stories about Samoa, where some had their first girlfriends, or New River, where we were all boots together when Chesty came on as our commander. We tacked their mess gear to the crosses and their ID tags if we had them and lay clean, fresh cut palm fronds over the raw dirt. I generally said a Hail Mary or Our Father or two. Sometimes afterward, we made our way down to the river to cool off for a while. At the river, men with heavies stood watch over us as we washed or sat on our utilities in the muddy shallows. We got all the news at the river. We could still sometimes hear the Navy battles at night and got the scores the next day at the river. Nobody really knew much unless they had buddies on board the ships. It seemed like we were winning because the bombardments weren't coming as often or lasting as long. We did hear of the sinking of the Jap battleship *Kirishima*. That was supposed to be a big deal and sent the message to Tokyo that we were trying to deliver for two months now—Guadalcanal was ours.

★

One year after Pearl Harbor, December 7, 1942, the First Division pulled out of the Canal. Two days later General Vandegrift turned command over to Gen. Alexander Patch. Scuttlebutt was we were being rotated out too, sometime in the next weeks. The Old Man was back on his feet, walking stiffly, with most of the metal pulled out of his legs. They didn't have any anesthesia for his operations and had to leave the biggest piece of metal in his leg, because he refused to get shipped out to Australia for the operation he needed to remove it.

We spent our last day on the island goldbricking in camp and at the river. The Old Man came with us. He still limped a bit. He got in the water and floated on his back below the small rapids where the few clear water holes were, exercising his legs. Scuttlebutt spread out that Radio Tokyo was calling us the Guadalcanal Butchers. We also learned that in the past few weeks the Navy had sent a lot of expensive Japanese warships to the bottom of Ironbottom Sound. There was news that Rommel was whipped in Africa. It was a different war now than it was when we arrived. The invincible Japanese infantryman was just a boogey-man story now. We killed over thirty thousand of them in four months and lost less than two thousand of our own men. We felt like we deserved to sit in the shallows and watch the river go by for a while. Most of us couldn't do anything else. We didn't have the energy to swim.

We went to chow in the afternoon. If you didn't already know who he was, you wouldn't have been able to pick him out from the rest of us. He had his head shaved that morning down at the river with a whole bunch of us. We all looked like new recruits, at least from the back. There he was as always, right with us in the thick of it even when it came to facing Marine chow. I thought he would always be there, that I'd always have him to show the way. But that was the last time I saw the Old Man. From now on, I'd only have what I learned from him in battle and what I remembered about him as a leader. I was lucky to know him and to fight with him. We all were. If we were going to be in combat, at least we had learned how to do it from the best battlefield commander who ever lived.

★

The transports wallowed offshore like big, fat whales sunning themselves on the surface. We had a sense that we'd broken the backs of the Japs but we also knew they were suicidal in their attacks, so we kept our ears open for the telltale sounds of Japanese air-plane engines overhead. By now we knew the different sounds of our own planes and enemy planes right away. We hadn't heard "Washing Machine Charley," the syncopated thrumming of the Jap high-altitude bombers, in a few weeks so we were figuring out slowly that things might be turning our way after all. Rumor was we were heading to Australia for rest and recuperation so that must have meant that at least this neck of the woods was safe for the moment.

The short ride to the transports in amtracs and small boats knocked us off our pins. It seemed like we lost our sea legs after being on the island for a few months but when we got out to the transports we saw the real problem. We were all just sick as hell. About half of us were too weak to climb the cargo nets to get on the damn ships. They had to hoist us up on cargo pallets like sacks of mail.

When we first got to Guadalcanal we thought we'd finish the job the early battalions of the First Division had started. It might take a few weeks and then we'd move on toward Japan together. Now we didn't even know if the First would survive as a fighting unit. We were leaving 1,242 of us in sandy graves on the island, another 2,655 wounded were in hospitals all over the Pacific and just about everybody else was so sick they couldn't fight even if they had to. The talk was that Topside thought it would be too much trouble to rebuild the First Division. They might just salvage what battalions were left and attach them to other units. The 1/7 might be one of those units that just disappeared in the shuffle. We had taken one of the biggest beatings. Ninety-three of us were in the ground.

It didn't seem right to just sail away and leave our boys behind under the sand, out in the sun and rain with guys who didn't even know them. They should be coming with us or going home where they belonged. It just didn't seem right.

★

We were under way, sailing through what the Navy swabbies called the Slot, the narrow straight between Guadalcanal and Florida Island over Ironbottom Sound. In a half hour we were passing Point Cruz where we first saw action and lost our title of the "first team." Tony Malinowski, my pal, the hero from Baltimore who volunteered to lay down in the path of the attacking Japs behind a log with only his Browning Automatic Rifle for protection and cover our retreat, was still there. He didn't even get a grave and a marker.

Then it was just palm trees and green hills in the distance sliding by like any other island in the world. It was a place where they grew coconut palms in plantations that stretched for miles. They harvested the coconut oil to make soap. That was the whole purpose of the island before the war, coconut oil for soap. It was already looking like just another place on the map, like nothing had happened there.

★

Every inch of deck space on the transport was covered with Marines lying out in the sun and enjoying the cool ocean breeze. The mosquitoes were gone, the stinging spiders were gone, the snakes, the rotten egg swamp gas and the crocodiles were all gone. Corpsmen made their way from one bag of bones in green dungarees to the next, taking down notes, peeking under wound dressings and handing out water and salt pills. Powell was somewhere on the ship nearby, but for now, I was laid up near a Marine who just started talking to me like we'd

known each other our whole lives. He was barely able to get himself
to the head to keep from crapping his pants, but kept telling me how
he was going to get four or five Australian girls to take a long, hot
bath with him.

We did almost nothing for two weeks on the transport except lie to
each other about our former lives and play cards. Dice took too much
energy. Soldiers shuffled around like ghosts on a haunted ship, some
falling down or wobbling around on their weak legs. I wrote a few letters but I was never very good at putting my thoughts down so they
were short. Just enough to let the folks know I was okay.

★

Our first port of call was Brisbane. It sure didn't look like much as
we heaved to at portside. Low, gray buildings and dusty streets ran
down to the docks. Maybe it was some kind of fishing port or a fron-
tier town. On the dock were two Army command staffers. They
worked for my old CO in the Philippines, Douglas MacArthur, who
was the top dog around there. The news spread fast, maybe even
before all of us were off the ship, that we were now under Mac-
Arthur's command and assigned to the defense of Australia. Old
Mac must have gotten himself into another fine fix if he was counting
on us. The word was he was up to his ass in New Guinea and didn't
have a spare man for Australia. One out of ten of us still couldn't
even make it down the gangplank without falling. The Army staffers
just stood there shaking their heads. We heard later that one said to
the other, "Well, there are your defenders of Australia." It got to be
a pretty popular joke in camp whenever some eightball fell on his
face or shuffled off toward the bushes trying like hell to get his pants

down before he unloaded in them. "Well, there are your defenders of Australia."

We were in no position to argue but what they called a camp, we called a swamp. And we knew all about swamps. We were dispersed in a swamp. More than a few of us took up another popular saying after we saw the place, "Hell, if this is the best they can do, why didn't they just leave us on Guadalcanal." The mosquitoes were bigger and hungrier and the damn place was soggy wherever you walked. Instead of the scratchy voice birds of the Canal, a gooney little bird called a kookaburra got on our nerves with a jarring call that sounded like a braying jackass. For a while, the kookaburras drew as much gunfire as Jap snipers. They'd come screaming into camp with that loud jackass sound and a half dozen of us would open up on them with whatever we had handy. If we'd had artillery, we would have used it. The Army staffers who were responsible for us issued strict orders against firing weapons at the birds that we ignored completely. After all, we were the defenders of Australia and no goddamn kookaburra was going to get the drop on us. We figured they were Jap spies.

Mosquitoes or kookaburras were forgotten as soon as we got handed our first liberty passes. We were on the first car, tractor or passing truck into town. Every man who could limp or drag himself or get a few buddies to wheel him in a wagon, made a beeline to the first watering hole we could find. It was a relief to meet the Aussie people who appreciated our need to get laid and blind drunk as fast as possible. Girls were in short supply for much of the task and booze was provided to make up for it. After a few hours, the main street of Brisbane was starting to look like the deck of our transport. Marines were lying all over it. Some were just sick and fell from exhaustion, the healthier ones were knocked down by the hooch. The tolerant people of Brisbane put up quite a few of us until we slept it off or returned us to camp by the truckload.

All of us, officers and enlisted men, gave Mac's staff officers a good piece of our minds about the swamp accommodations. Nobody did nothing. Orders came down that we were to start immediately on constructing the defenses of the Australian shore. To hell with that, we decided to do nothing too. We stayed in the swamp hunting kook-aburras and improving our skills for cheating at cards. Taking orders from the Army wasn't too much to our liking anyway.

A few weeks went by and a few replacements had come into our unit. Within a week they, too, were coming down with malaria even though no one else in the area besides us had the disease. That must have got a few people like Red Mike Edson or Chesty's buddy, the gray-bearded top gunny sergeant Lou Diamond, on the phone to Vandegrift. Within a few days Vandegrift had sent out his officers to find us a better camp. They scouted a place due south called Mel-bourne that was less tropical so they didn't have mosquitoes. They said they would be happy to have us. Then the Army said they couldn't spare the ships to move us. That's when the shit hit the fan. We didn't see much of it because officers weren't supposed to fight in front of the men, but we heard more than an earful. Rogers, Pen-nington and all of the others who were left from the Canal banged around the officers' quarters cursing like true, proud Marines. Any Army-issued order was immediately treated as erroneous or incom-plete and ignored and the Army colonels generally stayed away from the camp where it was clear that they weren't welcome. Finally a call must have gone out to the Old Man himself who was recovering from his wounds in a hospital in Noumea.

Then the Navy got involved. Admiral "Bull" Halsey heard about the fracas and immediately called up our command to let them know that he was sending transportation, "In tribute," Bull said, ". . . to what the First had done at Guadalcanal." It was the final slap in the face to the Army staff. They had to face our officers every day and make the arrangements to get us shipped out on Halsey's transport *West Point* and other smaller ships. It was best for everyone since the chain of command had broken down just about completely. We didn't pay a bit of attention to the Army staff. They were lucky we didn't mistake them for kookaburras. As we walked or were carried onto the ships bound for our new home the Army boys stayed clear of the docks for the most part. They didn't want to hear some of our comments on their hospitality.

*1/7 Division Band leads the welcoming
parade in Melbourne*

A Hero's Welcome

Melbourne was like a dream come true to us. We docked and looked at the first real city some of us had seen in two years. It had wide, paved streets with electric trolley cars and streetlights. Hundreds of people were at the dock to greet us because the newspaper had run a headline that day saying "The Saviours of Australia" were arriving. It was almost too much for some of us. I guess we just sort of lost our minds. Brisbane had only been a warm-up for Melbourne. We were so distracted, even though many of us still couldn't walk more than a few feet without resting, that dozens of us left our rifles on the *West Point*. For a Marine to leave his weapon behind he has to be either dead or crazy. And we weren't dead yet.

We marched through the city behind a Division band. It was almost as good as being on Broadway in New York City. People lined the streets, women in city clothes with perfume and their hair all done up were waving at us, cheering for us. We marched past hotels and barbershops, churches with steeples and a park. We marched through downtown and out to the area lined with neat row homes. If I squinted I could have said it was Raritan. It was home, or close enough.

The camp was already set up with dry barracks and clean bunks. To us it was paradise. But it was going to get even better. Those of us who could still walk after the parade lined up for liberty. We were wasting no time. Not long after we billeted, a steady stream of Marines swarmed into town. We were the first servicemen the Aussies had seen since the war started and we were their heroes. It was a free-for-all like I had never seen anywhere in my life. Strangers were buying us drinks, taxicabs gave us free fares and women came out of their houses to meet us. Now the women, what can I say about the women? To begin with they weren't shy. They stood up square to a man and told him straight out what they liked, didn't like and how they expected things to go. And things certainly did go. One of the things going around camp after that night was, "What they say about Atabrine ain't true." What I learned about nearly dying is that it gave me a hell of an appetite—for everything. The last time I had anything close to this much sex, I was nineteen years old and paying for it. I ate, drank and screwed like a wild pig and didn't feel bad for one second about any of it.

Maybe it was a good thing that just about all of the young men of Melbourne were fighting the Nazis in Africa and the Middle East on the side of the British, because the folks that were left in the city seemed to think it was all their contribution to the war effort. They'd find a bald-headed Marine dead drunk, planted face-first in their petunias and they'd bring him into their home, clean him up and introduce him to their daughter.

I woke up one morning on my bunk and had no idea how I got there. I didn't remember the trip back or how I got my arm all bloodied. Somebody had wrapped it in white gauze so I figured I must have been in the sick bay at some point. All I knew was my head hurt like hell, my mouth felt like mice had made a nest in it and my arm hurt almost as bad as my head. I got myself cleaned up and had to shave with my left arm because my right was so sore. I still couldn't remember how I had banged it up. At chow, Powell looked up at me over his coffee and smiled like the cat that just shit in the corner.

"Death before dishonor, Sarge," he said.

"What the hell was that?" I was thinking and didn't say anything.

"Let's take a look at it," he said.

"At what?" I still wasn't too fast on my feet before coffee. Then it started coming back to me. The drinking contest on Flinders Street, the cab ride and the little shop by the docks with drawings of dragons in the window. Powell nodded at my sore arm. Then I saw the rest: the tray of black inks, the needles and the bald top of a man's head bent over my arm as pain shot through me. Powell was kissing a very heavy brown-skinned girl and watching us. I peeled back the bandage on my arm and saw the scabbed-over letters in blue ink, "Death Before Dishonor" and some other design that was covered in dried blood. I liked it.

"Death Before Dishonor," I repeated to Powell. "Who paid for it?" I asked, because I didn't remember that part.

"Beats me, but somebody did," he said. It was done now and I was pleased with it. It seemed like a good choice considering how drunk we were.

For two weeks we crowded into every cab, bar and cafe in the city. Camp was nearly empty. There were no fights or problems with the local cops. It was a big, all-night block party—an open city for the "Saviours of Australia." Even the ladies weren't squabbling and getting jealous. There were plenty of men and they swapped us as fast as we swapped them. For a short time, it seemed like all the normal rules changed just for us.

Two weeks rolled by in a haze of singing, laughing, eating and everything else. We were out of the gates at one in the afternoon and usually due back by six the next morning. After a few weeks of filling ourselves with everything the city of Melbourne could offer and emptying ourselves of everything we could give, some of us found we were still hungry. We were hungry for our old lives. Outside the city lights and up the road from the neat row homes, were acres and acres of green farmland surrounding the city. The Aussies made a point of taking us in, opening up their homes to us. This was when we started to feel things that we forgot about. Things we had been trying to keep alive in our letters and our private talks together, the little things about living in a home with a family and working at something you loved to do. Pretty soon the cafes were empty and the kitchen tables of Melbourne were full. For me, kids were the best entertainment. Just like I spent all my time playing with Sally back in Reisterstown, I'd get down on the floor or the ground and just play for hours with any kid who would play with me.

We settled into a pretty soft routine. Duty was light and rest was generally the order of the day. It was garrison life, slow and quiet. A few of us had been adopted by local Aussie households and a few had enough faith in their future to ask girls to go steady with them.

The one thing all the Aussie girls seemed to want was the jitterbug. They wore us out with teaching them how to do it. Every pub had a few big-band records—Artie Shaw, Benny Goodman and Charlie Barnett—and as soon as the needle dropped the girls were up and grabbing any guy with two legs. In the States we heard somebody had turned all of Madison Square Garden into a jitterbug palace with fifteen thousand people at a time lighting up the place. We did our bit to keep the thing going but we were still wobbly and the girls had to change partners often to let us rest.

A lot of the guys disappeared almost completely. They bunked at camp when they had to but they were out of the gates at every chance. They worked at the nearby farms for free just to get the feel of doing useful work again. They picked grapes and baled hay. Some learned how to shear sheep and spent all day sweating over hundreds of bleating sheep. After their Liberty passes, they'd come back dirty, exhausted and pulling ticks out of their scalps. One gunny who had no intention of doing any work for as long as he was allowed to get away with it was invited to stay at a farmhouse about thirty miles outside of town. He said his hosts took such good care of him that they would gently rap on his bedroom door at noon and ask him if he wanted lunch in bed too.

Life floated along like a dream. The yellow jaundice faded in our eyes and skin. The malaria sweats and chills quieted down to the occasional ache in the joints and flush of fever. We rested and ate a lot of sheep. Mutton was on the menu just about every day and some of the guys with short memories started to complain. The locals didn't take offense at us singing at the tops of our lungs in their streets at all hours, they didn't seem to mind us passing out in their public parks or crowding them out of their own taxicabs but they didn't like us whining about the mutton. It was some kind of national pride or loyalty to the sheep who were everywhere in the country. Other than that we got along like long-lost cousins. That was until the Ninth Australia Division shipped in. These boys came back expecting things to be like they were when they left except that the girls would be starved for attention. It must have been quite a letdown when they furloughed in and found out Suzie was jitterbugging with two or three of us Yanks at the same time.

The fellas of the Ninth were a bit upset with us and so eventually it came to blows. This was pretty normal with two sets of fighters on the same piece of ground but what upset the apple cart a bit was that they fought in packs. They wouldn't let just one of their own settle his own matter, they all had to settle it. Of course that meant that all of us had to get involved and so things got out of hand.

The new CO who had taken over from Vandegrift sought the advice of the leader of the Division band, Capt. Leon Brusiloff. Brusiloff had led the way with his band when we first marched down the main street of town and had since played all over town at various jitterbug socials cooked up between the locals and our command. Brusiloff suggested the best way to smooth the ruffled feathers was a grand beer party. What a hell of a suggestion. We all considered the man a military genius from that point on. He was a damn good tactician as well because he told Topside that we should have the beer served in paper cups in case some bonehead wanted to toss a bottle to make trouble. The party went off without a hitch. All nine thousand of us piled into the Melbourne cricket grounds and drank beer and swapped lies until early the next morning. We even had a contest for lying called the tall-tale contest, which an Aussie won by telling us how he came to own a pair of moose antlers that he got without shooting the moose. According to his account, the moose had run in front of him on a wooded trail. Strangely enough he had a bucket of turpentine with him that he poured over the moose's rear end. The sticky moose ran to the nearest tree and began scratching his butt against it. "All I had to do," the Aussie said with a straight face, "was stand there 'til the moose rubbed himself down to his antlers." This must have been late in the party because we all roared with laughter. It was just so damn silly you had to laugh. Anyway, he won the tall-tale contest and everybody got along for the whole evening with no fights at all.

For the most part after that, things were quite a bit quieter in town. All we had to do if things got a little touchy was ask our Aussie brothers-in-arms if they'd seen that fella's antlers. It was hard for the Aussies to stay mad at us for long because we loved their country and city and their countrymen almost as much as they did. We knew we'd both be fighting again soon enough. For the Ninth, it was very soon. Their furlough was cut short and they shipped out to reinforce MacArthur in New Guinea. Once more Melbourne was turned over to us. We were part of the whole picture by then and it was almost like the fellas from the Ninth were leaving us to watch things until they got back. We heard all about New Guinea, with headhunters and poison darts and Japs who were spending months perfecting perfectly camouflaged booby traps that tore men apart and impaled them. Some guys just like to tell ghost stories. They liked to try and scare us or themselves, I don't know, but I got tired of it. I didn't want to trade places with the Ninth but I wasn't going to let some big mouth go to work on our minds. I saw how it got Hatfield running in circles back on the Canal and it didn't end up helping him any, so I shut it down. In my platoon, there was no weapon, no soldier and not even God himself who could stop a determined Marine. That was the law and the gospel according to Chesty and it was goddamn good enough for the rest of us.

We were out of the war and it was bringing on a change in the men. Nobody was in a hurry to go back on the line but we just weren't that good at being civilians. Those who weren't practically part of an Aussie family found themselves shuffling around the base and getting into trouble in town. We were back to our full strength with replacements. We'd had enough rest so that the dengue fever, malaria or whatever else, had either gotten us cashiered or back on full duty. The months rolled on with still no orders. The local cops were making more frequent calls to the base telling us to come and pick up some eightball who had gotten into a fight or stolen something. The Old Man always said you could usually find the real Marines in the brig and as usual he was right. Once you bloodied a man in battle, once they saw what we all saw, they were never exactly the same again. Some got quieter and kept to themselves more and some just turned hellish and couldn't be stopped from drinking, cussing and generally taking the fight to every other part of their lives. Down on Flinders Street in town was a handful of old drunks—broken men with ruined teeth, smelling like piss. They were all vets from the first war. I figured it was probably the same in every city in the world. There was a good chance any wino who couldn't remember his own name could recite his serial number and unit.

Liberty hours were restricted to put a damper on the police complaints but most of the men had run through all their money and all their credit anyway. A few of us were engaged to their steadies and marriages were planned. This was the only serious challenge to the wholeness of the unit I saw. A few of the boys were in love, head over heels in love, and would have done anything, and some did, for their girls. There was some concern about boys disappearing into the Australian countryside for good when our orders finally did come. Topside made sure all the particulars were recorded on who was shacking up with whom and where the parents of the girl could be found if needed. For the rest, like me, true love didn't stick. I sometimes wished it would but my inner compass wasn't pointing to Australia as my final destination. There was some other place I was going to end up. My fight with the Japs wasn't done and I couldn't get a sense of much beyond that, but marriage wasn't in the cards for me, not right then. I did love being with the ladies though. Maybe I loved them a little too much. Some guys just naturally have a bigger appetite, and I guess I was just one of those.

May came around and the weather turned sour—clouding over and rainy. The heat blew off, which was a relief, and some of the trees turned fall colors. The seasons were backward down here in the southern hemisphere. This was the fall and winter seasons starting up. Word came down that the Ninth had been just the ticket in New Guinea. MacArthur was all set to do a victory dance because they had finally kicked the Japs out. Nobody thought that the Japs were anywhere close to giving up, but at least we now had a few head-to-head matchups and we knew we could take them apart in a fair fight. We heard he was headed to Melbourne to make a show of his victory, which sounded just exactly like the Mac I remembered from the Philippines. He wasn't shy about getting what he wanted and taking the credit he thought he deserved. This was his first win since getting run out of the Philippines over a year ago, just as he warned it would happen, and he wasn't going to let anybody forget about it. This was just the second round in a fight he expected to win. He was going to fight the Japs, Washington or whoever else got in his way, until he was back in Manila again. Mac hated to lose and would never give up on a fight. Out of my three years in the Army, he was just about the only thing I remembered as being any good at all.

We were told to police the place up for a big celebration, so the mops and shoe polish came out and we went to work getting everything spit shined. Liberty was cut back so the troublemakers could dry out and get ready to parade around for the movie cameras. It was a big push to bring the good news to the folks back in the States. They needed good news and Mac was a bit of a blowhard, the perfect choice to deliver it. He was pretty well known after his grandstanding in congress about the sorry state of the Army before the war and people seemed to like the way he strutted around with his corncob pipe sticking out of his mouth. He looked confident, like he was taking a stroll, not fighting a war.

If he was coming to us, then maybe there was a plan to get us back in the fight. It was clear by now that if combat Marines like us weren't given somebody to fight, we'd pick a fight with the nearest people we could find. The Aussies were very forgiving people but it wasn't good for anybody to have us out of the action and hanging around much longer. It just wasn't in our nature to take it easy with a war going on. I hoped we were going to join Mac in a push to get Manila back. I thought of Lolita and her uncle's bicycle shop. She was probably married by now anyway.

I got the word that Chesty and Captain Rodgers had put me up for a medal for the nights on Bloody Ridge. It was all going to be part of the big party. A few other frontline guys like Mitch Paige were up for one too. Mitch was out on a ridge beyond the perimeter near the Matanikau. They came at him the night after they tried us. He knocked them back and then charged down his ridge right at them with a heavy in his arms. It burned him from wrist to elbow. If somebody was supposed to get a medal, he should be the one. And what about Powell and Evans? They were right there with me. It didn't make too much sense that they would give me a medal and the others, especially the boys that died on the ridge, didn't get one too. So I didn't make too much out of it. It wasn't like anybody else was making a big deal about me or anybody else getting pinned with tin by Topside. Save the brass buttons for the admiral, we were Marines and didn't much like the idea that one of us was better or braver than the rest.

May 21 came up and I wasn't on any duty roster for the day. All I had to do was hang around until the festivities started and see if they handed out liberty for the evening, which was usually the routine. Then I thought I might go into town and see if there was a new movie or maybe scare up a card game. We all got into our dress uniforms and put a last shine on our shoes. Rodgers came in and we fell into parade formation. He called me up front and center. I was told to fall in with the color guard that headed up the band and led the whole shebang toward the cricket grounds. Mitch Paige was there when I reported in. We looked at each other and said hello, heard a lot about you, that kind of thing. The CO called out the command and the band started in, almost knocking our hats off. The brass horns were only two feet behind our heads. I don't know how Brusiloff could hear at all after standing in front of these windbags for hours.

Then we were off, marching, heading up the whole unit. We made it out to the cricket grounds past the knots of Aussies who wondered what the hell the occasion was. Up on the reviewing stand were Red Mike Edson and the chief himself, General Vandegrift. We were marched right up there alongside them. The band knocked off and the chief stepped up to the microphone. He said a few words about honoring heroes throughout the Pacific theater, then started to read from the Presidential citation with Mitch's name on it. He went through the story of Mitch's stand on the ridge we called The Nose near the Matanikau, then put the Medal of Honor ribbon around his neck and saluted him. Then he started in on my story. He read the short account about holding off the Japs on the ridge, about repairing the guns and going back for more ammo. It seemed like he was talking about someone else. He didn't mention a thing about the boys, except that only two survived along with me. He made it seem like I had done it all by myself. It was over fast. Then he placed the ribbon around my neck and saluted me. I returned the salute and he moved back to the microphone. A lot of things were running through my mind, especially that five thousand Marine fighters were probably staring at me. Many of them had done as much as me or more. I always hated being in the spotlight. I stood up there and I was proud of what we did on the ridge but in my heart I knew nine other men should have been honored with me.

★

Back in the barracks the guys came up from all over the place and wanted to see the Medal. They crowded around and craned their necks. All of a sudden I was Manila John, not sarge or Basilone or shithead or whatever. Manila John, they said. They wanted to hear the story of the ridge and I wasn't telling anybody about the ridge just like that, like it was a bedtime story. I wanted to get out of there. I grabbed Powell and a few guys and we took off to town.

I can't stand gawkers, never could. They made me sweat. Sooner or later I would have to say something and I wasn't any better at speaking to groups of people now than I was as a kid. So I had to get away from the gawkers at the barracks. We headed straight to Flinders Street and got so drunk I'm surprised I didn't come back tattooed from head to foot. Maybe I was okay and maybe I wasn't, I don't know. All I know is they kept laughing at me because I couldn't get my cap on straight, so I gave up. They were all having such a laugh looking at me, I left it on across my head long-ways like somebody broke a toy boat over my head. Big laugh. Manila John, Medal of Honor, shit-faced drunk with his pisscutter on sideways. I guess I wasn't really okay. It wasn't like we were just regular guys having a good time because there was something missing and I was trying not to remember what it was, to block it out. If I did remember, I might just come apart or I don't know what. But you can't stop thinking of something just because you want to. So there they were, all nine of them. And then I knew I couldn't get away and I couldn't forget and so I decided what the hell, let them stay and have some fun, too. Them in their bloody shirts with dirt on their eyeballs. What the hell, I might be with them soon enough. We all might be. So we all had a little party. But it just didn't seem right. They got little wooden crosses and a hole on some stinking island and I got the Medal of Honor. I couldn't make any sense of that. Things just got funnier and funnier. It seemed to me like the shit was just starting to hit the fan.

★

June and July we were back on maneuvers, gearing up for some scheme they were cooking up with Mac's Sixth Army stationed up in Brisbane, probably in the same swamp we left behind. The wheels were turning again, slowly. Each day new equipment arrived and more young shaved-head "boots" a few weeks out of basic filled out our ranks. It was a good mix in a way because we could fill in the new boots on the real world of jungle warfare, not what they heard in scuttlebutt. I wished somebody like us had been there on the Canal to take us aside and tell us the real dope. I could tell we were going to keep a few of these kids from getting killed because they listened to every word and we never had to tell them something twice.

I got a letter from home that said George had joined the Marines. He was headed to the Pacific, too, so maybe we'd meet up some-where. Everyone was doing fine and they were praying for me every day. The whole town was. That was supposed to make me feel better because a lot of angels were watching over me. If that was true, I'd have a few things to answer for when I got to heaven. If I got there.

The day officer came in one day and handed me orders, separate from my unit. I was shipping out, going home. I was to report to Marine headquarters in New York City. No further instructions. Talk about coming from left field, I had to read the damn thing three times. I was going home. It didn't make any sense. My guys are gearing up for operations and I'm shipping out? Powell looked at me like I was Jesus H. Christ himself. He gave me his folks' address in New Haven and for a minute I thought he was going to cry. Nobody even thought seriously about home anymore. It was a faraway dream. But here it was in front of me and I was going. After I saw the effect it had on Bob, I didn't want to let too many others in on it. It would only make them feel bad. The orders said now, so I packed my sea bag. I went around and said my good-byes to the ones I knew, the ones who had been there. I found Evans but he was like someone I didn't even know anymore. He kept to himself more and more ever since the ridge and I took this one last chance to get through to him. I didn't want to tell him I was going home, I made something up, like Topside had something special for me all hush-hush. He didn't say much and that was it. I never saw him, spoke to him or heard anything about him again. The wisecracking kid who used to run around barefoot like me and fought like a tiger was left up there on the ridge with the others. The guy in front of me, who couldn't look me in the eye anymore, was just a ghost.

★ 10 ★

Hitting the Fan

Sergeant Basilone at a press conference

They swarmed over us, snapping pictures and yelling questions, everybody calling to me, "Manila John, how'd ya feel when you got the medal?" "Hey Johnny! Y'called home yet?" "How'd it feel to kill all those Japs? Were ya scared?" Talk about being in the spotlight, it was like the whole country turned its headlights on me and wanted me to tell them every last thing down to what I ate for breakfast.

"Hey Johnny, they're calling you Manila John, the Jap killer. How

ya like that?!" "Is it true you're going back into the ring after the war?"
On the flight into Roosevelt Base, the staff officer in charge of getting
my face in front of the public told me a few people from the papers
would be there when we arrived. He forgot to mention that everybody
from the papers would be there. This desk jockey officer, who was supposed to be my shadow for the next few months, told me to write a few
things down so I'd have something to say to the reporters. I'd never
talked to a newspaperman in my life and knew I wasn't going to be
much good at it. When we stepped off the plane it was like feeding
time at the zoo. When the questions started coming all at once, I froze
up—didn't know what to say. I just waved and my shadow nudged me
so I would say something. I managed to get a few words out, saying
that I felt fine and glad to be home. After everything I'd been through
in the last few years, I was still the kid in grade school who couldn't
stand in front of the class and speak. The steam rose under my collar
while I just stood there in the California sun grinning like a goddamn
idiot. My shadow threw the wolf pack a bone, promising them they'd
all get time alone with me, then I got pulled into a staff car. We took
off and headed to the staff offices. Roosevelt Base was on Terminal
Island just off of Long Beach. I was so embarrassed, I didn't say anything on the ride. I wanted to crawl under a rock. My escort tried to
make small talk, telling me I'd get the hang of it soon enough but I
knew I'd never be any good at this. I just looked out the window at the
giant loading cranes on shore and the freighters in the harbor. That
made me feel a little better. It was some connection to the real war.
This was the stuff that was going to keep us going. This was where a
lot of our gear came through. As long as these cranes and ships were
working, that was the important thing and my face being in the papers
was all tied up with that now. It wouldn't help the new Carolina or

Pennsylvania boys in the 1/7 to know what a Jap Nambu machine gun sounded like when it jammed so they could move safely, or remind them that Japs sometimes used firecrackers to draw their fire and reveal their position, or that the Japs threw smoke grenades and then yelled "Gas attack!" which was bullshit, or teach them a thousand other tricks to keep them from getting their asses shot off, but orders are orders and getting my face in the papers were my orders now. It didn't matter that I was just a stuttering monkey in front of people.

My orders were to sell war bonds. I was going on a tour and my specialty was changed from machine gunner to salesman. I couldn't imagine a worse pick than me to be a salesman. I was now under the command of a fast-talking, owl-eyed staff officer who must have sold popcorn or cotton candy before the war. He ran down the big plans they'd cooked up for this tour that was supposed to raise a few million bucks. All I could do was nod my head and keep saying that sounds fine, or whatever I could think of. It was all coming at me a bit too fast really and gave me a headache. Everything was turned upside down. August was summer again, like it was supposed to be, not winter like in Australia. I was supposed to be some kind of showboat hero, which I wasn't, and the one thing I knew how to do, that cost a hundred lives for me to learn, was how to keep men alive in a jungle firefight. I wasn't ever going to do that again. This was it for me. Even when we were starting to go on the offensive, when they would need me the most, I was out of the war.

★

George was in Camp Pendleton down in San Diego so I got a pass to go see him. I'd been lying around Roosevelt for a few weeks giving interviews to the newspaper and radio reporters. A few dozen guys, decorated vets from the Navy, Army and Air Force, were all billeted together and pulling the same duty as me. We were all happy to be off the front lines for a while but a few, like me, weren't too good at sitting on the bench and giving interviews. Especially if their units were heading into heavy action, us few who felt they should be helping out in the field started making trouble for the brass. It was the usual kind of thing of bringing women on base, being drunk and disorderly, telling our press officers to go fuck themselves, all the normal things fighters who aren't fighting do to pass the time.

We kept hearing that this bond tour was going to get going but one thing or another held up the show. First it was some movie star couldn't get away, and then it was a scheduled event, which was delayed and would throw the whole schedule off. So we ended up sitting in our barracks with absolutely nothing to do except wait to be called in for interviews with newspaper and radio people. They all pretty much asked the same questions. So I started telling them they could read the other newspaper and get the answers they wanted. My shadow lit into me after that. These were all important people from important places, he said. If I didn't toe the line, he said, he'd see about having me shipped back to the jungle. That was definitely the wrong thing to say. He said it like being in the jungle, fighting, was a place where you went if you couldn't get a soft desk job like him and his important people. That was a real bad thing to say. Some of the other guys said he had told them something like that too. We all decided it was a bad thing for him to say and that he needed to get an idea of what it was like for some of us fighting men in the jungle.

We were lucky to be let off the base often so we got to know Long Beach and could take the trolley up to Los Angeles in an hour. I secured a small cache of what we decorated combat vets called training ordnance from a few Mexican boys in East Los Angeles. Other people called this training ordnance fireworks. We were concerned with creating the most realistic training exercise possible for our press officer. Just after lights out, we placed the ordnance in strategic offensive positions around the press officer's sleeping quarters. At exactly 1100 hours, we conducted an aerial attack simulation on our sleeping officer. He responded exactly by the book. That meant that just after the first few explosions went off and we staggered in screaming with ketchup running down our faces and chests, that he panicked and ran where we told him to find cover. It was well known to us decorated combat vets that the only place a Marine is safe during an aerial attack is in the shitter. We were able to direct him to a safe place in spite of our wounds. He jumped in and saved himself, again exactly by the book. He was a fine Marine. The safe place was standing knee-deep in shit with his head just under the rim of the toilet seat. It was there that the MPs found him terrified and shivering when they came to investigate the attack. The exercise was a complete success and we received unit citations the following evening from the bartender at the Atlas bar in Long Beach.

I figured I better go see George and get away from these men who were a bad influence on me. On the train to Pendleton, I was just another Marine on his way back to base. The cut of my uniform was better because the press officers made sure we all had tailor-fitted uniforms and I was glad nobody noticed. This train ride was the first time I felt like myself, like I wasn't a goldfish in a bowl, in over a month. I was happy to just sit there and remember all the card games and crap shoots I'd had on trains all across the country. I probably made more money riding on trains than anyplace else I'd ever been.

The quiet time didn't last long. By the time I got down to Long

Beach and grabbed a ride from the train to the camp, my press officer had been on the phone. Reporters were at the gates and orders at
the gate for me indicated I was to give them my utmost attention. The
idea was that me going to see my brother George was some kind of
interesting story. I was starting to think that I would stop reading
newspapers soon if this was the kind of thing they spent their time
on. I lost a lot of respect for newspaper reporters or maybe I never
had any.

In camp it was almost as bad because the camp had its own paper and they wanted to talk to me too. All the young boots came out
to take a look at me while I was held up with the camp paper. I don't
know what they were expecting but they just stood there in the hot
sun gawking at me or giving me the high sign. Finally, I got to see
George who had just come back from a fourteen day leave he spent
in Raritan. He told me they were planning a parade for me.

"You're kidding," I said. I told him that the folks in Raritan must
know more about when I'm getting there than I do because our
schedule still wasn't set.

"Hell, Johnny. You ain't seen nothing yet. The whole country is
crazy about you. You're a hero and famous all over the world. Everybody from President Roosevelt on down is talking about you."

I thought George was just talking through his hat. I hadn't heard
about anything like that. There were a few dozen other frontline vets
like me and why the hell weren't they just as famous? He went on
and on about his visit back home and how everybody was clipping
newspaper articles about me. I was starting to see what he meant.
The newspapers were getting people all excited and making me look
like a hero and one thing was feeding the other. The more people

talked, the more the papers wrote and so on. George didn't get excited that often and was not one to exaggerate, so I got the picture that the story about us war bond salesmen was a lot bigger than any of us expected. There didn't seem to be any way I was going to avoid being in the spotlight for a long time to come. It was like being pulled out to sea in an undertow. There's just nothing you can do about it, you're fighting the ocean. Especially if you're a guy like me, who couldn't swim worth a shit in this ocean of questions and flash cameras, it was a real bad feeling.

As bad as I was starting to feel about my own future, I started to feel worse because of what we'd put my shadow, the press officer, through. From what George was saying, it sure looked like he'd been doing a bang-up job of getting the word out—and then we just went and put him in the shitter. Not that he didn't deserve it, but maybe we shouldn't have picked the shitter. At least now he would have more respect for what we did. But I was thinking, too, about when the boys in the 1/7 got the word that I was gallivanting around the country showboating for the brass. When they were laying in the rain eating a slice of Spam covered with dirt and gun oil from the hands of the men who had passed it down the line, what would they think of me?

I asked George if I put in a word and got him another pass, would he come back home with me. I knew I could swing a little weight and probably get my brother a trip home, especially if it would be a good newspaper story. Since this war bond mission was beginning to look like a life sentence, I saw how the angles might work for me too.

"I wouldn't feel right," he said. "I just got back." He didn't have to say any more. I knew he was thinking about the guys in his unit. He didn't want to have any special treatment either. That was why I wanted him to come, so we could make a joke of it. Because all I got was special treatment.

★

Finally orders arrived that the tour was starting and my first stop was to report to Marine Headquarters at 90 Church Street in New York City. I was being thrown right into the deep end. Nine A.M. sharp on September 4, I reported to the pressroom of Headquarters that was jammed to the rafters with reporters and every kind of camera there was. The lights were constant and bright in my face so that I couldn't really get a good look at anyone who was asking questions. The first thing I did was I told them the whole story of the ridge, real slow, from the beginning. I couldn't really tell them the whole story because of all the foul language we used and I couldn't really tell them about all the blood and guts either. I just told it like a storybook story and tried to get in the main things about what happened to me. I talked about the guns and being low on water and the Japs who just kept coming right at us. After that they let loose on me and wanted to know about what I was thinking and what I was feeling. Was I scared, yes. Was I in pain, yes. Was I thinking about my men, yes. It went on for an hour or two like that. They wanted to know about my family, did I have a sweetheart and other things that didn't have anything to do with the story. By the time the colonel who was in charge of this leg of the operation called it off, I was limp as a rag. My head was pounding and my mouth was bone dry. I kept drinking water but it only helped a little.

At noon I went to meet Mayor LaGuardia, down at City Hall. That was another mob scene with many of the same faces that were on me since the morning. Now this LaGuardia was a guy who knew how to work the press. He first mugged for the cameras, called a few of the reporters by their first names and shook a few hands. When he got to me he was all smiles and like he had met a long-lost son. He grabbed my hand and held on chatting with me like I was the most important guy in the world, all about how I was being treated. It was like he was giving me my last rites but all he was saying was, "You sleeping okay?" "How's the food where you are?" "How long you staying in town?" that kind of thing. He clung to my hand long after the shaking was done and wouldn't let go. Then I realized he was posing for the cameras. The look on his face, the handshake, all of it was just posed until he heard the flashes from the cameras die off. I could have said I was in love with a baboon and I don't think he would have heard a word of it. Then he turned with a great smile and held that position, too, for a long time. I didn't know whether to look at him or smile at the cameras or what the hell to do. I was just standing there staring at him until he noticed me and told me to smile at the cameras, so I did. He had a speech prepared for the reporters like I was supposed to do but I could never in a million years come close to what he said. It was like President Roosevelt or even MacArthur. Those guys knew how to put over a speech and this LaGuardia was no slouch either. He even had it all memorized. He said, "The Congressional Medal of Honor, as we know, is awarded only for conduct above and beyond the call of duty. In this coming bond drive all of us must do something above and beyond the call of duty. Buying a bond when one has money in the bank is only an investment. Buying a bond by depriving oneself of something is beyond the call of duty and it should give our citizens satisfaction to know that they have done that."

Then he turned to me while the reporters eavesdropped. "Sergeant, where did your old man come from?"

"Naples," I told him.

"Mine came from Foggia, but we are Americans," he said.

"You bet we are." That was the icebreaker and he gave me the wink. "I bet the Japs were happy to see you leave Guadalcanal?"

"I don't know about that," I said. I couldn't just stand here in front of fifty eavesdroppers and have a private chat like two buddies. I didn't know if he was being funny or what exactly. But it didn't matter because our meeting was over.

"Well, son," he said, "you at least have the satisfaction of knowing you've done more than your share." Then he offered his hand with a big smile and we shook again and he held on to it again and the flashbulbs popped again. He turned and went back into his office and the colonel led me down the hall at the head of the crowd of reporters. We stopped by a radio station where I told my story again. I was done for the day. The crowd of reporters dispersed and I was given a chit for lodging in a hotel near Headquarters. I asked for a pass to see my folks in Raritan and the colonel gave it to me with no problem at all. He said they'd have the tour schedule ironed out completely in a day or two but that I was to report next to Washington, D.C., where the tour was to start.

★

I called to let my family know I was coming and asked them please not to make a big deal of it. Just keep it in the family, I'd had enough of crowds already. On the train down, nobody paid any attention to me but as soon as I stepped off the trolley from Somerville it was like the second coming of Christ. Girls were yelling at me like I was Frank Sinatra. I should have known my family wasn't going to keep it a secret. I couldn't just wave and get into a car this time. I was trapped for an hour by everybody I ever knew growing up. Everybody wanted to touch me, shake my hand, tousle my hair, paw my uniform. I thought I was going to be sick. The crowd was getting bigger every minute and I just reached out to Carlo and held his hand.

"Let's go," I said and he knew I'd had enough. He pulled me and helped clear the way as we walked the last ten blocks to the house with a crowd buzzing around us like bees. Mama and Pop and most of my other brothers and sisters were at the front door waiting for me and I got to them as fast as I could. When I hugged Mama everyone clapped and laughed. They were spilling out onto the street in front of the house. "Johnny's home!" someone yelled and the crowd cheered. "Johnny Basilone, the Jap Killer!" someone else yelled and kids started making the sound of guns going off, shooting each other and falling in the street. I got inside as fast as I could and didn't look back.

Inside it was almost as wild, the questions kept coming, everyone giving me a hug and kissing my face all at once. I was passed around like a favorite doll for half an hour, and then I was allowed to sit down and rest. Until late at night people were outside the house. It was late summer and no one wanted to go home. They kept up a party of their own. Some brought beer. They came and went. They sat across the street on the curb and just watched the house. They kept looking at the house, waiting for me to come out or waiting for something to happen. Every half hour or so, a kid or someone who had enough beer to give them courage, knocked on the door. The first few times I went and said hello and waved outside to the others. Then I didn't come to the door anymore but they kept coming. Some we couldn't turn away, they were old friends. The living room slowly filled with people while we all had dinner at the table. Mama was trying to take care of everybody. We couldn't even eat in peace.

Pop finally laid his fork down and sat back at the table. It was too strange having neighbors in the house and not feeding them. It was a situation nobody ever saw before. Neighbors were acting oddly, like it was cold outside and we had the only fire. They kept interrupting us at dinner and none of us knew what to do. Finally, Angelo had to go out and ask people to leave. It was a hard thing to do and upset Mama terribly. Now it seemed like we were being rude. We just didn't understand how people could forget their common sense and manners. We finally got the house cleared out and had almost a full hour of just being with each other. I got the most satisfaction just studying everyone's face and listening to them talk. They wanted me to talk about myself but I'd already said everything there was to say. So many times I'd remembered their faces when I was in a bunk in a rolling troop ship or lying under the stars of the Southern Cross. A few times I thought I'd never see them again. Now I was storing up a new set of memories.

I was in my old bed again. All the windows in the house were open to let out the heat of the day and with luck catch a stray breeze. There was a strange new sound in the house. I could hear cars zooming by somewhere in the distance. I thought maybe I had learned to listen for engine sounds at night but that wasn't it. It wasn't me. Route 28 had been widened and paved smooth. It was always just under a mile from my window but now it seemed much closer because I could hear cars motoring along even late at night. I used to hear just crickets. Sometimes if the wind was blowing our way, I could hear the bullfrogs that lived in the pond across the pasture where Archie the bull lived. Route 28 was just a country road back then. I used to fall asleep to the chirping crickets. My bed used to be peaceful and quiet.

★

I was in the Navy Department's pressroom in Washington, D.C. Another tangle of reporters shot the same questions at me and flashed their cameras. Maybe my answers didn't sound right anymore because I had given them so many times and the reporters heard me being phony. They turned up the heat on me, trying to bait me into giving them something fresh. "Come on Sarge, level with us," they'd say. "What was it really like when you had a Jap in your sights? Didn't you want to make them pay for Pearl Harbor?" I knew they wanted stories of blood and guts and me saving the day. But the truth that they were never going to know was that I didn't save the day. The guys who really saved the day all got killed. I was just one of the guys who was left when the sun came up. That wouldn't sell many war bonds so I just gave them the answers I already had and they could tell I was hiding something. Fuck 'em. I turned to the press officer in charge and whispered to him, "This is worse than fighting the Japs."

"Just tell them what happened," he said. He didn't give a shit either. He was punching a time clock to retirement and I was just another sausage through the factory. So I started all over from the beginning. "It had been raining all day. A hard, tropical rain . . ." I just stayed to the story the way I always told it. I didn't see faces from that night on the ridge, or hear anything or smell anything. I wasn't going up on the ridge again for them, which is exactly where they wanted me to go. I just told the same story that every paper from Los Angeles to New York already heard. I made sure to put in a pitch to buy war bonds at the end, just like they told me to do. Orders.

They wanted more. The story of the ridge was getting played out.

They wanted to know what happened after the ridge. I told them about the Metapona and eighteen days in the field with Chesty Puller, the greatest battlefield commander in history. I could talk about Chesty easier than I could talk about myself. The problem was I couldn't quote most of what he said because he always used the words goddamn, fuck, ass and a few others that the papers wouldn't print. The only people I could really talk to were other Marines.

The colonel finally gave me my orders for the next few months. I was assigned to Flight number 5 of the War Veteran's Airmada. On the flight with me would be decorated Joes from the other services and a few movie stars. From the Army was Sgt. Schiller Cohen, the Navy man was Bosun's Mate Second Class Ward Gemmer and the Air Force threw in Machinist Mate First Class—which was their grade name for a pilot—Robert Creak. With us from Hollywood were Virginia Grey, Martha Scott, Eddie Bracken, John Garfield and Gene Lockhart. The tour started on the East Coast with scheduled stops in Newark, Jersey City, New Haven, Providence, Pawtucket, Manchester, Worcester, Albany, Utica, Rochester and ending up in Allentown, Pennsylvania. I didn't have to do much but say a few words at each place.

We kicked off in Newark where Virginia, John Garfield and Gene Lockhart released three carrier pigeons in Lincoln Park, each with part of a message for the CO at Fort Monmouth. They said, "One Down," "Two to Go," "For Victory." They were talking about Guadal-canal with "One Down," and Tokyo and Berlin with "Two to Go."

Lincoln Park was jammed with people coming out to see us. They spilled into the streets. A parade formed up and marched through downtown. I was hoping a few of my buddies from the gym where I used to train would come out and say hello. The next great Italian champ after Primo Carnera, Rocky Marciano, had bought the place and trained there all the time. These guys would know where the fun was after I was through playing Marine with the movie stars.

The Navy sent a blimp over the parade route. It dropped papier-mâché bombs on us. We ended up at a reviewing stand in front of City Hall where Mayor Murphy took the lead position. Everybody was excited and wanted to do their bit for the war effort. I had to give them that. When I saw all the people and how much they wanted to help, I saw that I could do some real good. After all, if I helped to keep the ammunition and supplies flowing over to the boys, that was something worth doing. I took some pride then in what I was doing. At least I wasn't trapped in a room with barking reporters and nothing very smart to say. Mayor Murphy made a good speech about everybody buying bonds until it hurt, and then buying one more. We all got our turn at the microphone. Bracken and Garfield were completely relaxed as they told the people how important it was that they support the boys overseas. They introduced the other fellas who stood up and told the crowd about what they had been through. We were all supposed to wear our medals but I didn't care to have the Medal of Honor around my neck all day. It drew too much attention. Virginia introduced me and turned to me with a look that was a little different than the look she gave to the other guys.

We did another event in Jersey City that afternoon and then had a few hours off. Virginia and I managed to separate from the others and slipped away to a hotel for a few drinks in a dark, back booth. She was from a show business family and grew up in Hollywood. I never met anyone even a little bit like her before. She was just about the funniest lady I'd ever run across, and beautiful with real movie star looks—honey colored hair and eyes that were deep blue, cornflower blue. She was thin, must have weighed just over a hundred pounds and had so much energy I thought she was going to get up and tap dance on the table. We laughed our heads off. She didn't take Hollywood glamour seriously at all since to her it was just the family business. She could tell dirty stories on all the big stars going all the way back to the silent movie days when her dad was a big shot.

She was too good to be true. I couldn't stop looking at her. What really got me was that she was the real McCoy—inside. The tour was more important to her than her Hollywood movies. It wasn't some put-up job just to get her face in the papers, she really put her heart into everything she said out there in front of the people. When I heard that from her and knew she was telling the truth, I was like a dog with a bone. It seemed like green lights all the way for Virginia and me. Being on the road like we were meant we were together every day.

At dinner in another fancy hotel, there were more speeches and toasts. This was a formal, sit-down dinner with business owners and bigwigs in the community. Of course, everybody was asked to dig deep for the war effort. I'm sure there wasn't one person in that dining room who didn't come out with a checkbook by the end of the evening. After dinner we were taken to Proctor's Theatre to see the movie, *Mr. Lucky*. Naturally, we all got in free, which I was starting to get used to. People got angry with me if I didn't let them pay for me. I couldn't reach into my pocket without half a dozen Joes going for their money rolls first. It was like a Wild West shoot-out, I'd go for my gun and they'd beat me to the draw. I finally gave up. In the movie, Cary Grant is supposed to be a gangster but falls for a dame and changes his ways. I hadn't seen a real movie in a long while and thought it was great. We laughed all the way through, even the sappy love story was okay. Virginia kept whispering funny comments all through the movie about Cary not knowing a lot about what a woman might want.

Virginia and me were falling hard and fast even though we'd only just met. It was easy to be around her when we were alone. She never put on airs. And I didn't treat her like some of the girls who just wanted to have a good time with soldier boys for an evening. She was a real first-class lady. She made her own money, a hell of a lot more than I did, and didn't need anybody. She was altogether a new deal.

Everything was still brand-new between us and we were surrounded day and night with wild guys like Eddie Bracken who was just about the funniest guy I'd ever met. He was like me, couldn't sit still. That took the pressure off us when we were out in public because Eddie was always there making jokes and playing tricks on everybody. It was the perfect setup. Nobody made a big deal about us. It must have seemed like the natural thing. We eventually got around to the talk about what I was planning for the future. I hadn't been with one woman in years and wasn't sure if I was one-woman material anymore. It was always love 'em and leave 'em, have a few laughs and then ship out or make it back to base. Now I was in a whole new ball game with Virginia, but I couldn't tell her. It would only have made us both feel bad.

After the movie, the movie stars, Virginia, Eddie and John Garfield walked up on the stage in front of the screen and introduced us vets to the other servicemen and people in the audience. The slogan was "Back the Attack" and we pumped a few more bond sales out of them. Virginia was a tiger and would have taken their gold teeth if she could. We left the theater, off for the evening. Orders were to report to the hotel lobby tomorrow morning. Virginia and I walked through the quiet streets for a while and didn't say too much. We got back to the hotel late and went up to our rooms. It was one of the only nights I didn't wake up around midnight and grab for a weapon. Just having her in the same building was enough for me. I slept.

The next day we had a police escort to City Hall where we were all formally greeted by the commissioners of Jersey City and posed for photos. Then we were off to the Hotel Plaza for an early lunch with about three hundred more of the top citizens of northern New Jersey and New York. Commissioner Potterton led the show and moved everything along so that we'd be out and on our way to another big rally in Journal Square Plaza by three. The rally was a huge success with people stretching as far as we could see and packed in like sardines. The story that always brought a hush over the audience and got the checkbooks flipping was when a new Navy man on the tour told his story. Seaman first class Elmer Cornwell told a hell of a good story about how he lost fifty pounds after his ship went down and he drifted around in a life raft for thirty-six days with rations for only fifteen. Even the pro Hollywood actors stood up and applauded when he got done. Virginia tipped me off to always go on and tell my story before Elmer. She said his story was a showstopper and never follow a showstopper.

We jumped in the cars after Jersey City and had a police escort all the way to Newark Airport, where we got in the Navy bombers of the Airmada for the flight to New Haven, Connecticut. In New Haven, the turnout was even bigger than in Jersey City. We headed up a military and civilian parade of over five thousand people including Grand Marshal Colonel F. W. Howe, the 79th Coast Guard Artillery band, a contingent of the Army Air Force Technical Command, the First Service Command with jeeps, tanks and scout cars. The State Guard followed them, then the Bradley Field Military Band, Boy Scouts, Girls Scouts and on and on. That evening there was another huge event at the Arena with speeches by Governor Baldwin, Mayor Murphy and Colonel Arnett.

I was starting to get my feet under me as far as saying my bit in front of people. Virginia coached me and gave me tricks like taking a few deep breaths before going up, and looking at one person in the middle of the crowd to help my concentration. All I had to do was look at her before I went up and trade a wink, then I was okay.

The next stop was Rochester, Bob Powell's hometown. His mother's house was at 98 Garfield Street so I planned a visit as soon as I could get away. Our first stop for the tour was Red Wing Stadium. We filled the place with cheering folks and by the time the rally was over, we knew we were way ahead of projections for the drive. I took off a little early from all the hand shaking and autograph hounds after the rally and went on my own over to Bob's house. His kid sister, eight-year-old Peggy, came to the door and then Mrs. Powell snatched the door open. Mrs. Powell pulled me inside with a hug that almost knocked the wind out of me. She showed me over to a chair in the living room and sat right down in front of me on the couch. She was so anxious to hear about Bob that she went right into asking me how he was. She must have asked me a half dozen times in different ways, trying to get the whole picture. After she was sure I wasn't trying to snow her about her son's general condition, she remembered that she hadn't offered me something to drink. Neither of us cared about the drink, it was just a time for her to catch her breath and start to believe that her son was really in good shape. I sat with her for hours telling her all the stuff that I knew wouldn't upset her but it wasn't easy. She sat where she could stare straight into my eyes, up close. I made it seem like a big camping trip with a lot of cutting up and hijinks. I told her the food was good, we got enough sleep and other guys did most of the tough fighting. I didn't say a word about the ridge or what I really saw and went through with her son. She was a smart woman and probably knew I was lying. She was as afraid to dig for more, as I was to tell it. It got pretty close to the bone for me when I was bringing up all the little details of everyday life on the line. I was getting close to the real memories and sometimes had to stop and breathe like Virginia taught me. Mrs. Powell dabbed at her eyes while she thanked me. I couldn't tell if it was from relief or that she knew how much I was lying and was imagining much worse. I didn't have that much practice lying through my teeth the way I did that night. I painted her a pretty picture, using all my poker training to keep my face from moving, while the real pictures where flashing just behind my eyes. It was a movie inside me that I couldn't turn off, I could only turn my mind's eye away from it.

I was saved when Bob's older sister, Vicky, walked into the house. She was twenty-two. She looked at me like she was going to jump me, like she hated my guts on sight. It must have looked bad when she saw me in my uniform talking quietly with her mother who was wiping tears from her eyes. The little sister Peggy announced that I was Bobby's friend and was telling them all about him. Mrs. Powell calmed her down right away, told her that I was Bobby's best friend and Bobby was fine. Vicky came over and sat down in front of me, a few inches from my face, like her mother. I went over the stories again. I liked talking about Bob and me. It made me feel almost like I was part of the unit again. It took a few minutes but she started to smile. When I saw that, I started to feel like I was coming unglued a little. She was as beautiful a girl as I'd ever seen, even counting Virginia. I felt like I was falling for her, too, and didn't even try to stop myself. My lies were bringing a smile to her face instead of a nasty scowl. Stories and stories and more stories I told, going back to New River, Parris Island, even all the way back to Cuba. That's how far back I went with Bob Powell. Soon the stories turned into bedtime stories as little Peggy dropped off while sitting on my lap. It was getting late but I didn't want to leave. I kept talking so that Vicky would keep looking at me. If I had to make a choice right then, I would have chosen to live there, in that house and never leave. I would live there with the Powell family. I would marry Vicky and wait for Bob to come back. It was my own bedtime story that I told myself after I handed the sleeping Peggy over to Mrs. Powell and then sat there quietly in the living room, alone with Vicky. For just a few more minutes, I sat there eye to eye with Vicky. There was nothing more to say. We looked at each other, into each other, and like I did with Virginia, I kept my thoughts to myself.

★

In Albany, I stopped in to visit Jackie Schoenecker's mother. Jackie was one of the old crowd like Bob. Jackie came off the line early, before the nights on the ridge. He was downed with malaria. In that way I guess it saved his life. I told Mrs. Schoenecker that he was being taken good care of in the hospital. I didn't mention that the hospital was a tent with shrapnel holes punched through it, or that it swarmed with flies and stunk like a slaughterhouse. I told her malaria wasn't that bad. I still had it and I was walking around fine. She showed me all his school medals that he won as a track star and the family photo album of Jackie from the time he was a baby. She wanted so badly to cry but held herself back, I'm sure, until I left. That was how it was with everybody. They held back, held their breath and held their tears until they saw either their loved ones or the telegram from the government. It seemed like everyone, including me, wanted to be with someone who couldn't be with them.

The tour marched on like the military operation it was. We didn't get much time to rest. It was into cars and out of planes, shaking hands, speaking to crowds, riding in parades and in and out of hotel rooms all day long and into the night. I couldn't complain, it was light duty compared to what everybody else in my unit was doing. The word came down to me that the 1/7 was in New Guinea now operating under "Dugout Doug" MacArthur. I didn't have to imagine much. I knew exactly what life was like for them. Everybody was saying the Japs were getting desperate now. We'd kicked their asses good on the water and knocked a lot of them out of the air, so they had to make a good show on the ground. They fought to the last man, no more retreats to lick their wounds like on the Canal. We all knew they tortured and executed prisoners. It was take-no-prisoner, hand-to-hand combat. I wondered how a new kid with seven weeks basic training could go into that and even if he survived, come out with all his marbles. Me and Bob and the others had almost two years of training and look what happened to us. There weren't many around like me, who could really help them when the shit started flying. I knew they needed me. It wore on my mind every day.

Once a few of the Hollywood papers got wind of Virginia and me, the tour didn't end when we finished for the day. We'd run into jokers in the hotel lobby where we were staying. They'd tell me they knew Rocco Fischetti or someone else in Raritan, trying to get my confidence. Then they'd get chummy all of a sudden and ask me, "What's up in the skirt department?" Some of these guys were real snakes.

They tried all kinds of tricks on us. Sometimes they'd spring out of nowhere, stick a camera flash in our faces and set it off. They were like the goddamn Jap snipers. I needed to get away from it and generally corralled Eddie Bracken or the Joes on the tour who didn't mind slipping away when we could. We'd find the local gin mill and make sure no reporters were drinking there. If the coast was clear, we'd let loose and turn the place upside down. It was just about the only time I had when I could stop talking about myself. If Garfield came at all he would generally drop out early but Eddie Bracken could hang on. It made the early morning calls tough but we figured it was our duty to keep the breweries and distilleries going. It was our extra war effort to support the booze industry.

Bracken stopped sneaking out with us after the second week or so and I had to recruit fresh troops to fill out our ranks. We might start the evening with a five- or six-man drinking squad and be down to two men by the time last call rolled around. We did our best in spite of overwhelming odds. There was just too much liquor for one drinking squad to hold the line. We were overrun almost every night. Virginia let me know she wasn't happy with me after a skirmish with the bottles that lasted for a few days.

I wasn't sleeping anymore like I had the first few nights. At midnight, I was wide awake. Midnight to 4:00 A.M. was the time I needed a little something to help me relax. One of the vets called it the Witching

Hour. He knew what I was talking about. We'd go out on night patrol
and always find some after-hours place open. It wasn't too hard to find
a friendly craps game on most nights.

September 19 was Basilone Day in Raritan and it slotted right
into our tour schedule. They came and got us at 8:00 A.M. at Marine
Headquarters on Church Street and drove everybody down through
New Jersey by car. I was getting to be such a famous so-and-so that
I couldn't even stay overnight in my own home before the parade,
nobody would have gotten any sleep. For a little town, it was supposed to be one of the biggest rallies on the tour, thirty thousand
people were expected. When eight o'clock rolled around I was just
back a few hours from night patrol. I must have looked pretty rugged. How Virginia managed to look glamorous at 8:00 in the morning was a miracle to me. She must have been up at 6:00, just after I
usually got in for the evening.

Basilone Day

We got to Raritan and the first stop was St. Ann's. In the crowd were
my old pals, Steve Helstowski and John Fasoli. Among all the hundreds of faces that were there, these two guys were easy to pick right
out. Helstowski had been on Guadalcanal, too, though in a different
outfit, and had been wounded there. At one point, we even ended up in
the same foxhole, praying to get out of that hole alive. I really didn't
think both of us would make it off the island and never expected we'd
be seeing each other back in Raritan so soon. I couldn't get over it, me
and Helstowski, both back home. Steve Del Rocco, my old pinochle

playing buddy and fellow caddy, was there too. Everywhere I turned there was some face I knew. It was the best party I ever had. It was almost too much. Everything was coming at me too fast.

I wanted my own parade to be different from the usual ones we had on the tour. When I first got the word about the parade, I asked Judge George Allgair, who was organizing it, if Father Russo would say a high mass for my boys. During the whole tour, I hadn't really been able to mention them or do anything in their memory. It was time for me to step aside and honor the true heroes. Father Russo had guided me as a young boy and young man. Maybe he could guide me now because I felt like I was losing my way again in all the hoopla. The feeling that had started back at Roosevelt Base was getting worse every day as I became more famous. Soon there wouldn't be a place in the whole country where I could hang my hat without having people tug on my sleeve and ask me about the ridge. The real heroes of the ridge weren't around to tell the story and I was getting worn out. Because I was under orders, I got up and told my story in front of thousands of people but I felt like a phony. I couldn't speak for my boys. I wasn't smart enough to tell everyone who they were and what they were really like. Even now, I couldn't help them. I needed Father Russo's help. He had helped me find my way before.

While Father Russo spoke of the boys up at the pulpit, I sat with everyone from my early life. I wanted them to know about these boys and help me pray for them. We all prayed while I saw those poor, dirty-faced boys, who trusted me to get them home safely. I needed everyone's prayers. I failed those boys. One by one they each came to me and I asked each one to forgive me. I asked them but they didn't answer. And why should they? They didn't owe me a thing.

The mass continued and Father Russo spoke. "Sergeant Basilone's life will be a guide to America's youth. God has spared him for some important work."

His words helped me. I remembered the last time I came to Father Russo and prayed for guidance. There was no answer then either, but it eventually came, just like he said it would. Then I knew that the boys' answer would come too. Maybe not now and maybe not soon, but it would come. I knew it would.

★

There were twelve bands in my parade that stretched for two miles from Somerville into Raritan. Pop and Mama rode in the lead car with me in the bright sunshine, under the perfect, jewel blue sky of New Jersey at harvest time. Steve Helstowski rode with us. He was wounded at Guadalcanal and deserved to be up front of this parade as much as me. Steve and me both being alive and riding at the head of a parade through our hometown tipped me off that this was more than just a special day. Father Russo's service loosened what felt like a tourniquet around my heart and now the day seemed to have magic in it.

We crawled along Grove Street from Somerville onto Main in Raritan through thousands of cheering folks all wanting to shake my hand or pat me on the back. This kind of thing might have given me the creeps before, but now things were different. It wasn't just about me. I was free somehow. God had given me a one-day liberty to enjoy the parade.

I was looking for Marion, my first girlfriend. Somehow I felt she would be there. She had to be there, somewhere. Thousands of faces passed by. Women hung out of the windows all along Main Street and waved. Even in a crowd of a million, I could have picked her out but she wasn't there. And Carla, the widow, who had caused such a scandal by being with me, she had to be out there somewhere too. I kept looking and thought I saw one or the other of them but it always turned out to be someone else.

We wound up in a field on the Doris Duke Cornwell estate where a large stage had been built. Mrs. Cornwell was the heiress of a to-bacco fortune and the subject of our endless kid's stories during the Depression. We all knew that she ate off of solid gold plates like King Cole in our picture books and wore emeralds as big as a jaw-breaker. We thought she might drive out of her long driveway one day and decide to adopt us because we were all such special boys. Today, she donated the use of her field for the stage where 250 of us were sitting.

A rising young opera singer, a local girl named Catherine Mas-tice, sang the National Anthem and I thought she was damn good. It made me think that maybe one of these times I would sing it. Father Russo gave the invocation and then Harry Hirschfield, the master of ceremonies, took over. He introduced George Allgair, who gave me a five-thousand-dollar war bond. He said, "As representative of the love and affection in which you are held by your own people." Every-body seemed to like that. They roared and clapped and whistled. Then it was my turn. I wasn't going to tell the story of the ridge. I was just going to stand up there and say what I felt. I wasn't afraid and I hoped Sister Mary Cordula, my last teacher who got me through the eighth grade, was out in the crowd listening because I finally wasn't afraid to stand up and speak in front of people anymore.

"I want to thank you, Judge Allgair, and these very good home folks of Raritan for this wonderful gift. For all my buddies overseas

on the front lines—that they really appreciate everything you wonderful people are doing by backing the attack and buying these war
bonds." I thought I was doing okay but then feelings just came up
and choked off the rest of the things I wanted to say. I just managed
to get out, "Today is like a dream to me. Thank you all for everything from the bottom of my heart." I couldn't say any more except to
introduce Steve to everyone. Then I sat down. I had to concentrate to
keep the feelings from taking over. I didn't want to cry here, in front
of everyone, on this perfect day, but I had a hard time holding back.
I didn't know what was going on with me anymore. My emotions were
all over the place.

The stage was crowded with governors, senators, mayors and
movie stars. As far as I could see were thousands of friendly faces.
Senator Frelinghuysen got up to speak. His son was a prisoner of war
in Europe. While he spoke, Angelo's daughter, Janice, snuck up on
the platform and sat on my lap. The crowd roared with laughter and
Frelinghuysen had to stop and start over again. She was just five and
we sat there on that perfect day. Maybe it was the happiest moment
in my life. At least it was the happiest I remembered in a long time.
I was home and everyone I loved was safe.

The former mayor of New York City, Jimmy Walker, got up and
gave a funny and very smart speech. Jimmy had a reputation as a
boozer, a crapshooter and a night owl. He would have fit right in with
my unit. He started off by saying, "I shall be eternally grateful to
Sam Kaplan for waking me up." You had to hand it to Jimmy, he
didn't strut around like these stuffed shirt politicians who wanted
you to think that when they weren't doing their jobs, they were home
saying the rosary. A bunch of phony bastards, most of them. At least
with Jimmy, you knew who you were dealing with. After the joke, he

got down to business and gave the best speech of the day. People loved him to begin with because he was one of us, but his speech really grabbed you by the heart. He said, "I used to think I came from an important and rather significant place, but I had to come out to Raritan, a little place with a normal population of six thousand, to see real enthusiasm and the biggest crowd I've seen in ten years." Everybody went nuts for him, cheering and whistling so that you couldn't hear yourself think. He went on and said a lot of nice things about Italians and what they did for the country and then he said a few nice things about me, that I was an inspiration to all Americans and so on.

Catherine Mastice came back and sang a song written by two local boys, one was Joe Memoli, the organist at St. Ann's. The song was called "Manila John." Now I had my own song like Bob Hope. Harry Herschfield called Pop up to the microphone from the front row. He nudged Pop to say something to everybody in Italian and Pop stood right up there and I think told everybody how proud he was to be an American, which was what he usually told everybody in English anyway. All his Italian Club buddies nodded their heads and people gave him a nice round of applause. He was as proud as he could be. We were selling bonds up in front of the stage as fast as we could take the money.

We all sang "God Bless America" and the rally ended. When it was all over we counted up $1.4 million worth of bonds sold. Virginia got in a car back to the city. She probably didn't want to confuse things by meeting my parents right now and I didn't try to stop her. I managed to slip back to the house.

In Pop's place, it was a madhouse again but we had the sense this time to post a few close friends as guards on the front porch so at least we wouldn't be constantly interrupted. I just wanted to lie on the rug and play with Janice. Everybody had questions and I answered some about how George was doing and where I was headed next. I didn't want to be rude but my head was still swimming with everything that had happened and I just wanted to be quiet for a while. Janice was fascinated with the blue ribbon and the Medal of Honor around my neck. We talked quietly while I answered her little-girl questions about war. My kid brother Donald, who was only fourteen, kept bouncing around us wanting attention, so I acted out the comic book version of the Battle of Bloody Ridge for him. I showed him how I mowed down the evil Japs on the Island of Death. My family let me relax with the kids for a while. We all knew it wouldn't last very long. I was due back in New York that night with an early report the next morning. Soon food was on the table and we all sat down together. I wanted to make everybody happy, but I wasn't feeling right. One minute I was okay, then the next I felt like I just lived through an ambush. Like I should have been killed but somehow they missed me. Then the next minute I felt like I did when I thought of guys who didn't make it. It was all mixed up together in my head. I couldn't tell what was going on. I didn't know if I was sad, happy or something else, maybe a combination. I was quieter than normal and that was fine. I didn't really have to say anything else. I was home.

The next day I was back on the money trail with Virginia and the Army, Navy and movie boys. For the next few weeks we were all over the East Coast. The tour ended and I was happy to get it over with. When we kicked off back on September 9, we had a goal of $15 billion. We raised over $19 billion by the time we wrapped it up on October 2. We did our job and then some, and we were all happy as hell. When they told me about all the money we got it was the first time I felt in my gut that I was helping the guys who were carrying the ammo. I also felt kind of like a spoiled brat. I remembered how badly me and the other guys had treated our first press officer back on Roosevelt Base and I felt a little ashamed. I always meant to write and apologize but I'm even worse at writing than I am at speaking.

Virginia and I had been together almost every day and night for the past month. We were close, the kind of close that happens when you are thrown together in the middle of a storm. The storm was over now and it was time for her to go back to her life and me to go back to mine. We both knew it but somehow I think we wished things were different. My life was the Marine Corps and until the Corps was done with me, I would go wherever they wanted me to. She had to make a living and that meant California for her. Maybe she would have left the movies, I don't know, I wasn't going to ask her. The idea of getting married must have crossed her mind, too, but when it came down to brass tacks, I didn't want to get married. We didn't have to talk about it. Everything was perfectly clear. Her flight was leaving from Newark. We held each other while the car waited with the engine running. We had one last kiss that said just about everything.

★

At Headquarters on Church Street the CO handed me a thirty-day pass and a smart salute and I was suddenly at liberty with nothing but time on my hands. Home was the place I needed to be. I headed south on the next train and just that quick I was back to being just another Marine sitting on a train.

There were only two bedrooms in Pop's house, one was for all the kids. I got the privilege of having a bed to myself since only Dolores

and Donald were left in the house. All the other kids had moved out.
For the first few days, I made a point of going out to see old pals in
town. I wore civilian clothes so people would start to see me again,
not the war hero. The knocks on Pop's front door at all hours died off
as people got used to seeing me around town again. This was just the
way I liked it. I didn't need any more special treatment.

The only people who kept coming around were the kids in town.
They came over and shuffled around on the sidewalk in front of the
house until there were enough of them to give them the nerve to call
for me. They'd stand out there and yell "Manila John! Come on out!"
None of them had the nerve to come and knock on the door, they
just stood out there and yelled. I'd always come out to see them.
Kids made me happy. When I came out they'd stand there, afraid to
say anything else until I started talking. I never had a problem talking in front of groups of kids. It wasn't anything like being with
adults. With kids the time just passed while they asked questions
and I told them stories. I talked to them about when I was growing
up and then, because they always wanted to know, what it was like to
be in the war.

At night friends and neighbors called to invite me to their houses
or out someplace for dinner. Women called all the time. One night I
gave a speech at Pop's Italian Club for a war bond night they put together on their own. Orlando's Tavern became a regular stop during
the first weeks at home. The owner, Tony, wrote to local boys who
were overseas and sent them packages with all kinds of stuff he
strong-armed out of his customers. He had just about all of our pictures up on his wall. All night Tony kept the drinks coming and I
did my best to keep up with him. The pictures on the wall kept me
company when the conversation died down around the bar. I knew

just about all these guys—DeLorenzo, Baldini, Al Matteis. All of them had their asses in the sling now. Not me. I was sipping my drink.

Sleep was still tough to come by. I couldn't sleep through the night, and if a car backfired or a screen door banged, I was flat on the deck in a split second. It was embarrassing and scared the hell out of people when I had to pick myself up and had the shakes. The only thing that helped me besides Tony's booze was talking with Father Russo. He said it would just take time to get myself calm again inside. He and I spent almost as much time together as when I was a confused kid who didn't know where I was headed in life. It seemed like the path I found in life was blocked now. I wasn't going any further in the Marines unless it was to a desk in an office somewhere. Goddamn I hated the thought of it but it was starting to be as clear as the nose on my face. I was going to end up as a desk jockey behind a pile of papers—the worst place in the world for me.

Ed Sullivan, the big-shot newspaperman, invited me to a big rally they were going to have at the Capitol Theatre in New York. Even though I was on leave, I wanted to go. I couldn't keep drinking Tony's liquor for free, he'd go broke with me hanging around. I showed up at Toots Shor's place before the show and Ed introduced me around. Toots was first in line and him and me hit it off right away. Everybody loved Toots, even women, which was hard to figure because Toots was no John Barrymore in the looks department. I had a few drinks and was feeling fine. The time came and we jumped in cabs and headed over to the Capitol.

The cab ride to the theater was something like a Jap shelling. New York cabbies are always in a hurry. I held on the best I could while the world banged and jumped all around me. We got to the theater and went in the back door. Ed was off in a second, taking care of last-minute arrangements, and I stood there in the dark listening to the people yakking in the audience. Then it started coming over me again, the feeling that I was ready to run. Everything around me was black, except for a faint light from a podium desk near the curtain rope. Faces came out of the black, faces from the ridge. My heart was going like I'd just run a mile. I heard our heavies firing and the goddamn mortars overhead. I started saying an Our Father, concentrating on every word.

I don't know how much time went by with me like that but it seemed like the next second when I heard Ed announce my name. I took the deep breaths like Virginia taught me and walked out into the bright lights. The whole place seemed to explode. Everybody stood up and cheered like it was the Army-Navy game. Holy shit, I thought, now what? I just stood there looking around, trying to get a grip on myself. Ed was clapping right along with the rest of them. It seemed like they weren't ever going to stop. They went on and on and on. I stepped right up to the microphone and started talking. I told them what I saw on the ridge. Terrible things. Things I'd never told anybody before. But here I was in front of a few thousand of the swankiest ladies and gents in the whole world and I was spilling my guts about what went on up there. I couldn't stop myself. I kept going and going and barreled right through the whole bloody mess. I don't think they were expecting that but there it was. I was soaking wet and out of breath. The place was quiet as a church. Then I just turned and walked off. I had to get someplace where I could be by myself. Somebody showed me to a dressing room where I laid down on a couch. I could hear them cheering for fifteen minutes. Ed came by the room later when all the noise died down and told me it was the longest standing ovation he'd ever heard. I was glad for his sake but I felt like I was coming apart. Whatever was going on with me, it wasn't getting any better. The shit had really hit the fan.

★ 11 ★

"I'm Staying with My Boys. They Need Me."

Even after the tour ended I was invited to speak at functions all over. Ed Sullivan and Toots kept inviting me to different nights they put together in New York. These nights weren't just private parties for having fun, these two guys could put the arm on people as well as any two shakedown artists I ever met. They worked like hell to squeeze money out of the swells. We were all over town, from Toots's place to the Copa and the Diamond Horseshoe. It was like being a guest of the mayor, even better. On the invitation list at a few get-togethers were several European families who escaped from the Nazis and were living in New York. The Rothschild family, who were wealthy bankers, and even an archduke named Franz Josef were happy to put their money into bonds. They shook my hand until I thought it was going to come off.

It was a good time running around with the Broadway boys. Toots was partial to dice and got us into ex-Mayor Jimmy Walker's floating craps game a few nights after we met our quota of bond sales. Ed didn't go for gambling, so he begged off early. Watching Toots operate in a nightclub and later at the craps tables in Jimmy's west side warehouse made over into a casino, reminded me of running Lolita's place in Manila years ago. It wasn't good to think about what probably happened to her when the Japs kicked Mac and my old army outfit out of the country, but what choice did I have? It wasn't something you can just put out of your mind. She was my first real girlfriend. Maybe if I was smarter I would have married her and got her out of there in time.

Outside of Raritan, everybody I knew was in the fight. Every minute of the day somebody or something reminded me of it. After the party was over with Toots for the night, it was just me and the voice inside that said people were in trouble. People I loved like my own family were facing the Japs. I kept getting the message that a lot of people needed me. It was the voice again, the whispering, telling me I was off the path.

The damn newspaper reporters never let up either. One after the other, they'd make the trip all the way to Raritan and show up on the doorstep. Of course they wanted to talk about one thing, trying to make me into some kind of Superman. What else could I say? This fella James Golden came down one day and I let him into the house.

He goes over the story again and again. He can tell I don't really want to talk about it but he doesn't let up. Finally I let him have it. "Look, Golden," I said, "forget my part. There wasn't a man on the Canal that night who doesn't own a piece of that medal awarded to me." This shut him up for a while. He excused himself and that ended the interview. Why didn't they ever want to know about the other boys? It was getting to be too much for me, everybody always wanting to put me on the spot. In the papers I read where even General MacArthur called me a "One Man Army." There was no getting away from it. All anybody wanted to hear about was the comic book story of me against the whole Jap army. I was feeling like nobody who wasn't on the ridge would ever know the truth, no matter how many times I said it. I couldn't sleep for shit.

Before my thirty-day leave expired I got a call from the CO at Marine Headquarters in New York. He told me I could have my pick of desk jobs but they wanted me posted in Washington. The War Department had more plans for me and they wanted to keep me close. The last place in the world I wanted to be was behind a desk. I told him no thanks, get me back in the action. Send me back to my unit. Or put me with the guys going to take back Manila. That was no dice, he said, and I blew my stack. It was like I was asking to move into the White House. Carlo was in the house and told me I should cool off.

Me and Carlo took a walk. We walked a lot, him and me. I needed to be walking to think straight and he would come right along with me. He always listened to me and he got an earful that day. I made a decision. I had to get back in the fight. It was the only way for me. He was having a hard time understanding why I needed to go. "Johnny, you can do anything you want now. You could even be a movie star if you wanted to." He always understood everything, ever since we were kids. But this one, he couldn't understand.

"Movie star? I'd hate to do that for a living," I told him. I didn't envy Eddie Bracken or Garfield. On our night patrols they told me plenty about the bowing and scraping they had to do just to feed themselves. Especially Garfield, who was a more serious type, a real artist. It looked to me like Hollywood was making him crazy. And in the end, he said, you get old and nobody gives a shit about your movies. But he couldn't stop now. He was going to make a pile of money before it was too late. If that was the best I could wish for, no thanks. I'd go back to Philgas before I went into the movies.

We walked over to Angelo's shop. He was the oldest and a cool head, so we always went over things with him.

"John, don't go back. You did enough for the war," Angie said. Always practical, that Angelo. It was a simple math problem for him. Once you put in so much, you're all done. Your bill is paid. I couldn't blame my brothers. It was the way most people thought.

But this was the way it happened. I was in Angelo's tailor shop that afternoon. My brothers Angelo and Carlo were both telling me every reason I shouldn't go back to the war. They went through everything they could think of, all the things I could have if I stayed—a family, any job I wanted, all the money I could ever spend. I'd be the most famous man that ever lived in Raritan, maybe even in New Jersey, except for George Washington when he crossed the Delaware. They laid it on thick but it was all crap to me. I didn't want to tell them this was what I was thinking. These were the best things they could imagine. They were what they wanted most in the whole world and I didn't want them to think I was making fun of it. But it was all just crap. All the time they were talking, in my head, I was already seeing myself back with my boys. Who could teach them how to set up a gun faster than me? Who learned from the best in the business, the Old Man, Chesty Puller, how to pull them out of a jam under fire? Everything my brothers said only made it clearer, until it was just as plain as day. I saw my path again. I could almost smell the gun oil.

I got my orders to report to the Washington Navy Yard. They gave me a job until they could figure out what to do with me next—guard duty at the Navy Yard, a desk job. Jesus Christ, I was so far out of the action I could have been in a coal mine. It was almost a year now that I'd been away from my unit. Only God knew what kind of mess they were in now and here I was guarding Washington, D.C. I was starting to understand why Chesty thought he could always find the real Marines in the brig. That's exactly where I was headed unless I got someone to start listening to me.

I walked along the yard talking with the welders and pipe fitters during the day and at night I got drunk as a skunk. Phyllis called me a few times from Reisterstown. She knew what it was doing to me to sit behind a desk all day. Complaining wasn't my style but she could always get it out of me if something was bothering me. I finally just had to admit I just hated this desk job like the clap. She didn't know what the clap was and I didn't explain it.

"I'm a damn museum piece," I just about yelled at her. To her it was most important to be safe and take care of other folks. That was her way. She was the oldest, even above Angelo, and always wanted to take care of everybody and get into everybody's business. I didn't even try to explain myself to her. My way was a Marine's way so there wasn't any use talking about it anymore—except to other Marines.

At the Navy Yard, I told the CO from the first day on the job that I wanted to go back to my unit. His job was to keep me available for pictures and speeches whenever they needed me. He wasn't transferring me out for anything in the world. Sometimes even other Marines, like this CO, didn't understand. A few weeks later, he came back and offered me a commission as an officer. My job would stay the same, I'd just get a bump in my pay grade.

"I'm a regular Marine. And that's how I want to stay," I told him. From the first day we weren't that friendly, now he thought I was looking down my nose at him. He was a career desk jockey as far as I could tell, how would he know how much I hated doing this desk job? I kept telling him in different ways that I was a guy who kept Marines alive in the field. That didn't matter. I was his goose that laid the golden eggs—a real, live Medal of Honor Marine from Guadalcanal. The clincher was that Guadalcanal was our first victory over the Japs and that made it a big deal. If it had been the second or third battle, I could have just kept doing my job.

I kept asking but the answer was always no. If they wouldn't send me back to my own unit, put me in the unit that was going to take back Manila. No. Pick a combat unit and put me in it. No. Bring in Bob Powell and give him a medal. No. Or Mitch Paige, he already had the medal. No.

The Navy Yard had a couple of bars nearby. Most looked and smelled like the bilge of a freighter—dark and oily. A few of the long-shoremen who made these places their second homes had been in the fight. I found a few of these guys who had seen action. There wasn't much to say to anyone else. Stumbling along the waterfront one night after guarding my nation's capital all day and unwinding with my new buddies, I saw I was likely to end up like the old beggars on Flinders Street in Melbourne unless something changed. Maybe I would sell my medal for a drink one day.

New orders came. I was supposed to be a guest at the National Association of Manufacturers' dinner in New York. It felt like a prison break. I was ready to go before I heard the end of the order. I belted on my tailor-fit, freshly pressed Charlies. They were snug in the waist and neck. A solid month of boozing along the waterfront had put ten pounds on me.

This New York get-together was the kingfish of them all. Tycoons from textile, steel, rubber and all the big industries filled the grand ballroom of the Waldorf-Astoria. A few movie and radio stars were in the mix including Ed Sullivan, who made sure I met everybody in the room. It was okay meeting all the important people but the guy I really wanted to talk to was my old CO, General A. A. Vandegrift, who had put the Medal of Honor around my neck back in Australia. He was one of the five servicemen who was going to be on the stage with me. I made a beeline for him. He was a good guy and gave me all his attention once I started in on what I wanted. It was pretty simple. After a little warm-up where I brought up the name of Chesty Puller and explained what I did all day, all I said was, "Sir, I want the fleet." He was one Marine who knew what the hell I was talking about.

"I'll see what I can do," he said. That was good enough for me. The ceremony kicked off and me and the general and everybody else got to say their bit. Checkbooks came out and I don't know how much we raised that night but it wasn't chicken feed, that's for sure. Sullivan and I made the rounds to a few joints including Toots's place that night. It was a good night. It was the first time in almost a year that I thought I might get my job back.

Ten days after I got back to the Navy Yard my new orders came through. I was shipping out to Camp Pendleton. I was going to bring a platoon of young boots up to snuff. There was another island in the Pacific that needed our attention.

Amphibious exercises—
Oceanside, California, 1944

Pendleton

It was coming up to Christmas. My orders were to ship out on December 27. I had a few days' liberty to get my affairs in order so I spent them mostly in Raritan. The nights were easier for me now. I wasn't down at Orlando's Tavern every night. My course was finally set.

I had time to think about how things happened to me. Just like I'd seen trouble with the Japanese when I was a young caddy and I saw the war coming when I returned from Manila, I started to see something else now. I started to see the end of the war. I saw that we would win. Ever since the Canal, we beat the Japs every place we matched up. In most fights it was about ten of their dead to each one of ours. These were my thoughts, my sort of daydreaming during the day.

At night, when the voice in my head let me know if I was on my path or not, if I was being a fool or not—I never got a fix on where my path was going after the war. I thought to myself I'd stay in, join

Chesty and make the Corps my career, but I got no answer to that. I listened but nothing came back. This didn't worry me the way it used to. I knew everything would be clear when the time was right.

Days went by quickly as we got ready for Christmas 1943. Angelo and Phyllis had children now and Donald and Dolores were still young enough so that we had enough kids to make it a real Christmas. Being around the kids gave me the feeling that it might be time for kids of my own. If I could find some way to pay for them, I thought I'd like to have lots of kids, maybe ten. It was the marriage part that made me wonder if I was cut out for it. I loved women, maybe too much. I loved all colors, all sizes. They were a tough habit to live without. Plenty of times I couldn't walk down the street without looking at every skirt that passed by. I never said anything, of course, I gave them respect, but I did look at an awful lot of them. Maybe I'd always be like this and what wife could put up with that? Especially if they found out that my wild oats were spread halfway around the world and back. I didn't like to think that maybe it was too late for me, but maybe it was.

We went to midnight mass on Christmas Eve and prayed for George back in Pendleton, who was due to ship out any day and for Alphonse, who was with Patton's tank corps in Europe. Having three of us in the war was wearing on Mama and Pop. Mama said the rosary constantly. She saved all our letters and postcards in a special box that she kept in with the fine linen. She read our letters over and over. Catherine and Mary looked in on her almost every day and Phyllis called from Maryland on Sundays. They knew she was suffering in her quiet way. They made us boys promise to write to her every week. We knew our letters were the only comfort she had.

The day after Christmas I went on another long walk with Carlo.

Over the holiday I looked hard at what it was to have a big family like mine. Something was telling me that was the way to go, to find that kind of love for myself. My days as a lady killer were fun but they were going. It was easy to have a girl in every port when I was with the boys and we didn't know if we were going to even be alive next week. But now, at home, where I could be quiet and think about what I really wanted, I knew something inside me was changing. Carlo was married, Angelo was married. Everybody in the family had their special one, except me. Me and Carlo took off walking again, way out beyond the country club, while I sorted out my thoughts. Maybe I'd track down Marion, my childhood sweetheart, if she wasn't married already. Maybe I'd meet a few of the girls my sisters knew.

As we're coming back to the house, we saw Phyllis on the front porch. A feeling came over me. It was one that I couldn't shake. I got the feeling that my life was like a card game where a run of luck had come along and helped me sweep the table. I was holding all the chips now. Any card player knew the odds after a run like I had. My luck had to end soon. It was just like the vision I had on the golf course that said I would have trouble with the Japs. As much as I didn't like what I saw, then or now, I learned not to ignore it. It was plain, right in front of my face. I wasn't coming back. That was clear.

We stayed out of the house and talked on the tiny porch. The wind whipped up as the sun dropped. I was thinking hard, trying to decide whether this new, terrible feeling was one I wanted to tell them. I'd always told Carlo and Phyllis everything. Even my silly ideas about trouble with Japanese people, I told them. But that was nothing compared to this feeling that I would never come back. There was no way around it. They should know. The conversation got around to me shipping out tomorrow and it being nice that I was going to be on the same base as George. There wasn't any real clever way to say it that I could think of, so I just came right out with it.

"I won't be coming back," I said. They both looked at me. They didn't know what I meant until a few moments passed and I didn't say anything else. Then they got upset as hell.

Carlo came right back at me. "Johnny, what are you saying such a thing for? Don't say that." Phyllis looked me over real close, and then decided she didn't want to hear it. "No," was all she said. She was smart, maybe the smartest in the family. She knew about intuition, female and otherwise. Since my two earlier predictions had been true, she caught on right away that I wasn't just talking through my hat. Somehow, someway, I saw things that other people didn't see—things in the future. All my sister could do was deny it and hope she was right. There was no sense in me repeating it. I didn't like it any more than they did. It was either true or it wasn't. Repeating it would only upset everyone more and maybe put the jinx on me even worse. Maybe Phyllis was right and I was wrong this time. She turned her back on me and walked into the house. Our little talk was over.

★

I got to the front gate of Camp Pendleton early in the morning before the sun had a chance to burn through the morning chill. The dry grass hilltops of the camp poked through a white blanket of ocean mist. They looked like a woman's knees surrounded by the soft, white bedsheets of a good hotel like the Waldorf-Astoria. I was leaving that life of luxury for good, but it was okay by me. At the gate, the guards snapped to and waved us through. For the first time in over a year, I knew I was where I belonged. The ride in told me that things had changed a lot since I came to visit George a few months ago before the war bond drive. Acres of tents stretched out on either side of the main road where only empty fields had been before. The sun was barely up, but jeeps and trucks were already raising clouds of yellow dust as they moved down the long rows of crates, vehicles and Quonset huts. It was a sprawling military boomtown with tacked-up road markers at dusty crossroads pointing to various headquarter buildings and supply depots. The drive took twenty minutes from the gate to the barracks area of my new unit, the Fifth Marine division, 27th Marines, First Battalion, C Company. Washington had boosted me to platoon sergeant and given me orders to whip a machine gun platoon into shape for an amphibious assault in the Pacific. They didn't know where, they just knew it was going to be rough. The Japs were fighting like cornered animals. There wasn't going to be any surrender. It looked like every last man and boy in Japan was going to die before they would give up.

I reported to company HQ, checked in and was directed to the sergeants' billet. This area of the camp looked like the boomtown had just gone bust. The hills that looked soft and brown from the coast road were dry and dusty up close. The barracks were just a shade different than the dust, a drab yellow. What was supposed to be the mighty new Fifth Division was a ghost town. On first inspection of the barracks I found a few young boots who had arrived ahead of the others. They looked happy as hell to see me. They had been there a few days already and were bored silly. They jumped to attention when I walked into the big, empty barracks. I gave my first command under my new rank. "At ease men." I introduced myself and got their names. They were just a couple of skinny young kids who couldn't have been more than twenty years old. It was good to be back. I could help these boys.

I saw right away they needed something to do so I put them to work getting the place squared away before the others arrived. The first military equipment I requisitioned were buckets, mops and pine oil floor cleaner. This was going to become the home of the fearsome C Company. It took two days of cleaning to bring the barracks up to snuff.

The muster roll started to fill out with the first shipment of boys from the Paramarine Training Battalion, parachute troops. Right away there were problems with these guys. They thought they were the elite fighting force of the Corps and didn't mind saying so. This took a few direct talks, face-to-face, actually nose-to-nose, to get my point across that they were now part of the finest naval assault force ever assembled and all their candy-assed parachute training wasn't going to help them here. Soon enough they got the picture.

A young sergeant, Biz Bisonette, checked in at the same time as the paratroopers and assisted with the training of the company. He was a tough cookie and an expert in hand-to-hand combat. When it came to jungle fighting, we learned our lesson on the Canal. Any frontline jungle fighter would need hand-to-hand skills as much as any weapon in the arsenal. The first order of business was getting the boys on the firing range with the .30 cal. machine guns—the old water-cooled Brownies and the lighter, air-cooled version. The air-cooled version weighed only thirty-six pounds compared to over ninety pounds for the heavies when they were filled with water and loaded with ammunition. Troops were still issued the old Springfield bolt-action rifles as their personal weapons but the Garand M-1s that we had liberated from our Army guests on Guadalcanal were starting to replace the Springfields.

I drilled the boys on the mechanics and took them through the book, my book, on machine gunning. The effective range of the M1919A4 machine gun was a thousand yards. The flat trajectory mode meant the rounds would travel parallel to the ground and not rise above the height of a man for six hundred yards. They operated by recoil and were assisted by expanding powder gas.

The care and maintenance and of course, blindfolded setup, repair and tear down, were all chapters in my book that my new boys would learn better than anything they ever studied in their lives. These new boots would also know how to operate all the weapons on the battlefield, ours and the enemy's, in case they had to use them. We practiced "snapping in" or setting up various pieces of equipment until everyone in the company could recognize any piece of a weapon by its feel and set it up in the dark.

A vet sergeant, Ray Windle, came on board in the next week or so. He'd seen plenty of action and knew the score on a jungle battlefield. He was a tough talker like Chesty and a hothead, so I knew he'd be an easy mark in a card game and this gave me hope for off-duty entertainment. I couldn't fraternize with the boys to the point of gambling with them, so I was left with the noncoms. This cut my chances for extra income in half. But I was glad to have Windle with us. He was the kind of battle commander we needed around these boys. They looked so damn young, some of them. They looked like the sons or the kid brothers of the boys in the 1/7. Malaria and combat hadn't touched these boys yet.

Entire battalions started arriving. Many were boys who had trained to be paratroopers, like the earlier group. Once Topside caught on that you can't parachute into a jungle, where most of our work was going to be, it became our job to retrain them in amphibious assault tactics and jungle warfare. All these paratroop boys, from the first ones I had my nose-to-nose discussions with, to the latest arrivals, all griped when it came time to get their nice shiny paratrooper boots muddy and take their bloused pants out of their boot tops. The shiny boots and bloused pants were what told everybody that these guys were special. Now, because bloused pants in a jungle would only funnel water and mud into their boots, I ordered them to wear their pants outside their boots and loose like everybody else. And their bright, shiny boots that told everybody that they arrived at a fight from the air without getting their feet dirty, were about to get scuffed and covered with dust. It was humiliating and took a few days for most of them to get over it. They also had the pleasure of humping heavy steel guns on sweaty twenty-mile marches instead of floating through the air under clean, green silk. Things moved slower in a machine gun company and would move even slower in a jungle. It took some getting used to for them. I cut them some slack except for the real hard cases. I was part of an elite force once myself. We were just like these guys.

★

Even on base, I couldn't get away from the women and the truth was, I didn't want to. At the mess hall, three times a day, the staff who served us was mostly women. They were Marines and were given every bit of respect they deserved, but even dungaree utility uniforms couldn't hide all their curves. There was plenty of whispering about me being a war hero and all but I still wasn't too good at getting special treatment, even from ladies.

It had to happen, me being like a pig in a pastry shop when it came to females. I saw her as I came down the serving line. She was dark—Italian or Spanish kind of dark. Black hair, dark eyes and she walked around like she owned the place. Damn, I had to get to know that one.

At first, it was just a look between us. There was nothing on it. No wink or smile like we knew something special between us. It was just her looking at me from a distance, taking stock of me, and me looking back at her. I nodded and she might have nodded, or not, but she wasn't falling all over herself to get to know me. I liked this girl. She was tough. And she was a sergeant, so the rules against fraternizing didn't apply. That little look and nod was all it took to get the rumor mill started up.

Sgt. Lena Riggi heard from her lady friends all about me. They went on and on about what a hero I was, how brave I was and that I knew all the movie stars. Sgt. Riggi waited for them to tire out, looked at them and said, "So what." She was the girl for me. When she saw me again she pretended like no one had told her a thing about me and that was just the way I liked it.

The pace of training picked up. With so many men and so much equipment piled into the camp, exercises went on twenty-four hours a day so that everyone would get some time at the various gunnery ranges, obstacle courses and in the pools. The boys had to take a twenty-five-foot plunge into icy water in an exercise that simulated abandoning a ship. They had to tread water and practice rescuing a disabled man in the water. This was nothing compared to some open ocean exercises including one where they were dropped off a rubber dingy about a quarter mile from the beach, wished good luck and told to swim back. My focus stayed on the gunnery range. Everything I learned on the ridge and in the jungle, these boys were going to know.

It was clear to everybody because of all the buildup that we were headed toward a hell of a fight somewhere. We practiced beach landings and assaulting fortified positions. My machine gunners needed steady hands and cool heads for the work we had assigned to us. Our most important assault exercise was providing covering fire for a demolition man in an attack on a fortified position. We drilled by laying a line of covering fire about a foot above a man's shoulder as he ran toward an objective. One slip or a half second of distraction meant we would shoot our own man. It was a tricky maneuver on a firing range. Under bombardment on a beach it would be ten times worse and fatal for both the gunners and the demo man if it failed.

We worked the boys hard every day so that most of them just dropped on their bunks when the day was over. But not always. If they had the energy, they might head to one of the slop chutes—beer joints—off base in Oceanside or go to one of the movies we showed every night at a big outdoor theater in camp. Some were too young to get beer, like eager young private Tom Nass, so I got it for them if they asked me. I figured if they were old enough to die, they were old enough to try and get drunk on 3.2 beer.

My off-duty angle was to get Lena to come to the movies with me, so I asked for her phone number one day when I saw her at the mess. It wasn't anything like the love scenes they show in the movies. She wrote down her number like she was filling out a requisition form for more beans. There wasn't any giggling or doe eyes as she handed it to me, just a little smile and a polite warning not to call too late. She was all right, I thought.

Even better than the movies, there was a celebration planned to inaugurate our division. The Fifth Marine Division was going to receive its regimental colors, our battle flags, one for each regiment, the 26th, 27th and 28th. A big ceremony was planned and was going to be followed by "holiday routine" which meant the rest of the day after the ceremony was liberty on base for most of us. It was going to be a tough morning for Lena because of the special menu that day, but she would be free in the afternoon. The dedication ceremony was attended by all the top brass including our commanding general, Keller E. Rockey, and Brig. Gen. Arthur Warton. We all assembled on the main parade grounds, the band played and we saw our standard unfurled for the first time. I generally don't go in for much parading and such but this gave me a moment where I was proud as hell. We were at our full strength now with all muster rolls full and we were completely equipped. We had trained hard for weeks and if the call came, I knew we were ready. We all faced the flags and presented a smart salute as the band played.

We even had movie stars Edmund O'Brien and Ann Blyth there to celebrate with us. There was no way in hell I was going to get up in front of these twenty-five thousand Marines and give a speech and I'm glad they didn't ask me to. I felt happy as hell to be one of the faces in the crowd again. The rest of the day was filled with baseball, football and basketball games where I am sure all of the money in camp changed hands at least once. These gyrenes, like everyone I ever met, were crazy as bedbugs for gambling. Technically, it wasn't allowed, but I never saw a thing when it came to endless card and craps games that went on, and I don't think anybody else did either. I was the last guy in the world to tell anybody they shouldn't gamble. If they were old enough to die, they were old enough to piss their money away if they wanted to.

Lena met up with me and I got a good look at her for the first time. She walked easy, like a girl walks when she's on her way somewhere important. She didn't have the kind of sway girls can turn on when they want to impress a guy. She walked right up and stood square on her feet with a beautiful, big smile. Damn she had a big, beautiful smile with a mouthful of teeth you could see a mile away.

We probably walked several miles going from one ball game to the next, talking all the way. She came from a big Italian family, onion farmers up near Portland, Oregon. That accounted for the stance she had that I recognized right away. She grew up working hard like the farm kids I grew up with. It generally made for a strong back and square shoulders, even on women. She didn't ask me a thing about the medal. She didn't even seem much interested in war stories. That was good because I wasn't the guy to tell any. We just walked and talked like any other two people getting to know each other. Both being Italian and Catholic, there was a lot we already knew and didn't have to say. Mostly we talked about our families. She didn't mind walking, which was a good sign because I always had to walk to think clearly. We walked past rows of parked tanks, trucks and all kinds of artillery. She joined the Corps because she wanted to be with the top outfit in the war effort. It wasn't hard to figure out with all this hardware around us and only a few hours left of liberty that we didn't have all the time in the world to get to know each other. The talk always circled back to family and how much we missed them.

That was in February. Through March and April we got to see each other once or twice a week. Her barracks were over a mile from my sergeants' billet and our schedules made it tough to have more than a few hours together at any one time. We went to the movies on base when we could and if we could get in, we had sodas at the PX. I had pretty much stopped boozing except for the few times I went with the boys into Oceanside and ended up crowded into a bar with a bunch of hooting youngsters. The 3.2 beer these places served was so weak you'd get dizzier going back and forth to the pisser than from the alcohol in it. This kind of party didn't have the kick for me that it used to. I didn't have all the steam to blow off like these younger guys and I couldn't take their money playing cards, so I was just sitting most of the time chewing the fat. With all the live fire exercises we were doing, the last thing I wanted were gunners with the shakes, so I steered clear of drinking contests and encouraged my boys to do the same. We were heading into a real shooting war. Anybody who came back could get good and drunk then. They didn't listen. Neither did I when I was their age.

★

The months rolled by with training continuing at the same pace. We worked a lot on physical training, getting our lungs and legs to the point where we could hump steel and supplies uphill or through deep sand all day. It was hard to have energy left over to see Lena even though I was thinking of her all the time now. She was thinking of me, too, and wasn't shy about telling me how she felt. May rolled around and George and the 4th Division got their orders. They were first at bat, we were on deck. My time with Lena was almost up. There were some things I wanted to know before it was all gone.

I wanted to know what it was like to love somebody the way Pop loved Mama. At least I wanted a few days, or weeks if I could get it, to know what it was like to be married. I wanted to be able to say I love you a few times and mean it. Maybe it was something we wouldn't have done if we weren't in a rush, but Lena agreed to marry me. We set the date for July 10, 1944. Within a day of saying yes, she started spinning out lists of things that needed to be done and I got an early taste of married life. She had always wanted a big, white wedding with all the trimmings. All I had to do now was come up with the money somehow.

The camp chaplain told Lena he needed two weeks to give her instruction. It was a Catholic Church requirement. All brides-to-be must have instruction on the details of Catholic married life. He was strict with her and insisted she start right away before she got swamped with planning the wedding. She told him she couldn't give him two weeks and he insisted. She refused and held her ground just like she did the first time we laid eyes on each other. To me the back and forth between her and the padre was funny. The way she stood up to this man, who spoke for the Catholic Church, made me laugh whenever she told me about it. She didn't see it that way and I had to wipe the smile off my face when she started in talking about it. She finally had enough of the good father's advice and told him so.

"What are you going to tell me?" she said. "You've never been married." That was the end of her Catholic instruction. We found Father Paul Bradley of St. Mary's in Oceanside to marry us. One thing that was getting clear was I liked this girl more every day.

The afternoon of the tenth came and I was in the church waiting for her. The time scheduled for the ceremony was three o'clock. At quarter of, all the twenty-five guests had arrived, including my CO, Colonel Duryea, Lou Plain, the executive officer for the outfit, Lena's officer-in-charge, Sgt. Frank Budemy, and all the ladies from her reserve outfit. Three o'clock came and went. I didn't think she was the type to get cold feet but after fifteen minutes I started thinking maybe it was all a bit too fast for her after all. Twenty minutes went by. The best man went out to the steps of the church to wait for her. Twenty-five minutes late and in tears, my bride showed up in the one cab that operated in Oceanside. The cabbie had forgotten about her on her wedding day.

After a few moments for Lena to dry her eyes, she walked down the short aisle of the little church. She told me she had always wanted a big, fancy wedding with lots of people and a big pipe organ playing, but what she got was kind of small and plain. With our twenty-five guests there were a few extra from camp and a few local people who had heard about it and came to pay their respects. A few reporters came down from Los Angeles. As she walked down the aisle the church organist played on a small, electric organ in the corner. She stared straight ahead, nervous as a cat on Frank's arm. He was standing in for her father. She admitted later that she was glad it wasn't a big, long aisle, with a blasting pipe organ and thousands of people watching her. She might have fainted.

At the altar all the hoopla didn't matter anymore. Father Bradley recited the vows and I looked into her eyes like I never looked at a woman before. These were the eyes that I wanted to remember when the dark nights closed around me in a jungle somewhere. They were big, beautiful brown eyes. We said our vows. Father Bradley said I could kiss the bride. I did. Then I told him that he could kiss her, too.

Our reception was at the Carlsbad Hotel, just down the road. This was the place the Hollywood crowd stayed when they were around town making war movies. The reception wasn't fancy, with meat and everything else being rationed, but even so we managed to have a pretty decent dinner with some of the people from our units. Most of them didn't stay, making up excuses about a night maneuver or something they had to get back to in camp. None of us had much money. Everybody knew that I was pretty well tapped after paying for the ceremony and I'd have to pay for them if they stayed to eat. A few of Lena's girlfriends stayed and the few fellas from my unit got a drink at the bar and sat with us, saying they weren't hungry. After dinner, we spent our honeymoon night in a room upstairs. We were happy together. Even though it was a rush, I knew I did the right thing. I think she felt that way too.

We were on the train early the next day to see Lena's people in Portland. The train was hot, crowded and dirty. We managed to get a seat while most of the Marines and sailors on board had to stand. We traveled until late the following morning, over twenty-four hours, with no place to sleep except our seats. I thought a lot about the fancy private cars and having our own airplane on the bond tour. I wished I could give Lena some of that kind of treatment. She wanted all the fancy stuff that women want for their weddings and it was a shame she didn't get most of it. But she didn't complain, I had to give her that. She didn't make a peep and I started to feel lucky I married her. That was our honeymoon, a stopover in Los Angeles on the way and a few days in her parents' home in Portland.

When we got back, Lena looked for an apartment off base that we could afford but all the cheap places were taken by officers and their wives. Together we only made about seventy dollars a month so we didn't have a lot of choices. Lena got pissed off after a few days and wanted to use my name and status to pry open a place for us to live. I was having none of that. I wasn't going to trade on the medal for anything. It wasn't completely mine anyway. Nine boys also owned it with me. I thought this might be a hard idea for her to understand and expected we would have our first big fight, but she surprised me again. I said what I had to say about it and we never talked about it again. She was a Marine, she understood what I was saying. It was then that I knew I married the right one for me. We continued to live in camp in our separate barracks.

In the next few weeks, we had one seventy-two-hour pass. We hopped the train to Los Angeles, where we did the town on a bank-roll of under a hundred dollars. Most places were open to servicemen and women without a cover charge. The first place we tried was Slapsie Maxie's on Beverly Boulevard. Maxie was a fighter from New York who didn't have much of a punch. Sometimes he looked like he was just slapping the other fighter, that's how he got the name. Maxie's was the place to go because he had all kinds of acts there—singers, dancers, comics—so it was the place for fun. We got in the line that stretched down Beverly and waited our turn. Somehow word got around about me and all of a sudden people are turning around, whispering and looking sideways at us. I'd been through it enough now to know what was coming but I just hoped it would die down and we could be like anybody else. Lena didn't know a thing about what it was like with me being famous, so I didn't know how she would take it. The next thing we know some blowhard is spouting off about the Medal of Honor and pulling us up to the front of the line. I didn't like the attention and I didn't like the way the fella was talking about the Medal, like I won a beauty contest. So I said thanks but no thanks. I didn't feel like explaining and I didn't have to as far as Lena was concerned. She knew what it was all about. We left and never did go back to Maxie's place. We ended up at the Trocadero on Sunset. This was a little bit more of a class joint. Joe E. Lewis, the comic, was there. His routine was all about boozing and losing money on horses. He had everybody in the place almost crying with laughter. A few people who said they were somebody in the movies came over to our table and said hello.

They left business cards, telling me to give them a call. They wanted to introduce me around town to movie people. Joe pointed me out from the stage and I had to stand up and take a bow while everybody clapped. Joe was a real patriot. He was close to fifty but he did shows for a lot of the fighting boys who were stranded on islands out in the Pacific. The brass didn't want to let him go but he needled them until he got himself flown out on a cargo transport. All he brought along was a change of clothes and a few cases of good scotch. He made a lot of friends and brought a little bit of home out to us. He was a real good guy, so I stood up for Joe and fried under the spotlight for a while. He was a good comic for Marines since his two favorite subjects—drinking and gambling—were pretty much what we liked to do too. Lena didn't mind all the attention, it was new to her, so I stood up there and let her enjoy it. It was our best night together, we ended up walking back to our hotel as the sky turned from black to deep blue and the stars faded out. We were getting used to each other. That seventy-two hours was our best time together. Our last day was just rest. We didn't get out of bed until dinnertime.

Two weeks after our seventy-two hours together word came down. The 5th Division was shipping out, destination unknown. Lena's friend, Ruby Matalon, our maid of honor at the wedding, gave us the keys to her apartment in Oceanside for our last night. The details on our embarkation came down that C Company was to report to the assembly area for transport to the docks at 4:00 A.M. At that time in the morning there was no transportation back to camp from town. I couldn't stay at the apartment. We didn't get our last night alone. That last night I stayed with her in the mess until late. We talked of our life after the war—what we would name the first boy and the first girl. She held up pretty well while we talked. She didn't cry and pretended she was okay but she was no poker player. But I was. I told her, "I'm coming back," and she believed me.

Our first port was Hawaii, our first bivouac, Camp Tarawa. Our ship over, the USS *Baxter*, was like the trains on land—hot, dirty and crowded. The food was the worst I'd seen since the Canal when the menu was Spam cold out of the can. You couldn't tell what the vegetables were since they had been cooking for hours. The meat was dry as leather. The only thing that looked like it was supposed to was the canned fruit. There wasn't room belowdecks for all the men, so the deck became a tent city. Every square foot was somebody's front porch. We muscled into a clear patch where I drilled my fifty-eight boys on their weapons and did our PT— physical training. There was still nobody who could beat me when it came to assembling the old Brownie .30 cal. blindfolded. I made a contest out of it—beat the sarge and win the pot. Anything with gambling got the boys interested. The rest of the time we spent in one line or another. It took two hours to get through the chow line and a half hour to get to the head. General quarters sounded one afternoon when one of the ships in the convoy picked up the sound of a Jap sub that was shadowing us. Other than that, the weeklong trip was spent mostly writing letters and staring out to sea. This was the first time most of my boys from the parachute outfit had a chance to get their sea legs. Plenty of them spent the first few days at the rail puking even though the seas never got much above a foot or two. In a storm, these guys would be useless. The process that would break them down and strip them of their spirit was starting. All I could do now was guide them through it and help them stay alive.

I thought a lot about George, who went with the 4th Division into Saipan on June 15. The operation went on for almost a month, ending right before Lena and I were married. We heard casualties were high, over 25 percent—that meant somewhere around ten thousand men got killed or wounded. Ten thousand. The number sank into my gut. That was the last we heard.

We sailed into Hilo Harbor on the morning of August 18. Our first bivouac was in the city park along Maume Beach on Hilo Bay. The whole battalion was quarantined in the park until further notice. Scuttlebutt was that a Marine was sick with something they couldn't diagnose. Until they figured that out, we sat in the park. Tents went up to shield off the rain that came once or twice a day and latrines or "1,2,3s" one foot wide, two feet deep and three feet long were dug in the nice green lawn. We were camped there three days until the mystery illness was cleared up. Hawaii was a different part of the Pacific than I was used to. The temperature wasn't too hot or too cold. Other than the rain that came down in short showers, it was what you might think of as paradise. Every hour I thought of Lena and how much she would like it here. Maybe I'd bring her back here for a proper honeymoon, if things worked out for us. Drills continued. We were on an accelerated training schedule and our holiday in the park didn't slow that down.

Somehow a newspaper reporter tracked me down in camp and asked for a few minutes of my time. It wasn't like I could point to something I had to take care of right then. We were penned up in the middle of a city park like chimps in the zoo. He was nice enough and I said okay. He wanted to know how I was getting along after my successful war bond tour. I told him, "I'm not a good speech maker, though they say I'm a fair instructor. But instructing a bunch of kids on machine guns and sounding off to a bunch of civilians in a war plant are two different things." He stayed on to chat for a while and I let him. I generally clam up after I've said my bit and soon he saw the well was running dry.

On the fourth day, we broke camp and moved out about a half mile down the road to the narrow gauge railroad that the plantations in the interior of the island used to get their supplies from the ships in the bay. We piled onto the flat, open freight cars for our sixty-five-mile trip up the cliffs and through the jungle to Camp Tarawa. The jungle in Hawaii was full of life and color, completely different from most of the Guadalcanal jungle that I remembered. Once we had scaled the cliffs on switchbacks that took us a few hours, we moved into the dry interior of the island. We headed out across the "Great Hawaii desert" and crossed into Parker Ranch that they said was a quarter million acres. In the distance were the snowcapped Mauna Loa and Mauna Lea volcanoes.

Camp Tarawa, some called it the Dust Bowl, was about fifty thousand acres of barren desert where winds kept the air filled with red volcanic dust night and day. Even in one of the most beautiful places on earth the Marines managed to find an uncomfortable place to camp. Pendleton was beginning to look like the Waldorf compared to this place and that's just how I wanted it. My boys were going to be sharp as a razor when the call came and I didn't want any distractions from their training. The beach in Hilo was twelve miles away over rutted roads and the nearest town, Kamuela, had one tin-roofed shack called the Aloha Sandwich shop and a tiny restaurant with less than a dozen seats.

We lived in the standard twenty-by-twenty-foot tents, an eight-man squad to each one. The tents had one flap to get in and out and one sixty-watt lightbulb hanging on a wire from the center pole. The great luxury was the wooden floors that allowed us to get out of the dust for a while.

Word came back about Chesty and the 1/5 on Peleliu. They said the 1/5 was finished as a fighting unit. They'd taken 50 percent casualties mostly due to the caves and tunnels the Japs dug into solid rock. Fifty percent casualties rang in my ear. I thought right away about Bob Powell, the poor bastard. If he was still alive, he must be awfully tired by now. The news was like hearing your hometown just burned down. This was the 1/5, Chesty's outfit, the heroes of Bloody Ridge. If that could happen to them, it wasn't good news for the rest of us.

Our tactics against fortified positions took a turn after Peleliu. A new weapon in our attack arsenal was introduced—the flamethrower. We had demonstrations and some training with it at Pendleton but now it was a key part of our tactics. It was the best weapon to get the Japs out of their holes. This ugly war just got uglier. We made plenty of jokes about the thing, but the truth was we cursed the damn Japs for this. We were going to have to burn them in their holes like bugs. There was plenty of talk about how it must have been different fighting the Germans in Europe. It made me think about Alphonse in his tank with George Patton's 2nd Armored Division. The word was that at least the Germans knew when they were beaten. The Japs didn't care. We had to kill them one by one, every last one of them.

The standard drill was now modified to include a beach landing and coordinated movement against a fortified blockhouse. The lead weapon was still the machine gun supported by a squad of riflemen. Machine gunners then provided the covering fire for the demolition man—a jackrabbit who was supposed to run up to the front door of a bunker and deliver a satchel charge. The charge was to open a breech in the bunker wall. Then the same covering machine gun fire that flew a few inches from the demo man's ear was directed to within a few inches of the Zippo or flamethrower's ear. By the book. We did this drill over and over again.

A month or two into our stay at Camp Tarawa the men were getting stir-crazy. There was no entertainment or distraction of any kind. Not even a regular newspaper. Someone smuggled in the local paper with the interview I gave down in Hilo printed in it. That was all the news we'd had for weeks. The only big event was the return of the 4th Division.

George's 4th had moved from Saipan to Tinian and defeated the Japs in both engagements. I still had no word on whether he made it or not. All I knew was that casualties were heavy on Saipan. When the 4th returned to Hawaii, they camped on Maui, a nearby island. I expected somebody to give me the word sooner or later. Within a day or two, the word came from HQ. George made it. He was on Maui.

I got a twenty-four-hour pass. I didn't know if I wanted to laugh or cry all the way over to see my old boxing coach and sparring partner. I got over there and waited for a while at the HQ. The 4th had a nice spot compared to our desert outpost. They were only a mile or so from Haiku, a decent-size town with stores and a movie theater. A few days before I got the word that George was okay, the newspaper article with my interview caught the attention of Dr. John Fox, the superintendent of a local high school near Hilo. The doctor was a native of Raritan and got word to me in camp with an invitation to dinner at his house. That nearly knocked me over to hear from an old neighbor out there in the middle of nowhere. With the news about George, it was like Christmas. I figured George could hitch a ride on my ticket and both of us could get a good feed out of the deal. Most Marines after a few months of field rations and transport ship mess halls would sell their boots for a good meal. I couldn't wait to tell him.

The guy that walked up to me looked a bit like George but not much like the brother I remembered. I'd seen plenty of this kind of look before but it hit extra hard because I knew by heart every crease and bump of the face that used to be there. I was afraid to shake his hand too hard in case he fell over. He looked like he had been starved for a while. The worst part was the way he wouldn't look at me except to glance at me and then look down again. George used to be the guy who would be happy to tell you exactly what you were doing wrong whether you were doing something wrong or not. Now he seemed like he didn't care to speak up at all. He talked about the letter I wrote to him from Guadalcanal. He said now he knew what I meant. I didn't want to ask him about what went on over there. I had a good idea. We made it to Dr. Fox's house by late afternoon and had one of the best dinners I ever tasted. George talked a little more but he wasn't himself, not by a long shot. He joked about getting locked up in the brig in New River for coming back late from liberty. They gave him only bread and water but he said he ate twenty-five loaves of bread in five days.

"They lost money on me," he joked. That was the best thing he could have said as far as I was concerned. It meant he still had a bit of his old self and wasn't too far gone. Time and quiet would bring him back to himself, at least that was Father Russo's remedy. I thought a little bit of prayer couldn't hurt either. George was more likely to go to the booze when the night sweats started.

★

The boys in my squad were just about as sharp as they were ever going to get. They could operate every weapon on the battlefield and could perform everyone else's job in the squad if they had to. They could march twenty miles with full combat loads of gear, then attack any target. They'd been shot at with live ammo, dunked in the ocean and left to bake in dusty foxholes for days at a time. The only thing we didn't know was how they would react once the blood started flying. That was something only God knew.

We taught them everything we knew and all we could do now was keep them sharp until the word came down. I took a page out of Chesty's book and did something that we did on the Canal after Bloody Ridge. It made us feel like we were still a unit and still fierce even after all we went through on the Canal. We shaved our heads bald. To these new boys it was like graduation, especially after I was the first one to get my head cleaned off. They all followed me. Now we were the C Company cueballs and we were as tough an outfit as there was in the Marine Corps. I remembered seeing Chesty after the ridge sitting at chow with his bald head. All of us baldies sat around him and apart from the other units. It was just us, the 1/7, and Chesty was our center. He was one of us. I wanted my men to see me and feel that way. If we were going to hell, we were all going together and I was the one who knew the way. Corporal Brookshire's squad tried to outdo us by wearing earrings, like pirates. Plenty of tough talk passed between our squads. They were challenging us. We had to keep an eye out that words and practical jokes, that were often elaborate and painful, didn't go too far. Some of these boys were on a hair trigger. We'd been in camp, kept away from the civilized world for four months. All that time, night and day, all we did was train and clean our weapons. The only thing these boys wanted to do now was get out of this dust bowl and go "slap a Jap." It was December 1944. We were ready.

On December 27, the Division started loading out equipment. Topside wasn't saying where we were going but we had a pretty good idea. The whole Pacific campaign was a series of stepping stones up to Japan's front door. We heard scuttlebutt and read a few news reports that we were bombing an airfield on an island that was only seven hundred miles from Japan. The place was called Iwo Jima.

SULFUR ISLAND

The diary of Maj. Yoshitaka Horie, aide to Lt. Gen. Tadamichi Kuribayashi, commanding general of Iwo Jima:

"After General Kuribayashi's appointment as commanding general of Iwo Jima in May, 1944, he devoted his time to the problem of defending it by starting construction of underground fortifications.

"In October, he began to make pillboxes, using several battalions for labor. After three months he made 135. In order to connect with each defensive position of Motoyama District, we planned to make 28,000 meters of underground tunnels and began the work in December, 1944."

Iwo Jima, although 700 miles from the Japanese mainland, was considered to be a district of Tokyo, the Motoyama District. If captured by American forces, it put the capital within range of B-29 bombers. The defense of the island was critical to the survival of the Empire.

The island is five miles long, two and a half miles wide at the

northern end, tapering to a point on the southern end. Mount Suribachi forms the southern tip of the island and is the remnant of a
fountain of lava that spilled northward, cooling in the seawater to
form the rest of the land mass. Suribachi stands 555 feet high and
is an irregular lump with a ragged top edge. The name Iwo Jima
means Sulfur Island in Japanese.

Sixteen miles of tunnels were dug through the hot, sulfurous
rock underneath the black pumice sand. Fully equipped soldiers
could run without crouching through this network of tunnels that
were lit by electric lights and supplied with fresh air by a system of
conduits. The tunnels connected many of the 150 fortified firing
positions that faced the roughly one mile beachfront where the
Americans were forced to land. Forty-six feet underground a field
hospital operated with its own air and electricity supply. Beds were
carved into the solid rock walls. Commanding General Kuribayashi's command post was located seventy-five feet underground. Suribachi itself was riddled with tunnels that connected elevated gun
emplacements with supply depots. These tunnels were fortified with
concrete and the walls often finished with plaster. Supporting systems of ventilation, water, electricity and steam powered the entire
seven-story defense complex buried inside the mountain. Japanese
gunners looking down from protected gun emplacements dug into
the sides of the volcanic rock were close enough to identify the in-
signia arm patches on the uniforms of the attacking Americans.

In every blockhouse and fortified underground position throughout the island was posted General Kuribayashi's "Sacred Battle
Vows." All 22,000 of the Japanese defenders understood the vows
as the logical end of their service to the Emperor under the warrior's code of bushido that instructed them, "Death is lighter than a

feather but duty is weightier than a mountain." After a year of being defeated by the Americans on every island battle, no Japanese soldier expected to leave Iwo Jima alive. The general's posted note read, "Kill ten Americans before you die."

Iwo Jima, February 19, 1945—0945 hours.

They tore us up while we were lying on the beach but me and Lou Plain finally got this show on the road. We kicked their asses and dragged boys up by the scruff of their necks. "Get the fuck off the beach! Move out!" we yelled at them over the incoming fire. They were moving over the terraces now and were finding whatever cover they could in shell craters on the flat land. Bulldozers had punched a gap through the terraces and tanks were on their way up from the beach to support us. A few mixed squads of C and B Company boys were now at the edge of Motoyama One airfield, our first objective. Once we took out the bunker that was slicing open the 4th Division with their cannon, we only had to worry about the snipers, the dug-in artillery looking down on us from Suribachi and the constant hail storm of mortars that fell straight down from the sky. Other than that, things were looking up. At least we were off the water's edge. That place had turned into a killing field. We were dug in at the edge of the airfield, but we were only a narrow salient, about eighteen men, and could be outflanked at any moment. I had to get going and bring up armor and reinforcements. From our position at the south end of the runway, we could see Japs dart across the tarmac, retreating to their fallback positions, giving me some idea of where I could direct fire when the bigger guns moved up. For now riflemen took potshots at the running targets. Dead ahead on the airfield was a graveyard of wrecked aircraft.

We moved out of our positions up a slope and onto the runway. The plan was to cut the line of retreat and sweep to the north, taking the whole runway. When we cleared the south end and started our advance, the big guns from Suribachi swung over from the kill zone on the beach to us. The Navy was also lobbing shells into our sector from offshore. We were too far ahead of our lines and into an area the Navy targeted as enemy territory. Then mortars started dropping on us from the north end. We were in at least three sets of crosshairs now and headed toward a real unhealthy future if we continued on. Our line fell back and the men took cover in deep craters in the airplane junkyard. Over a dozen of them fit into one crater, a handful into smaller craters close by.

"Dig in and hold this ground, come hell or high water. I'll go back for more men," I ordered. Jesus, did they look like a scared group of boys when I told them that.

Tanks were coming through the breech in the terraces when I got out to the flat land between the beach and the airfield. They were moving straight ahead and didn't seem to have any idea where the enemy was. I signaled the lead tank and pointed out the target areas to the right, at the north end of the runway where the mortars where coming from. They caught on quick and directed fire there. That would help my boys at the airfield hold on for a while until I could round up more firepower.

Lou Plain, our executive officer, was bringing up boys from the beach and directing them to covered positions in the flats with one hand and showing tanks the way to the breech in the terraces with the other. I took a few dozen of his boys and told them to follow me. We leapfrogged from one shell hole to the other, gathering boys from these holes as we went and then pushing on to the next. We were making progress. When we got across these flats and up the slope to the airfield, the plan was to flank the north end positions and secure this first objective.

Even though they had slaughtered us a dozen at a time on the beach, we weren't stopped anymore. Armor was coming up and soon my boys would be reinforced. I knew this wasn't the seventy-two-hour turkey shoot that Topside tried to sell us, but now I knew we weren't going to get run off either. We would take Motoyama One today. The boys who died on the beach this morning paid for it in advance and we intended to collect.

I rubbed the bible in my breast pocket. The word was that a bible had stopped a bullet for some lucky Marine somewhere, so a lot of us carried them. The other superstition was that as long as you could hear the mortars falling you were okay. When your luck ran out, you wouldn't even know it, because the word was that you never heard the mortar round with your name on it.

Epilogue

★

Sergeant John Basilone was killed by an enemy mortar round at approximately 10:45 A.M. on February 19, 1945. He suffered massive abdominal wounds but lingered for approximately twenty minutes before succumbing from shock and loss of blood. Four Marines died from the same explosion. His last words were spoken to a Navy corpsman who attended to him following the explosion. That corpsman has vowed never to reveal those final words.

For his fearless leadership, his daring attack on the enemy bunker and successful capture of the first objective of C Company on Iwo Jima, he was awarded the Navy's highest honor, the Navy Cross. He also received the Purple Heart for wounds received that day. Sergeant Basilone is buried in Arlington National Cemetery in section 12, grave 384.

Sergeant Basilone's wife Lena never remarried. She continued to be active in veteran's affairs until her death in June 1999 at age 86. Brother Carlo Basilone still lives in Raritan, New Jersey, and brother Donald Basilone lives in Florida. Sister Phyllis Basilone Cutter, who wrote the original, *The Basilone Story*, the basis of this book, passed away on August 14, 2004. No other siblings of John Basilone still survive.

Sergeant Basilone has become, like his mentor Chesty Puller, a legend in the Marine Corps. At the entrance to his hometown of Raritan, New Jersey, a bronze statue of him stands silent guard, on a small median strip. The section of Interstate Route 5 that passes by Camp Pendleton in Oceanside, California, is called the Basilone Memorial Highway. His heroic exploits are recounted for every new Marine as a part of their education in the finest traditions of the Corps.

Sergeant Basilone, in his personal humility and unwavering dedication to the men who served with him, became a true hero of the American people during World War II. His courage eased their fears during many dark hours when the outcome of the war was uncertain. His cheerful, good nature in spite of his own psychological and physical suffering gave them hope. His tireless service, whether fighting or rallying support for the troops, helped Americans bear the hardships of wartime.

America owes a debt of remembrance to Sergeant Basilone and all the thousands of men and women who served to protect the country against the determined enemies of World War II. To remember their sacrifices is to honor them.

Acknowledgments

★

There are many people to thank for their generous efforts in making this book possible: The Sgt. John Basilone Foundation for its support; Kelly and Susan Murphy for their generous efforts copyediting; Col. Ken Jordan, USMC (ret.), for his technical advice and encouragement; Sergeant Basilone's nephew, Jerry Cutter, for his research, financial expertise and wise counsel; the Basilone family, including Bill Brownson—a nephew, Sergeant Basilone's sister and two brothers—Phyllis Basilone Cutter, Carlo and Donald Basilone— for providing personal materials and memoirs; the people of Raritan, who were so generous with their time and the use of the Raritan Public Library. Special thanks to residents in the Raritan area and those who continue to honor Sergeant Basilone, including Peter Ippolito, Anthony Cucci, John Pacifico, Marie Porcaro, Rocco Fischetti, Charles Franchino, Jim Foohey and fellow Basilone author Bruce Doorly. Thanks also to Jordan Jaffe Schneider of the Basilone Stamp Campaign for her dedication to the memory of Sergeant Basilone and her assistance with locating people for this book. Ed Schwallie deserves special thanks for his early support of the book.

As always, many veterans shouldered the burden. This time instead of fighting the war, they volunteered to make this account of it as accurate as possible by answering lots of late-night phone calls about small details of equipment and tactics and by reading early drafts of the manuscript. Sincere thanks to Tom Nass, Adolf Brusa, Warren Sessler, Don Richter, Roy Roush, Kevin Henry, Art Karin, Bryon Doenges, Bob Hansen, Col. Jerry Brown, John Blankenship, Frank Taylor, Chuck Tatum, Dr. Gary Solis—Chief of the Marine Corps Oral History unit, Fritz Gemeinhardt, Charlie Bateman, Woody Williams, Clifton Weathers and Bernie Dobbins.

Warmest personal thanks to my wife, Adoley Odunton Proser, and JoAnn Cutter, wife of my partner, Jerry Cutter, for their loving support and time given to reviewing the manuscript, fielding phone calls and listening to problems.

Most importantly, as Sergeant Basilone would insist, special thanks and gratitude to the men and women of the armed forces who endure the hardships, fight, suffer and die for each other and freedom. We, the free, salute you.

Sergeant John Basilone's Decorations and Memorials

★

DECORATIONS

Congressional Medal of Honor
October 24–25, 1942, Guadalcanal

★

Navy Cross
February 19, 1945, Iwo Jima—posthumous

★

Purple Heart
February 19, 1945, Iwo Jima—posthumous

★

Presidential Unit Citation
1942 Guadalcanal
1945 Iwo Jima—posthumous

★

American Defense Service Medal
1941, Culebra, Cuba

★

Asiatic-Pacific Campaign Medal with two Bronze Stars
1942–43 Guadalcanal
1945 Iwo Jima—posthumous

★

World War II Victory Medal
1941–1945—posthumous

★

American Campaign Medal
1945—posthumous

★

New Jersey Distinguished Service Award
1951—posthumous

MEMORIALS

USS *Basilone*—U.S. Navy destroyer 824 commissioned in 1949.
No longer in service

★

Basilone Memorial Bridge, New Jersey, 1951

★

Seventeen miles of Interstate 5 outside of Camp Pendleton in
Oceanside, California, named Basilone Memorial Freeway

★

Basilone Day, February 19, 2004, has been proclaimed
in Maryland, New Jersey, Pennsylvania, South Carolina,
Texas, Virginia, West Virginia, Rhode Island, Oregon,
Colorado, South Dakota and Iowa

★

Commemorative statue in Raritan, New Jersey

★

Annual John Basilone Day Parade in Raritan, New Jersey

★

Commemorative U.S. postage stamp, pending

Bibliography

★

Bradley, James. *Flags of our Fathers*, New York: Bantam Books, 2000.

Conner, Howard. *The Spearhead*, Nashville, TN: The Battery Press, 1987.

Cutter, Phyllis Basilone. *The Basilone Story: The Life of Sgt. John Basilone, Medal of Honor-USMC*, Port St. Lucie, FL: Phyllis Basilone Cutter, 1961.

Davis, Burke. *Marine! The Life of Chesty Puller*, New York: Bantam Books, 1968.

Doorly, Bruce. *Raritan's Hero, the John Basilone Story*, (self-published).

Hersey, John. *Into the Valley; A Skirmish of the Marines*, New York: Schocken Books, 1942.

McMillan, George. *The Old Breed: A History of the First Marine Division in World War II*, Nashville, TN: The Battery Press, 1949.

Newcomb, Richard. *Iwo Jima*, New York: Bantam Books, 1995.

Richter, Don. *Where the Sun Stood Still! A Story about Those Who Fought in the Historic Battle for Guadalcanal*, Agoura Hills, CA: TAWE California, 1992.

Ricks, Thomas E. *Making the Corps*, New York: Scribner, 1997.

Roush, Roy. *Open Fire!* Woodland Hills, CA: Front Line Press, 2003.

Tatum, Charles W. *Iwo Jima; Red Blood, Black Sand; Pacific Apocalypse*, Stockton, CA; Charles W. Tatum Publishing, 1995.

Wells, John Keith. *Give Me Fifty Marines Not Afraid to Die*, Abilene, KS: Ka-Well Enterprises, 1995.